0-
3.95

The complete paintings of

Rembrandt

Introduction by **Gregory Martin**

Notes and catalogue by **Paolo Lecaldano**

Harry N. Abrams, Inc. *Publishers* New York

Classics of the World's Great Art

Editor
Paolo Lecaldano

International Advisory Board
Gian Alberto dell'Acqua
André Chastel
Douglas Cooper
Lorenz Eitner
Enrique Lafuente Ferrari
Bruno Molajoli
Carlo L. Ragghianti
Xavier de Salas
David Talbot Rice
Jacques Thuillier
Rudolf Wittkower

*This series of books is
published in Italy by Rizzoli
Editore, in France by
Flammarion, in the United
Kingdom by Weidenfeld and
Nicolson, in the United States
by Harry N. Abrams, Inc.,
in Spain by Editorial Noguer
and in Switzerland by
Kunstkreis.*

© Copyright by
Rizzoli Editore, 1969
Library of Congress
Catalogue Card No. 72–2264
ISBN 8109–5528–8
Phototypeset in England by
Keyspools Ltd, Golborne, Lancs.

Printed in Italy

Table of contents

Gregory Martin   **Introduction**   **5**

Paolo Lecaldano   **Early documents on Rembrandt**   **8**

The paintings in colour   **15**

List of plates   **16**

The works   **81**

Bibliography   **82**

Outline biography   **83**

Letters and inventory   **89–90**

Catalogue of works   **91**

Table of concordance   **126**

Other Rembrandtesque works formerly considered autograph by some critics or in public collections   **127**

Appendices   **1 Drawings by Rembrandt**   **134**

2 Etchings by Rembrandt   **136**

3 Pupils of Rembrandt's   **139**

Indexes   **Subjects**   **141**

Titles   **141**

Topographical   **143**

Photographic sources

Colour: Blauel, Munich; Carrieri, Milan; Dulwich College, London; Flammarion, Paris; Frick Collection, New York; Held, Ecublens; Lord Chamberlain's Office, London; Mauritshuis, The Hague; Metropolitan Museum of Art, New York; Meyer, Vienna; J. W. Middendorf II, New York; Museum Boymans-van Beuningen, Rotterdam; National Gallery of Art, Washington, D.C.; National Gallery of Scotland, Edinburgh; National Gallery of Victoria, Melbourne; Nationalmuseum, Stockholm; Rijksmuseum, Amsterdam; Staatliche Kunstsammlungen, Cassel; Steinkopf, Berlin; Wallraf-Richartz-Museum, Cologne; Witty, Sunbury-on-Thames.

Black and white illustrations: Annan, Glasgow; Acquavella Galleries, New York; Art Gallery of Ontario, Toronto; Art Institute, Chicago (Ill.); Bayerische Staatsgemäldesammlungen, Munich; Blomstrann, New Britain (Conn.); Bowdoin College Museum of Art, Brunswick, Maine; Brunel, Lugano; Bührle, Zurich; Bullaty-Lome, New York; Chomon-Perino, Turin; City Art Museum, St Louis (Mo.); Cleveland Museum of Art, Cleveland (Ohio); Columbus Gallery of Fine Arts, Columbus (Ohio); Cooper Ltd, London; Corcoran Gallery of Art, Washington, D.C.; Demanega, Innsbruck; Detroit Institute of Arts, Detroit (Mi.); M. H. De Young Memorial Museum, San Francisco (Calif.); Dingjan, The Hague; Faringdon, Buscot Park, Berkshire; Fine Arts Gallery, San Diego (Calif.); Frick Art Reference Library, New York; Frick Collection, New York; Fundaçao Calouste Gulbenkian, Lisbon; Giraudon, Paris; Glasgow Museum and Art Galleries, Glasgow; Held, Ecublens; Herzog Anton Ulrich-Museum, Brunswick; Houghton Jr, New York; Hyde Collection, Glens Falls, (N.Y.); John J. Johnson, Philadelphia (Pa.); Joslyn Art Museum, Omaha (Ne.); Kaplan, New York; Kleinhempel, Hamburg; Konstmuseum, Göteborg; Kunsthistorisches Museum, Vienna; Kyle, Leighton Buzzard; Lord Chamberlain's Office, London; Los Angeles County Museum of Art, Los Angeles (Calif.); Memorial Art Gallery of the University of Rochester, Rochester (N.Y.); Metropolitan Museum of Art, New York; Middendorf, New York; Minneapolis Institute of Arts, Minneapolis (Ind.); Montreal Museum of Fine Arts, Montreal; Musée Jacquemart-André, Paris; Musées Royaux des Beaux-Arts, Brussels; Museum Bredius, The Hague; Museum of Fine Arts, Boston (Mass.); National Gallery, London; National Gallery of Art, Washington, D.C.; National Gallery of Canada, Ottawa; National Gallery of Ireland, Dublin; National Gallery of Victoria, Melbourne; Nationalmuseum, Stockholm; Nelson Gallery of Art, Kansas City (Mo.); Newbery, Liverpool; North Carolina Museum of Art, Raleigh (N.C.); Norton Simon Foundation, Fullerton (Calif.); Oeffentliche Kunstsammlung, Basle; Olson, Knislinge; Photo Studios Ltd, London; Pracownia Fotograficzna Muzeum Narodowego w Krakowie, Krakow; Pushkin Museum, Moscow; Reinhart, Winterthur; Rheinisches Bildarchiv, Cologne; Rijksbureau voor Kunsthistorische Documentatie, The Hague; Rijksmuseum, Amsterdam; Ringling Museum of Art, Sarasota (Fla.); Rizzoli Archives, Milan; Schiff, New York; Scott, Edinburgh; Service de documentation photographique, Versailles; Six Collectie, Amsterdam; Soprintendenza alle Gallerie, Florence; Staatliche Graphische Sammlung, Munich; Staatliche Kunsthalle, Karlsruhe; Staatliche Kunstsammlungen, Dresden; Staatliche Kunstsammlungen, Cassel; Statens Museum for Kunst, Copenhagen; Stearn & Sons, Cambridge; Stewart Gardner Museum, Boston (Mass.); Stickelmann, Bremen; Studly, New York; Szépmüvészeti Múzeum, Budapest; Taft Museum, Cincinnati (Ohio); Toledo Museum of Art, Toledo (Ohio); Waggaman, La Jolla (Calif.); Wallace Collection, London; White, Cowdray Park.

Introduction

No one would deny Rembrandt a place in the inner sanctum reserved for the great. His is a household name that must rarely fail to evoke some response. Such posthumous fame speaks of a man of great understanding, warm sensitivity, and high imagination, who found expression in the manipulation of a brush, pen or pencil and etcher's needle.

But the admiration, which Rembrandt so obviously deserves, brought in its wake undesirable offshoots. The delicate task of removing authentic but wrongly attributed works and imitations from Rembrandt's painted œuvre has only recently been undertaken. The result has been to reduce it to a little over 400 paintings. This total does not greatly exceed the number of the designs which he etched independently and to which he devoted a good deal of his energies.

In many ways, Rembrandt sums up the virtues of his native country, which – as the United Provinces – achieved its independence after a long struggle against its traditional ruler, Spain, in 1648, when the artist was forty-two. For his art is at once outspoken, uncomprising and frank, and expresses tolerance, charity, commitment and independence of spirit. Every work by Rembrandt marked a renewed dedication to the reality and quality of life. And it is his unwavering humanism that ensures his wide and lasting appeal.

Painting and etching brought Rembrandt early fame in his native Leiden and then prosperity in Amsterdam where he settled in 1631. But after the death of his wealthy wife, Saskia, his life gradually slipped away from the mainstream and took on a troublesome course. Extravagance and a decline in commissions brought financial disaster in 1656; two years later, the law having pursued its slow progress, Rembrandt's possessions were put up for sale, and, in 1660, he was forced to move to a poorer part of Amsterdam. The chief (but not the only) supports at this difficult time were his common-law wife, Hendrijcke Stoffels, and his son, Titus, who formed a company to manage his business. Both pre-deceased him; and thus it was a rather lonely, needy and neglected Rembrandt who died in 1669 aged sixty-three.

Rembrandt was probably the least publicly orientated of men. It is difficult to envisage this pudgy-faced man with small, alert eyes and a large nose desiring much from society after his heyday in the 1630s. His circle of friends was probably made up of intellectuals – both Jewish and Protestant – preachers and doctors, or fellow artists and connoisseurs. With the exception of Constantijn Huygens, an early admirer, who through his position at court brought Rembrandt into a prolonged but intermittent contact with the Stadtholder, and Jan Six, the dilettante with whom Rembrandt was on close terms in the 1640s and '50s, his friends were not wealthy or well-born.

Rembrandt had little interest in public affairs – in politics or war. He never painted a battle scene, and his attempt at describing the political aims of the state resulted in a confused and over-complex oil sketch, which he did not further pursue. His hatred of bloodshed is reflected in the extraordinary *Oath of the Batavians* (no. 415) executed for the Town Hall of Amsterdam, which has a brutal realism and fierce drama that his contemporaries could not stomach.

It was the Bible that chiefly attracted him. In Christ's life and parables, and in various Old Testament scenes, usually involving women, Rembrandt found the subject-matter which stirred his emotions and over which his imagination could range, fed by a sympathetic and enquiring understanding. And it was his sympathy for his fellow beings that made him a consummate painter of portraits.

But the motive force that geared his manifold, humanist qualities was the sheer instinctive drive that compelled him to self-expression. This force charged every situation with dramatic significance, which Rembrandt made pointfully articulate by a dedication to expressive detail and draughtsmanship. His imagi-

5

native power was thus shatteringly vivid, and his visual language was encyclopaedically rich in sharply observed detail that is always relevant.

This force was both dominant and demanding. And Rembrandt was as determined as he was imaginative. Unlike Rubens, the other giant of seventeenth-century painting who constantly surprises by his prolific speed and inventiveness, Rembrandt's search for meaningful solutions at the behest of his imagination was slow and painstaking. This applies both to his etchings and paintings. However unfinished some of his later paintings may appear, their surfaces are richly various and encrusted – the result of a long, concentrated effort.

It is thus hardly surprising that Rembrandt was no prodigy. His earliest dated painting was executed when he was twenty-one, probably after he had completed his training with his most influential teacher, the competent Amsterdam figure painter, Pieter Lastman. In Leiden, he was to find his confidence through his friendship with the slightly older and daring Jan Lievens, and to abandon the bright, metallic colour range favoured by Lastman. In its place, Rembrandt modified a then fashionable Caravaggesque idiom, by concentrating light in one focal point and for the rest working in a muted tone, which gave maximum effect to resonant colour. He was always to rely on this inherently dramatic use of light.

In his Leiden years and for about a decade in Amsterdam, Rembrandt's vision was both exuberant and tempestuously dramatic. Caravaggio and Rubens were probably his heroes, and their lessons, combined with his sense of characterization and unerring narrative gift, make such grandiose works as *Belshazzar's Feast* (no. 180) and *Samson Blinded by the Philistines* (no. 184) intensely and frighteningly effective.

Such genius brought new life to the staider requirements of portraiture for which Rembrandt was soon in demand after he settled in Amsterdam. In his hands, and after a sideways glance at Van Dyck, his sitters relaxed and were endowed with a lively and natural alertness. His imaginative powers and his ability to establish an emotional focal point particularly suited him to group portraiture. His first – *The Anatomy Lesson of Dr Tulp* (no. 81) – records not only a group of men and a notable anatomist, but also the excitement of scientific discovery. The group of men are made to take part in an event. And thus, too, in his most famous painting, the *Militia Company of Captain Frans Banning Cocq* (*The Night Watch*) (no. 246) executed ten years later in 1642, Rembrandt avoided the usual monotony of describing a serried row of amateur soldiers, by showing all the bustle and palaver of their setting out on patrol.

By the 1640s, Rembrandt had forsaken outspoken eloquence for a subtler and serener poetry. Love and tenderness are the keynotes of this decade, which saw the death of his wife, and both are epitomized in the "Hundred Guilder Print" – a passionate evocation of the gentleness and humanity that Christ brought to his ministry and in the two renderings of the *Holy Family* (nos. 270 and 271). These paintings are delightful variations on Raphaelesque themes, and as such are indications of Rembrandt's increasing interest in the art of the Italian High Renaissance. It was this new orientation that led to a return to the grand scale with this time a different, calmer sense of monumentality, in which a growing resonance of colour and freedom of handling replace his concentration on supporting detail. The pregnant, gorgeous grandeur of his vision in the 1650s gave the Louvre *Bathsheba* (no. 317) a grave sensuality, and charged the deeply moving *Jacob Blessing Joseph's Children* (no. 344) at Cassel with a mass of glowing reds, golds, browns and white which are laid on with a thickly loaded and controlled brush.

After the formal splendour of the *Equestrian Portrait* (no. 427) in the National Gallery and the hymn to civic decency and bureaucracy of the *Sampling Officials* (no. 424), Rembrandt's style grew increasingly detached and adventurous. Structure and form are almost cruelly established in the *Oath of the Batavians* (no. 415) and nearly dissolve amidst the dazzling colours of the *Jewish Bride* in the Rijksmuseum (no. 434) and the *Family Portrait* (no. 448) at Brunswick.

Appropriately, after the long sequence of self-portraits which was begun early in his career, one of his last works is the *Self-Portrait* (no. 449) in the National Gallery, painted in the year of his death. After the dashing pride of his youth and the splendid majesty of his maturity, Rembrandt conveys here the alert isolation and dogged introspection that had pervaded his last years.

GREGORY MARTIN

Early documents on Rembrandt

We are giving below – as the biographical and critical sources on which all subsequent research was based – the texts of the first six basic documents referring to Rembrandt's life and art. They were published as part of the artistic literature of the seventeenth century and the first two decades of the eighteenth, and were written by Johannes Orlers, Joachim von Sandrart, Filippo Baldinucci, André Félibien, Roger de Piles and Arnold Houbraken.

Rembrandt van Rijn, son of Harmen Gerrits zoon van Rijn and Neeltgen Willems van Suydtbrouck, was born in the city of Leiden on 15th July of the year 1606. His parents sent him to school so that he would learn latin, and intended later on to send him to the university of Leiden so that once he was of age he could, with his knowledge, serve the city and the country as best he could, and help in their development; but as he was showing signs of having not the slightest inclination or talent for such purpose, and as all his impulses were directed towards painting and the art of drawing, they were compelled to remove him from his school and enter him as an apprentice to a painter so that he could learn from him the basis and principles of these arts. So they sent him to the knowledgeable painter Iacob Isaacxsz van Swanenburch so that he could be taught by him; he stayed with him three years and in that time made such progress that all connoisseurs in art marvelled at it: it was clear that in time he would become an exceptional painter. For that reason his father decided to send him to the famous painter P. Lasman who lived in Amsterdam, so that he could be taught by him in a better and more profound manner. But after spending six months with him he decided to practice painting on his own: and thus he was fortunate enough to become one of the most famous painters of our century. His art and work were so much in demand with the burghers and citizens of Amsterdam, and as he travelled thither many times to execute portraits and other pictures, he decided to move from Leiden to Amsterdam, and indeed did so in the year 1630, and settled in that city where he still lives today, in the year 1641.

JOHANNES ORLERS, *Beschrijvinge der Stadt Leyden*, Leiden, 1641 [2]

It is a matter of wonder that the great Rembrand von Ryn, though the scion of a simple family of country millers, should have been inclined by nature towards the noble career of an artist and have attained its highest reaches through hard work as well as through his inclination and natural talent. He took his first steps in Amsterdam, with the famous painter Lastman and his natural genius, his indefatigable energy and con-

tinuous hard work were such that all he needed was a visit to Italy and to other countries where he could have learnt classical art and art theory: this lack was all the more serious in virtue of the fact that he knew only Dutch and therefore could learn little from books. As a result he always remained tied to his own conventions and he did not hesitate to oppose and contradict our own artistic laws – such as those of anatomy and the proportions of the human body –, perspective, the study of classical sculpture, the drawing and pictorial composition of Raphael, as well as the academies which are so necessary for our profession. He asserted that one should let oneself be guided by nature alone and by no other law; thus, in a painting, he would put light, shadow and the outline of objects as he thought fit, even if they were in opposition to elementary laws of perspective. And for that reason, as the outlines should rightfully have been placed differently, in order not to take undue risks, he would cover them with thick black shadows and consider them only as a contribution to the general effect. In this he was extremely clever and not only was he able to draw from nature with great skill but also to imbue his work with natural vigour and a powerful strength, particularly in his half-bust portraits and his heads of old people, but also in smaller pictures, in the elegant clothes and other pretty baubles he painted.

Apart from that he etched on copper very many subjects which were then made into prints. From all this one can see that he was extremely active and indefatigable: he was also favoured by fortune in that he had ample financial means and his house at Amsterdam was filled with a quantity of youths of good families who flocked around him to be taught and instructed in the art of painting. Each of these paid him an annual sum of one hundred florins; to this must be added the profit he made from the sale of his pupils' paintings and etchings, which amounted to two thousand or two thousand five hundred florins, quite apart from what he made from the sale of his own works. It is certain that, had he been able to keep on good terms with every one and look after his business properly he would have increased his fortune greatly; instead of which, though he was not exactly extravagant, he had no idea of the importance of social rank and was forever rubbing shoulders with people of inferior classes, which was detrimental to his work.

He was very skilful in the mixing of colours according to their own particular characteristics, so that his paintings are imbued with the vividness and harmony of life itself. In doing this he opened the eyes of all those who, following the accepted norms, become colourists rather than painters, placing colours one next to the other without any feeling or sensitivity, with the result that there is nothing of nature in their paintings; they are rather like those boxes of colours which are sold in shops, or clothes which have just returned from the dyer's.

Apart from this he was fascinated by every manifestation of art, whether painting, drawing or etching and also by every kind of exotic object of which he owned a great number and in the choice of which he showed knowledge and taste. Many people respected and praised him for this.

In his works this painter made little use of light except where he wanted to give greater relief: in the rest of the work light and shade was carefully balanced. He also made skilful use of reflexions by which means light could be made to penetrate areas of shadow; his colours are vigorous and luminous; and in everything he displayed good judgement. In his paintings of old people, their skin and hair, he showed great patience, ability and experience and they are very life-like. Few of his pictures were inspired by classical poetry, allegory or history, but his subject-matters are usually taken from everyday life, subjects which pleased him or which to him were full of *schilderachtig*, as they say in the Netherlands, altogether full of fascination and close to nature.

He died in Amsterdam, leaving one son who, according to rumour, is also skilful in matters of art.

JOACHIM VON SANDRART, Teutsche Academie,
Nuremberg and Frankfurt, 1675–9

About the year 1640, there lived and worked in Amsterdam Reimbrond Vainrein – which in our language means Rembrandt of the Rhine – who was born in Leiden, a painter of greater reputation than merit. He painted a vast canvas [*The Night Watch*, no. 246], which was housed in the barracks of the foreign guards and in which he depicted a company of Civic Guards; this painting made his name more famous than that of any other painter of his country. The reason for this was above all that, among the other figures, he had painted a captain with his foot raised, as in the act of walking, with a standard in his hand which was so exquisitely rendered in perspective that, though barely half a yard long on the canvas, it seemed displayed in its entire length; the rest of the painting, however, was so crowded and confused that one could barely make out the other figures from one another, though they had all been painted from life and with great care. This painting which made such a great impact upon its age brought him four thousand crowns – corresponding to about 3,500 of our Tuscan currency. He also painted many oil pictures representing scenes from the tales of Ovid on the walls of the house of a magistrate. As far as we know there are two paintings of his in Italy: one is in Rome, in the picture gallery of Principe Pamfilio, a man's head with a beard and a turban; the other is in Florence, in the Royal gallery, in the room where the portraits of painters are exhibited; it is a self-portrait [today in the Uffizi, no. 430]. This painter belonged at that time to the Menistic religion [the Mennonite sect; but it is doubtful whether Rembrandt ever belonged to it] which, although a heretical sect, is nevertheless opposed to Calvinist doctrines; its members do not receive baptism until the age of thirty; they do not elect literate preachers but men of low class who are given the same honours as gentlemen and men of wisdom; as for the rest, they live as they please. This painter being quite different from the others as far as intelligence and mode of life were concerned, was just as

peculiar in his painting and his style can only be described as entirely his own, without any outline, external or internal, and consisting entirely of roughly applied and repeated brushstrokes with an emphasis on areas of shadow, but without any really deep shadows. And what is almost impossible to understand is this: how it is that with such quick brushstrokes he worked so slowly and painstakingly. He could have painted many portraits thanks to the reputation he had acquired through his use of colours but which his drawing did not live up to; but the knowledge that his prospective client had to sit for him for two or three months, caused few people to commission him. The reason why his work took so long was that no sooner was the first sketch dry than he covered it with fresh brushstrokes so that the paint was sometimes up to an inch thick; thus he toiled ceaselessly and painted much but few works; nevertheless his reputation was such that one of his drawings in which little or practically nothing could be seen – as reported by Bernard Keillh of Denmark [Monsù Bernardo], a very fine painter, now working in Rome, who worked in his school for eight years – fetched thirty crowns at an auction sale. Rembrandt's extravagant style was equalled by his mode of life, for he was a first-rate joker and laughed at everyone. He had an ugly, plebeian face and dressed in tatty, dirty clothes in which he worked, cleaning his brushes on them and other such things. When he was hard at work not even the foremost monarch on earth would have managed to be granted an audience, but would have had to come back again and again until he had finished his work. He often went to public sales where he bought ancient and old-fashioned clothes which he found bizarre or picturesque; and though sometimes they were filthy, he hanged them on the walls of his studio, among the many beautiful objects which he delighted in: all manners of ancient and modern weapons such as arrows, halberds, daggers, sabres, knives and other such objects; an enormous quantity of exquisite drawings, prints and medals, and many other things which he thought a painter might need for his work. He deserves, however, great praise for his generosity, extravagant though it may have been, for he thought so highly of his art that when similar things were auctioned – especially paintings and drawings by great artists of his own country – he raised the initial price so high that there was never a second buyer: he said he did this in order to raise the status of his profession. He was also very generous in lending his possessions to other painters whenever they needed them for their work. The area in which this painter really excelled was a curious method which he invented of etching on copper; in this his technique was entirely his own and has neither been adopted by others nor ever seen again; it consists of strokes and smaller strokes, and irregular lines without a general outline, which nevertheless produce a deep and powerful effect of *chiaroscuro*. And in truth the teachers of art praise Rembrandt far more for his etching than for his painting in which he seems to have had more luck than talent. Most of his etchings are signed with the name Rembrandt in badly formed characters. These etchings brought him a fortune which went to his head; thinking that his works did not fetch the price they deserved, he decided to increase their desirability and at incredible cost he started to buy them back throughout Europe, wherever he could find them and at whatever price: he bought, among others, an etching of his at an Amsterdam auction sale for fifty crowns; it was a *Resurrection of Lazarus* and, in time, he also bought back the original block which he had etched. In the end he so depleted his fortune through his extravagance that he had nothing left: and what rarely happens to other painters happened to him: he was bankrupt; he left Amsterdam and offered his services to the King of Sweden and died there in misery about the year 1670. This is all we have been able to gather about this painter from those who knew him well. We do not know whether he persevered in his chosen religion. There are still several painters who were once his pupils: the above-mentioned Bernard Keillh of Denmark and Guobert Flynk of Amsterdam: these showed the master's influence in their use of colour but the outline of their figures was better; finally among his pupils was the painter Gerard Dou of Leiden.

FILIPPO BALDINUCCI, *Notizie de' professori del disegno da Cimabue in qua*, Florence, 1681–1728

"Rembrandt was still alive [in 1666]: he was a painter who dealt with all subjects and executed many portraits. All his pictures are painted in a very personal style, quite different from the usual highly polished style of the Flemish painters. He often used nothing but sweeping brushstrokes, applying the colours close together but not bothering to blend them together. Nevertheless tastes vary and his works are admired by many. It is true, however, that he has great talent and that he has painted some very beautiful heads: although his brush does not flatter them, they are very powerful and when looked at from a distance their effect is pleasing and striking."

"Certainly," said Pimandre, "the portraits by this painter are quite different from those of Van Dyck: the qualities which one looks for in a fine head and which you mentioned yourself, are not, in my opinion, to be found in Rembrandt's heads. Not so long ago I was shown one where all the colours had been applied separately and where the brushstrokes were so thick that the face itself looked horrific when you looked at it closely. And as one should not need to look at a simple drawing from a distance I fail to see how one can get any satisfaction from looking at such badly finished pictures."

"This is not the case with all the works of this man," I replied. "He is so skilful in putting together tones and half-tones and has such feeling for light and shade that even when he has painted a picture so gross as to make one believe that it is only half-sketched, the picture becomes a success when, as I said before, one looks at it from a slight distance. In fact from a distance the thick brushstrokes which you have noticed become thinner and merge together to produce the intended effect.

The distance needed to look properly at a painting is not just in function of the greatest space and ease which the eyes have to gather the objects and comprise them together, but also because it puts a greater density of atmosphere between the eye and the object.

"Do you mean," interrupted Pimandre, "a greater density of atmosphere will make all the colours of a painting appear merged together, to use your own words?"

"What happens", I replied, "is that whatever the amount of care which goes into a painting, each part of it will necessarily be composed of an infinity of different tones which will always remain, to some extent, distinct and separate; these tones will have difficulty in blending together, just as some natural bodies do. And it is equally true to say that when a picture is painted to perfection, it can be looked at from a lesser distance and will only

seem more intense and beautiful, as is the case with Correggio's paintings. But it is for this reason that I have pointed out to you that the skilful blending of colours contributes greatly to the power and truthfulness of a picture, as does a greater or lesser distance.

"Let us please go back to that painter; his style which is so far removed from that of others has removed us from him."

"Not only is his painting different from that of others," I replied, "but he has also produced etchings which are entirely personal in style. From these have been made many extremely original prints and, among other things, some really beautiful portraits, quite different, as I have said, from the usual kind of prints. He died in 1668."

ANDRÉ FÉLIBIEN, *Entretiens sur les vies et sur les ouvrages des plus excellens peintres anciens et modernes*, Paris, 1685

The name Van Rein came from the place where he was born, a village on that branch of the Rhine which passes through Leiden. He was the son of a miller and the pupil of a modest painter of Amsterdam, called Lesman; but such was the quality of his spirit and talent that he acquired a great reputation in his profession. Nevertheless one must not expect to see in his works any precise drawing or a taste for the antique: he himself said that his art was the imitation of nature and, since this included everything, he collected ancient suits of armour, ancient musical instruments, old clothes and a multitude of ancient, embroidered cloths, and he used to say that they were his antiques. In spite of his peculiar style he never stopped to show an interest in the beautiful Italian drawings which he collected, as well as fine prints, but he never learnt from them: which only goes to show how education and habit are the major influences on our lives. Nevertheless he painted many portraits of amazing intensity, grace and truthfulness.

The manner in which his etchings are done is very similar to that of his paintings: it is expressive and spiritual, especially in the portraits which suggest flesh and life. There are about two hundred and eighty prints by him: they are mostly self-portraits and their dates indicate that he was born at the beginning of the century: of all the dates engraved by him on the prints, none goes further back than 1628 nor later than 1659 and four or five show that in 1635 and 1636 he was in Venice.

He was married in Holland and has made an etching of his wife with himself.

He retouched several of his prints up to four or five times in order to change the light and shade and arrive at a finer effect. It seems that he did not much care for white paper as far as the etchings were concerned, for he had a great number of proofs printed onto half-tinted paper, mostly China paper which is reddish in colour; and these proofs are particularly sought after by collectors.

The technique he used in his etching is one which, to my knowledge, has not yet been developed; it has something of the so-called "black" style which, nevertheless, is later than this.

Although he was a man of great intelligence and had become quite wealthy, he was inclined by nature to have dealings with people of humble extraction; and when once someone who was worried about his reputation mentioned this fact to him, he answered: "When I want my spirit to be lifted, I do not turn towards high honours, but towards freedom." And when, one day, he was criticised for his peculiar use of colours which made his paintings so thick, he replied that he was a painter, not a dyer.

He died in Amsterdam in the year 1668.

NOTES ON THE PAINTINGS OF REMBRANDT

Natural talents benefit most from the way in which they are cultivated and the case of Rembrandt is a perfect example of the influence that education and habit have on man. This painter was born endowed with natural genius and powerful spirit; his output was fertile, his thinking subtle and original, his compositions expressive and his feelings intense; but since, with his mother's milk, he had also imbibed the very taste of his own country, and since he had been brought up with an uninterrupted vision of a rather heavy nature, although he later discovered a more perfect truth, his art turned towards the traditional, despite the good seeds which had been implanted in his spirit. Thus does one find in Rembrandt neither a taste for Raphael nor a taste for the antique, neither poetic abandon, nor elegance of design; all one finds is what the character of his country, filtered through a vivid imagination, is capable of producing. This is sometimes redeemed by some brushstroke of genius, but having had no training in the rules of divine proportions, he only too easily falls back into his usual bad taste.

This is the reason why Rembrandt has not painted many historical subjects, although the sharpness of his vision in many of his drawings is as good as can be seen in the works of some of the greatest painters: the great number of drawings which I myself have under my eyes can prove this to anyone desirous of judging for himself. And although his etchings do not have the breadth of vision present in the drawings, they are nevertheless uncommonly beautiful and show a wonderful use of light and shade.

It is true that Rembrandt's talent did not benefit from a selective vision of nature; however he had a wonderful talent for reproducing concrete subjects, as can be seen in the various portraits he made and which can outclass the works of the greatest masters.

Even though his outlines may not be correct, his drawings themselves are full of sensitivity and one can see, in the etched portraits, that each line, just as each brushstroke in the paintings, adds a vivid, life-like character which bespeaks his genius.

He had a supreme feeling for *chiaroscuro*, with the various areas of colour gaining mutual advantage through their very juxtaposition. In his works the roses and reds are no less true to nature or fresh or delicate than in the works of Titian. Both these painters were convinced that certain colours kill one another when too well mixed and therefore one should blend them as little as possible. So they would first of all lay onto the canvas a range of colours harmonious in relation to one another and as close to the true colours of nature as possible; then, by means of light brushstrokes in neutral colours, they would imprint upon this first layer the modelling and freshness of nature. Where they differed was that Titian blended his brushstrokes more carefully whereas Rembrandt kept them virtually separate, as can easily be seen when one looks at his painting closely; if, however, one looks at them from a suitable distance, the brushstrokes and colours appear smoothly blended. This is a method particular to Rembrandt and it is a convincing proof that his talent was not a

matter of chance, for he was supreme master of his colours.

ROGER DE PILES, *Abrégé de la vie des peintres, avec des réflexions sur leurs ouvrages*, Paris, 1699

The year 1606 which produced so many good artists also saw the birth of Rembrant, on 15 June, at Leiden on the Rhine. His father was called Herman Gerritzen van Ryn and owned a mill on the Rhine, between Leyendorp and Koukerk. His mother's name was Neeltje Willems van Zuitbrock, and both parents earned enough to live comfortably.

This Rembrant was an only son and his parents wanted him to learn Latin and become a cultured man, so they sent him to school at Leiden. However his own leaning towards drawing caused them to change their mind and they sent him instead to learn about art from Jakob Izakzen van Zwanenborg, with whom he spent three years; and his progress was such that everyone was amazed and convinced that great things were to be expected from him; thus, so that he would have every opportunity of having a solid base in art, his father took him to P. Lastman in Amsterdam. He stayed there six months after which he spent another few months with Jak. Pinas. At this stage he decided to set up on his own and was rewarded with extraordinary success from the very first. Other critics claim that Rembrant's and Jan Lievensz.'s first teacher was Joris van Schooten.

In those days, while he progressed in his career and lived in his parents' house, he was occasionally visited by art collectors; he was once given by them the name of a nobleman from The Hague to whom it was suggested that he should show and offer to sell a painting which he had just finished. Rembrant went to The Hague on foot, carrying the canvas, and sold it for one hundred florins.

This brilliant beginning made him see the possibility of making money and his output increased and earned him the admiration of all the experts; he had, as the expression goes, his hands full. Later, as he was often compelled to go to Amsterdam to paint portraits and other pictures which he was commissioned to do, he thought it more convenient to settle there, as the city seemed particularly kind to him and his success there was ensured. His move to Amsterdam took place about the year 1630.

Commissions for pictures flocked in from every part of the city and a crowd of pupils started to gather around him: to cope with this he rented a warehouse in the Bloemgracht in which each pupil was given a room, often divided from the others by a paper wall or a curtain, so that they could each work in privacy and without disturbing the others. But young men often play tricks, especially when there are a lot of them living together, and this was the case even then. When one of them happened to have a female model he would take her to his room; his friends, burning with curiosity, would file on bare feet to look at them through a gap which had been arranged for that very purpose in the dividing wall. And so it happened on one warm summer day that both the painter and the model had stripped off their clothes, and the jokes and pleasantries they exchanged were easily heard by the other apprentices. In the meantime Rembrant, who had come to check on the progress of his pupils and give them his advice, came up to the room where these two were sitting close together in a state of nature. He found the door locked but was told by the others what was going on and observed them at play through the gap in the wall, until he heard them say among other things:

"Here we are, naked like Adam and Eve in the Garden of Eden." At this point Rembrant banged on the door with a stick and shouted, to the culprits' terror: "But because you are aware that you are naked you must come out of the Garden of Eden." Then he forced his pupil to open the door, putting an end to the Adam and Eve duet, and turning the comedy into a drama, he chased them with his stick so furiously that they had hardly time to slip into some clothes as they ran down the stairs.

As an artist he was imaginative and this is why one often sees several sketches by him for the same subject; he was also prolific in painting facial expressions and costumes. In this he deserves greater praise than anyone else, especially when one compares him to those who are eternally reproducing the same faces and costumes in their pictures, as if all men looked exactly the same. I know of no other artist who has introduced so many variations and so many different aspects of one and the same subject. This was the result of careful observation of various passions and these are recognisable in the facial expressions and in the attitudes of his characters. Collectors of drawings may be familiar with the various sketches – not including the prints – of the scene in which Christ is recognised by his two disciples at Emmaus; there are also several sketches of the amazed disciples as they realise that it is Christ who has appeared before them. I have myself etched and reproduced here, as an example to young and inexperienced painters, one of these sketches which I admire particularly for the extraordinary expression of amazement which is imprinted on the faces turning towards the empty seat in which Christ had just been sitting before he disappeared.

It is, however, to be deplored that Rembrandt, with his tendency to change and turn to some new experience, only half-finished a great number of his paintings and a still greater number of his etchings; only the ones he did finish can give us an idea of the beauty we could have expected of his works had he completed them as he had started them: this is particularly evident in the "Hundred Guilder Print" whose technique leaves me breathless, unable as I am to understand how he was able to complete it after such a cursory sketch. This technique can also be seen in his *Portrait of Lutma* of which there exist a first state, a second state with added background, and finally a completed state.

His paintings are created in a similar way; I have seen several examples in which certain details are painted with the utmost care, whilst the rest of the picture looks as if it has been painted with a whitewashing brush, without the slightest regard for the drawing itself. But he pretended by way of justifying himself, that a picture is finished when the painter feels that he has expressed his intention in it; he carried this concept to such lengths that, in order to concentrate the maximum effect on a single pearl, he deleted from one of his paintings, the whole figure of Cleopatra . . .

With regard to this I should like to report an example of his extravagance. One day he was working on a large collective portrait representing a husband with his wife and children. He had almost finished it when his pet monkey died: as he did not have another canvas at hand he added a portrait of the dead monkey to the picture he was painting. Naturally the couple who had commissioned their collective portrait could not bear to see that repulsive object depicted next to themselves; but the painter was so taken with the effect produced by the monkey's dead

body that rather than delete it to please his clients, he decided to keep the painting for himself without completing it and he used it for long as a dividing wall between two of his students' cubicles.

Nonetheless many of his paintings, carefully executed and finished, can be seen in the foremost collections; several of these which were bought at high prices, were brought to Italy and France a few years ago.

I have noticed among other things that he took greater care and patience over his paintings as a young man than he did in later life. This is particularly evident in the well-known picture of St Peter's boat [no. 102] which was hung for a long time in the office of the burgomaster Jan Jakobzen Hinloopen in Amsterdam: the attitudes and expressions of the characters are painted with the utmost faithfulness to nature and at the same time the painting as a whole is executed with much greater care than is usually seen in this painter's works. There is in the same collection another painting by Rembrant, *Ahasuerus, Esther and Haman at Table* [perhaps no. 390] which was praised by a discerning connoisseur, the poet Jan Vos.

Of similar execution is the picture *The Woman Taken in Adultery* [*Christ and the Woman Taken in Adultery*, no. 256] which belongs to Willem Six, Dean of the Council of the city of Amsterdam; also the picture representing St John the Baptist preaching [no. 140], painted in monochrome and admirable for the lifted faces of the people listening and for the variety of costumes; this painting belongs to the Director of Posts, Johan Six of Amsterdam.

In spite of this I must point out that he lent great importance to the things I have mentioned and did not worry about the rest; I am certain of this for many of his pupils told me that quite often he would sketch a face in ten different ways before painting it onto the canvas, or that he would spend a whole day or even two arranging the folds of a turban until he was satisfied. As far as nudes were concerned he was not usually so careful and generally painted them rapidly; it is rare to see in his works a beautifully painted hand because, especially in portraits, he would put the hands in shadow or simply reproduce the hand of some lined old woman.

In his female nudes – a most wonderful subject and one which has always fascinated the most famous artists – he has produced such pitiful things that they are hardly worth mentioning: they are invariably repellent and one can only ask oneself with amazement how a man of such talent and intelligence could be so stubborn in his choice of models.

Karel van Mander reports that Michelangelo [da Caravaggio] used to assert that a painting, whatever its subject-matter and whoever its author, is a fatuous and childish thing if it is not painted from nature; that there is nothing preferable to following nature: and for this reason he never attempted a single brushstroke without a living model before his eyes. Our great Rembrant was of the same opinion and was indeed faithful to the principle that one must follow only nature: anything else was worthless in his eyes.

Rembrant could never have been bound by rules dictated by others, nor could he have followed the example of the artists whose way of reproducing beauty has made them famous; he was content with imitating nature as he saw it and without any pedantry . . .

In his lifetime his works were so highly valued and sought after that, as has often been said, one had not only to pay him, but to beg him as well. For years he was so overwhelmed with commissions that his clients had to wait for a long time although, especially in the latter part of his life, he worked so fast that, upon close inspection, his paintings seem to have been executed with a builder's trowel. Visitors to his studio were often prevented from looking too closely at a painting by Rembrant saying: "The smell of the paint may do you harm." It is said that he once painted a portrait so thick that the canvas could be lifted by holding on to the nose on the face of the sitter. In his paintings one can see precious stones and pearls on necklaces and turbans, and these are applied so thick that they seem to have been done in relief; it is for this reason that his paintings have such strong effect on people, even when looked at from a distance.

Among his many superb portraits is a self-portrait [no. 436?] which belongs to Jan van Beuningen, painted with such skill and vigour that the most splendid paintings of Van Dyck or Rubens cannot come near it: the head seems actually to stand out from the painting and turn towards the onlooker. Just as powerful is the self-portrait [no. 430] which is in the Grand Duke's Gallery in Florence.

Enough has been said about the paintings. I should now like to discuss – although this biography is longer than has been allowed – his peerless etchings which alone would have been enough to make him famous. Several hundreds of them are known to print collectors, and a similar number of pen drawings on paper. . . . Among many, one of the most extraordinary is *The Last Supper* which I saw when it belonged to the collector van der Schelling and which now belongs to Willem Six whom I have often mentioned; it is valued at more than twenty ducats although it is just a pen sketch on paper. . . . He etched many comical subjects, figures, portraits, as well as a great number of male and female faces, by means of a single needle, not usually very accurately, and had them made into prints to be sold to his admirers.

He also invented a personal method of elaborating and finishing the blocks he etched; as he did not teach his pupils this method, it is impossible to establish how it was done. Thus the invention was buried with the inventor, just as it happened with the method of painting on glass, used by Dirk and Wouter Crabet of Gouda.

For instance three different versions of the Portrait of *Lutma* are known: one barely sketched, another slightly more elaborated, in which can be seen the outline of a window, and finally the finished version which is very carefully and vigorously done. In the case of the *Portrait of Silvius* too, one can see that it was first etched as a sketch, then the shading and stronger strokes were added in such a way as could have been obtained with half-tones.

These works brought him great fame and a sizeable fortune, especially thanks to his method of putting in slight changes or small additions so that his prints could be sold as new. In fact there came to be such a demand for them that no true connoisseur could possibly be without both versions of *Juno* – with and without the Crown – or *Joseph* with his head in the light and with his head in shadow and so on. All connoisseurs had to have *The Woman by the Stove* – which in itself is one of the less important etchings – in both versions, with and without the key, although he himself had sold the etching through his son Titus as he considered it too unimportant to deal with himself.

Apart from this he had such a vast number of pupils – each of whom paid him one hundred florins a year – that Sandraert who knew him personally, asserts that he can value the income he received from his students to over 2,500 florins a year. Yet his love of money was such (I do not mean by this that he was particularly greedy) that his pupils would often for fun paint onto the pavement or elsewhere on his way, coins worth one or two bits or a shilling, so that he would try to pick them up, and it was without the slightest embarrassment that he discovered his error. Truly having money does not appease the desire for it.

We must add to this all that he earned with his brush; for he asked exhorbitant prices for his paintings. Undoubtedly he saved vast sums of money, especially as he did not spend much in taverns or banquets, and still less for his house where he lived very simply, often eating just bread and cheese, or salted herring. Nevertheless he does not seem to have left a large inheritance when he died.

His wife was a countrywoman from Raarep or Ransdorp, near Waterland, quite short in stature but with a well-defined face and plump figure. Her portrait can be seen next to the artist's in an etching.

Towards the end of his life he frequented practically only lower-class people and fellow artists. Perhaps he was acquainted with the principles of the art of living as expressed by Gracian: "It is a good thing to frequent people of distinction so as to become one oneself; but once this aim has been reached, it is a good thing to mix with common people", and for this he gave the following reason: "If I want to improve my mind I shall seek not honours but freedom."

ARNOLD HOUBRAKEN, *De Groote Schouburg der Nederlantsche Konstschilders en Schilderessen*, Amsterdam, 1718–1720

The paintings in colour

List of plates

PLATE I
Tobit, Anna and the Kid (no. 4)
1626

PLATE II
Two Scholars Disputing (no. 17)
1628

PLATE III
The Risen Christ at Emmaus
(no. 22)
1628-9

PLATE IV
Self-Portrait with a Gorget
(no. 29)
c. 1629

PLATE V
The Apostle Peter Denying Christ
(no. 21)
1628

PLATE VI
Rembrandt's Mother as a
Prophetess (no. 40)
c. 1630

PLATE VII
Jeremiah Foreseeing the
Destruction of Jerusalem (no. 53)
1630

PLATES VIII–IX
The Anatomy Lesson of Dr Tulp
(no. 81)
1632

PLATE X
Scholar Reading (no. 56)
1631

PLATE XI
Scholar in Meditation (no. 57)
c. 1631

PLATE XII
The Descent from the Cross
(no. 145)
c. 1634

PLATE XIII
Portrait of a Young Lady with a
Fan (no. 89)
1632

PLATE XIV
Bust of a Man in Oriental Costume
(no. 176)
1635

PLATE XV
Samson Blinded by the Philistines
(no. 184)
1636

PLATE XVI
Belshazzar's Feast (no. 180)
c. 1635

PLATE XVII
King Uzziah Stricken with
Leprosy (no. 177)
1635

PLATE XVIII
Tobit Healed by his Son (no. 183)
1636

PLATE XIX
Portrait of Saskia Laughing
(no. 111)
1633

PLATE XX
Portrait of a Man in Polish
Costume (no. 205)
1637

PLATE XXI
Portrait of Saskia in a Hat
(no. 158)
c. 1634

PLATE XXII
The Entombment of Christ
(no. 224)
1639

PLATE XXIII
The Holy Family (no. 227)
1640

PLATE XXIV
Portrait of Cornelis Claeszoon
Anslo with a Woman (no. 236)
1641

PLATE XXV
Portrait of Maria Trip (no. 221)
1639

PLATE XXVI
Portrait of Agatha Bas (no. 238)
1641

PLATE XXVII
Portrait of Saskia with a Pink
(no. 239)
1641

PLATES XXVIII–XXIX
The Night Watch (no. 246)
1642

PLATE XXX
Allegory of the Concord of the
State (no. 243)
1641

PLATE XXXI
Young Girl at a Window
(no. 267)
1645

PLATE XXXII
The Adoration of the Shepherds
(no. 272)
1646

PLATE XXXIII
The Risen Christ at Emmaus
(no. 287)
1648

PLATE XXXIV
Portrait of Hendrickje in Bed
(no. 285)
c. 1648

PLATE XXXV
Girl at a Window (no. 308)
1651

PLATE XXXVI
The Man with the Golden
Helmet (no. 299)
c. 1650

PLATE XXXVII
Aristotle Contemplating a Bust of
Homer (no. 316)
1653

PLATE XXXVIII
Old Man in Sumptuous Dress
(no. 309)
1651

PLATE XXXIX
Portrait of Nicolas Bruyningh
(no. 315)
1652

PLATE XL
Young Woman Bathing in a
Stream (no. 334)
1655

PLATE XLI
Bathsheba with David's Letter
(no. 317)
1654

PLATE XLII
Portrait of Titus Studying
(no. 335)
1655

PLATE XLIII
Jacob Blessing Joseph's Children
(no. 344)
1656

PLATE XLIV
Portrait of Titus Reading
(no. 351)
1656-7

PLATE XLV
Portrait of Hendrickje at a
Window (no. 350)
1656-7

PLATE XLVI
The Waiting of Tobit and Anna
(no. 371)
1659

PLATE XLVII
Jupiter and Mercury Visiting
Philemon and Baucis (no. 370)
1658

PLATE XLVIII
Self-Portrait with a Stick
(no. 366)
1658

PLATE XLIX
Portrait of Titus Dressed as a
Monk (no. 384)
1660

PLATE L
Self-Portrait at the Easel (no. 380)
1660

PLATE LI
The Apostle Peter Denying Christ
(no. 392)
1660

PLATES LII-LIII
The Sampling Officials of the
Draper's Guild (no. 424)
1662

PLATE LIV
St Matthew and the Angel
(no. 407)
1661

PLATE LV
Two Negroes (no. 414)
1661

PLATE LVI
The Oath of the Batavians
(no. 415)
1661

PLATE LVII
Portrait of Titus in a Beret
(no. 429)
c. 1663

PLATE LVIII
Juno (no. 432)
1664-5

PLATE LIX
The Jewish Bride (no. 434)
c. 1665

PLATES LX-LXI
Family Portrait (no. 448)
1668-9

PLATE LXII
Portrait of a Man in a Tall
Hat, with Gloves (no. 443)
c. 1668

PLATE LXIII
Portrait of a Lady Holding an
Ostrich-Feather Fan (no. 444)
c. 1668

PLATE LXIV
Self-Portrait Laughing (no. 436)
c. 1665

Cover Illustration Detail of *Young
Girl at a Window* (no. 267)

PLATE I   TOBIT, ANNA AND THE KID [no. 4]
Amsterdam, Rijksmuseum (39.5×30 cm.)

PLATE II TWO SCHOLARS DISPUTING [no. 17]
Melbourne, National Gallery of Victoria (72.5×60 cm.)

PLATE III   THE RISEN CHRIST AT EMMAUS [no. 22]
Paris, Musée Jacquemart-André (39×42 cm.)

PLATE IV   SELF-PORTRAIT WITH A GORGET   [no. 29]
The Hague, Mauritshuis (37.5×29 cm.)

PLATE V   THE APOSTLE PETER DENYING CHRIST [no. 21]
Tokyo, Bridgestone Museum of Art (21.5×16.5 cm.)

PLATE VI REMBRANDT'S MOTHER AS A PROPHETESS [no. 40]
Essen, Von Bohlen und Halbach Collection (35×29 cm.)

PLATE VII JEREMIAH FORESEEING THE DESTRUCTION OF JERUSALEM [no. 53]
Amsterdam, Rijksmuseum (58×46 cm.)

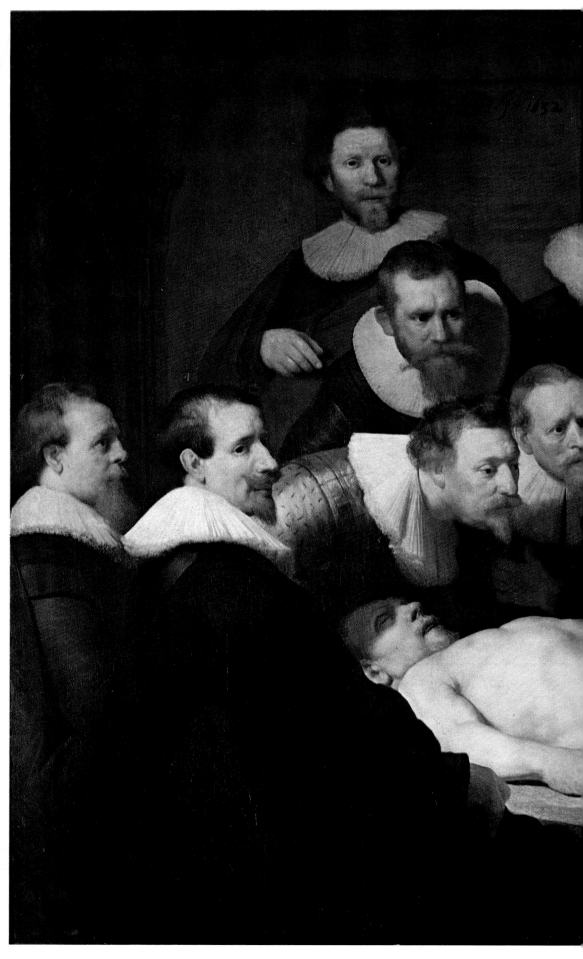

THE ANATOMY LESSON OF DR TULP [no. 81]
The Hague, Mauritshuis (169.5×216.5 cm.)

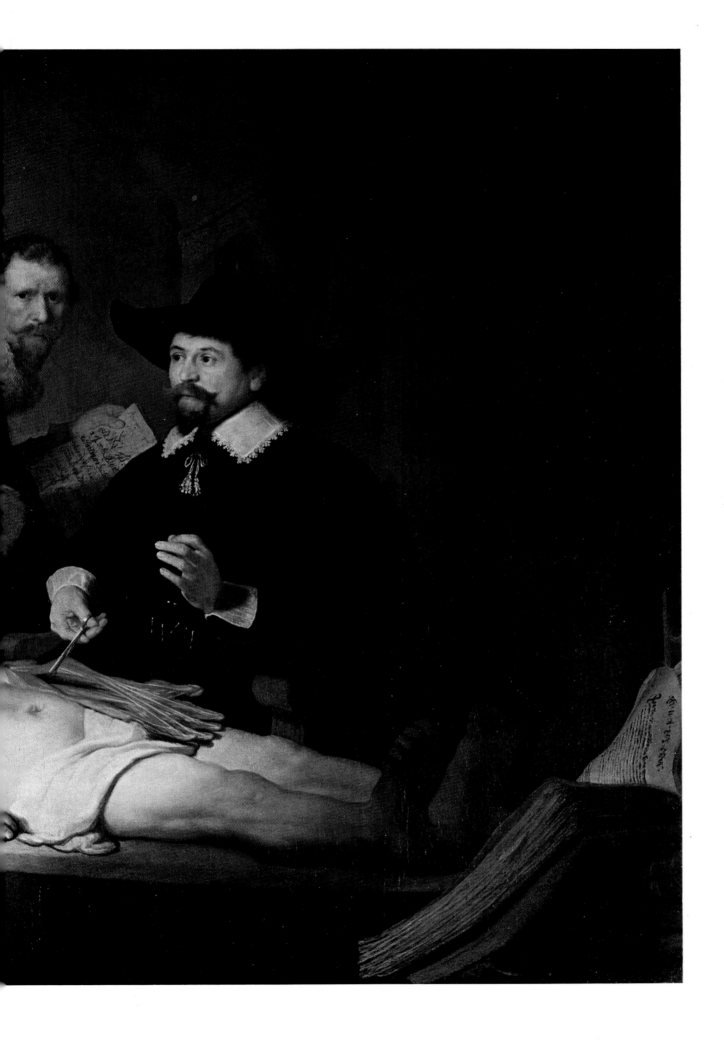

PLATE X   SCHOLAR READING   [no. 56]
Stockholm, Nationalmuseum (60×48 cm.)

PLATE XI SCHOLAR IN MEDITATION [no. 57]
Paris, Musée du Louvre (29×33 cm.)

PLATE XII   THE DESCENT FROM THE CROSS   [no. 145]
Munich, Alte Pinakothek (89.5×65 cm.)

PLATE XIII   PORTRAIT OF A YOUNG LADY WITH A FAN   [no. 89]
Stockholm, Nationalmuseum (72×54 cm.)

PLATE XIV   BUST OF A MAN IN ORIENTAL COSTUME   [no. 176]
Amsterdam, Rijksmuseum (72×54.5 cm.)

PLATE XV   SAMSON BLINDED BY THE PHILISTINES [no. 184]
Frankfurt, Städelsches Kunstinstitut (236×302 cm.)

PLATE XVI   BELSHAZZAR'S FEAST [no. 180]
London, National Gallery (167.5×209 cm.)

PLATE XVII   KING UZZIAH STRICKEN WITH LEPROSY [no. 177]
Chatsworth (Derbyshire), Devonshire Collection (101.5×77 cm.)

PLATE XVIII   TOBIT HEALED BY HIS SON   [no. 183]
Stuttgart, Staatsgalerie (47×39 cm.)

PLATE XIX   PORTRAIT OF SASKIA LAUGHING [no. 111]
Dresden, Staatliche Kunstsammlungen (52.5×44.5 cm.)

PLATE XX   PORTRAIT OF A MAN IN POLISH COSTUME [no. 205]
Washington, D. C., National Gallery of Art (97×66.5 cm.)

PLATE XXI   PORTRAIT OF SASKIA IN A HAT [no. 158]
Cassel, Staatliche Kunstsammlungen (99.5×79 cm.)

PLATE XXII   THE ENTOMBMENT OF CHRIST [no. 224]
Munich, Alte Pinakothek (92.5×69 cm.)

PLATE XXIII   THE HOLY FAMILY [no. 227]
Paris, Musée du Louvre (41×34 cm.)

PLATE XXIV   PORTRAIT OF CORNELIUS CLAESZOON ANSLO WITH A WOMAN   [no. 236]
Berlin, Staatliche Museen (176×210 cm.)

PLATE XXV PORTRAIT OF MARIA TRIP [no. 221]
Amsterdam, Rijksmuseum (107×82 cm.)

PLATE XXVI   PORTRAIT OF AGATHA BAS   [no. 238]
London, Buckingham Palace (105.5×84 cm.)

PLATE XXVII PORTRAIT OF SASKIA WITH A PINK [no. 239]
Dresden, Staatliche Kunstsammlungen (98.5×82.5 cm.)

THE NIGHT WATCH [no. 246]
Amsterdam, Rijksmuseum (359×438 cm.)

PLATE XXX   ALLEGORY OF THE CONCORD OF THE STATE [no. 243]
Rotterdam, Museum Boymans-van Beuningen (74.5×101 cm.)

PLATE XXXI   YOUNG GIRL AT A WINDOW [no. 267]
London, Dulwich College (77.5×62.5 cm.)

PLATE XXXII   THE ADORATION OF THE SHEPHERDS   [no. 272]
London, National Gallery (66.5×55 cm.)

PLATE XXXIII   THE RISEN CHRIST AT EMMAUS [no. 287]
Paris, Musée du Louvre (68×65 cm.)

PLATE XXXIV   PORTRAIT OF HENDRICKJE IN BED   [no. 285]
Edinburgh, National Gallery of Scotland (81×67 cm.)

PLATE XXXV   GIRL AT A WINDOW [no. 308]
Stockholm, Nationalmuseum (78×63 cm.)

PLATE XXXVI   THE MAN WITH THE GOLDEN HELMET   [no. 299]
Berlin, Staatliche Museen (67×50 cm.)

PLATE XXXVII   ARISTOTLE CONTEMPLATING A BUST OF HOMER [no. 316]
New York, Metropolitan Museum of Art (143.5×136.5 cm.)

PLATE XXXVIII   OLD MAN IN SUMPTUOUS DRESS [no. 309]
Chatsworth (Derbyshire), Devonshire Collection (79×76 cm.)

PLATE XXXIX   PORTRAIT OF NICOLAES BRUYNINGH   [no. 315]
Cassel, Staatliche Kunstsammlungen (107.5×91.5 cm.)

PLATE XL   YOUNG WOMAN BATHING IN A STREAM [no. 334]
London, National Gallery (62×47 cm.)

PLATE XLI   BATHSHEBA WITH DAVID'S LETTER   [no. 317]
Paris, Musée du Louvre (142×142 cm.)

PLATE XLII   PORTRAIT OF TITUS STUDYING   [no. 335]
Rotterdam, Museum Boymans-van Beuningen (77×63 cm.)

PLATE XLIII   JACOB BLESSING JOSEPH'S CHILDREN [no. 344]
Cassel, Staatliche Kunstsammlungen (177.5×210.5 cm.)

PLATE XLIV PORTRAIT OF TITUS READING [no. 351]
Vienna, Kunsthistorisches Museum (70.5×64 cm.)

PLATE XLV   PORTRAIT OF HENDRICKJE AT A WINDOW   [no. 350]
Berlin, Staatliche Museen (86×65 cm.)

PLATE XLVI   THE WAITING OF TOBIT AND ANNA [no. 371]
Rotterdam, Stichting W. van der Vorm (40.5×54 cm.)

PLATE XLVIII   SELF-PORTRAIT WITH A STICK [no. 366]
New York, Frick Collection (133.5×104 cm.)

PLATE XLIX   PORTRAIT OF TITUS DRESSED AS A MONK   [no. 384]
Amsterdam, Rijksmuseum (79.5×67.5 cm.)

PLATE L   SELF-PORTRAIT AT THE EASEL   [no. 380]
Paris, Musée du Louvre (111×85 cm.)

PLATE LI   THE APOSTLE PETER DENYING CHRIST [no. 392]
Amsterdam, Rijksmuseum (154×169 cm.)

THE SAMPLING OFFICIALS OF THE DRAPERS' GUILD   [no. 424]
Amsterdam, Rijksmuseum (191.5×279 cm.)

PLATE LIV   ST MATTHEW AND THE ANGEL [no. 407]
Paris, Musée du Louvre (96×81 cm.)

PLATE LV   TWO NEGROES [no. 414]
The Hague, Mauritshuis (78×64.5 cm.)

PLATE LVII   PORTRAIT OF TITUS IN A BERET   [no. 429]
London, Dulwich College (73×60 cm.)

PLATE LVIII   JUNO [no. 432]
New York, Middendorf Collection (127×123 cm.)

PLATE LIX   THE JEWISH BRIDE [no. 434]
Amsterdam, Rijksmuseum (121.5×166.5 cm.)

FAMILY PORTRAIT [no. 448]
Brunswick, Staatliches Herzog Anton Ulrich-Museum (126×167 cm.)

PLATE LXII   PORTRAIT OF A MAN IN A TALL HAT, WITH GLOVES [no. 443]
Washington, D. C., National Gallery of Art (99.5×83.5 cm.)

PLATE LXIII   PORTRAIT OF A LADY HOLDING AN OSTRICH-FEATHER FAN   [no. 444]
Washington, D. C., National Gallery of Art (100×83 cm.)

PLATE LXIV   SELF-PORTRAIT LAUGHING   [no. 436]
Cologne, Wallraf-Richartz-Museum (82.5×65 cm.)

The works

Key to symbols used

Grade of authenticity

⊞ Autograph

⊞ Widely attributed

⊞ Perhaps with collaboration

⊞ With collaboration

⊞ With wide collaboration

⊞ Included with reservations because of poor state of painting

⊞ No judgment possible because painting inaccessible

▨ Recently published, no critical opinion available

⊞ Doubtful authenticity

⊞ Widely excluded

Technique and support

⊘ Oil on panel

⊘ Oil on canvas

⊘ Oil on paper

⊘ Oil on copper

⊘ Information given in the text

Other data

▤ Signed

▤ Dated

▤ Signed and dated

▤ Mutilated (or fragment)

▬ Mutilated (or fragment), signed

▤ Mutilated (or fragment), dated

▤ Mutilated (or fragment), signed and dated

▤ Work in which none of the above signs apply

Whereabouts

⦙ Public collection

⦙ Private collection

⦙ Whereabouts unknown

Bibliography

General catalogues of Rembrandt's paintings in their order of publication

JS 1836   J. Smith, *A Catalogue raisonné of the works of the most eminent Dutch, Flemish and French painters*, vol. VII, London 1836
BH 1897–1905   W. Bode and C. Hofstede de Groot, *Rembrandt: beschreibendes Verzeichnis Gemälde mit den heliographischen Nachbildungen*, Paris 1897–1905
V 1909   W. R. Valentiner, *Rembrandt: des Meister Gemälde*, Stuttgart 1909
HdG 1915   C. Hofstede de Groot, *Beschreibendes und Kritisches Verzeichnis der Werke der hervorragendsten Holländischen Maler des XVII Jahrhunderts*, vol. VI, Stuttgart 1915
V 1921   W. R. Valentiner, *Rembrandt: wiedergefundene Gemälde*, Stuttgart 1921
B 1935   A. Bredius, *Rembrandt: sämtliche Gemälde*, Vienna 1935 (second edition, London 1936)
B 1966   K. Bauch, *Rembrandt Gemälde*, Berlin 1966
G 1968   H. Gerson, *Rembrandt Paintings*, New York 1968
BG 1969   A. Bredius, *Rembrandt, The Complete Edition of the Paintings*, revised by H. Gerson, London 1969

General catalogues of the etchings and drawings
M 1952   L. Münz, *The Etchings of Rembrandt*, London 1952
B 1954–7   O. Benesch, *The Drawings of Rembrandt*, London 1954–7

General works
A 1952   R. Avermaete, *Rembrandt et son temps*, Paris 1952
B 1957   O. Benesch, *Rembrandt*, Geneva 1957
BH 1969   B. Haak, *Rembrandt: His Life, His Work, His Time*, New York 1969
G 1948   H. E. van Gelder, *Rembrandt*, Amsterdam 1948
H 1932   A. M. Hind, *Rembrandt*, Cambridge 1932

H 1948   R. Hamann, *Rembrandt*, Potsdam 1948
K 1956   G. Knuttell, *Rembrandt*, Amsterdam 1956
M 1893   E. Michel, *Rembrandt: sa vie, son oeuvre et son temps*, Paris 1893
M 1954   L. Münz, *Rembrandt Harmensz. van Rijn*, New York 1954
M 1968   J.-E. Muller, *Rembrandt*, Paris 1968
N 1902   C. Neumann, *Rembrandt*, Berlin 1902
R 1948   J. Rosenberg, *Rembrandt*, Cambridge (Mass.) 1948
V 1877   C. Vosmaer, *Rembrandt: sa vie et ses oeuvres*, The Hague 1877
V 1906   J. Veth, *Rembrandt Leven en Kunst*, Amsterdam 1906
V 1956   A. B. de Vries, *Rembrandt*, Baarn 1956
W 1926   W. Weisbach, *Rembrandt*, Berlin 1926
W 1964   C. White, *Rembrandt and his World*, London 1964

Particular studies
B 1959   J. Bruyn, *Rembrandts keuze van bijbelse onderwerpen*, Utrecht 1959
B 1960   K. Bauch, *Der frühe Rembrandt und seine Zeit*, Berlin 1960
C 1966   K. Clark, *Rembrandt and the Italian Renaissance*, London 1966
E. 1967   F. Erpel, *Die Selbstbildnisse Rembrandts*, Vienna 1967
G 1961   H. Gerson, *Seven Letters by Rembrandt*, The Hague 1961
HdG 1906   C. Hofstede de Groot, *Die Urkunden über Rembrandt*, The Hague 1906
HdG 1922   C. Hofstede de Groot *Die holländische Kritik der jetzigen Rembrandtforschung*, Stuttgart 1922
L 1932   A. P. Laurie, *The Brushwork of Rembrandt and his School*, London 1932
S 1953   S. Slive, *Rembrandt and his Critics 1630–1730*, The Hague 1953
T 1968   C. Tümpel, *Studien zur Ikonographie der Historien Rembrandts*, Hamburg 1968
V 1931   W. R. Valentiner, *Rembrandt Paintings in America*, New York 1931

Abbreviations

Various articles mentioned in the text
Authors
AB   A. Bredius
CHCB   C. H. Collins Baker
CJH   C. J. Holmes
CT   C. Tümpel
EK   E. Kieser
EP   E. Panofsky
FE   F. Erpel
HdG   C. Hofstede de Groot
HEG   H. E. van Gelder
HFW   H. F. Wijnman
HG   H. Gerson
IB   I. Bergström
IHE   I. H. van Eeghen
JH   J. Held
JIK   J. I. Kusnetzow
JR   J. Rosenberg
JZ   J. Zwarts
KB   K. Bauch
KC   K. Clark
LM   L. Münz
MK   M. Kahr
OB   O. Benesch
SS   S. Slive
VB   V. Bloch

WB   W. Bode
WRV   W. R. Valentiner
WS   W. Scheidegg

Reviews
AiA   *Art in America*
ABu   *Art Bulletin*
BCP   *Bulletin of the California Palace of the Legion of Honor Museum*
BM   *Burlington Magazine*
BME   *Bulletin du Musée de l'Ermitage*
BMML *Bulletin des Musées et monuments lyonnais*
DIAB   *Detroit Institute of Art Bulletin*
JPK   *Jahrbuch der preussischen Kunstsammlungen*
KCH   *Kunstchronik*
MA   *Maandblad Amstelodamum*
NKJ   *Nederlands Kunsthistorisch Jaarboek*
OH   *Oud Holland*
P   *Pantheon*
SZK   *Studien zur Kunstgeschichte*
ZBK   *Zeitschrift für bildende Kunst*
ZFK   *Zeitschrift für Kunstgeschichte*

Outline biography

1606 15 July Traditional date
(according to Orlers' statement,
see p. 8) of Rembrandt's birth
in the university city of Leiden.
The city numbered about
40,000 inhabitants and was
situated 43 kilometres south-
west of Amsterdam, on the
banks of one of the minor
branches of the Rhine, which
was itself divided into two
branches, the Oude Rijn, or
Old Rhine, to the north of the
city, and the Nieuwe Rijn, or
New Rhine, to the south; the
river was subdivided further
into canals and re-formed itself
within the city. Rembrandt
Harmenszoon (literally, "Son of
Harmen", usually abbreviated to
Harmensz.) was the son of
Harmen Gerritszoon van Rijn, a
wealthy miller who had been
converted from catholicism to
calvinism, and of Cornelia
Willemsdochter (literally
"Daughter of Willem", usually
abbreviated to Willemsdr.) van
Zuytbroeck, nicknamed Neeltje
or Neeltgen, a baker's daughter.
The couple had been married
on 8 October 1589 in a
reformed church and lived in a
house which they owned, in
the Weddesteeg.

Rembrandt was the last but
one of nine children; these
were: Gerrit who, like his
father, became a miller;
Adriaen, who became a shoemaker; two girls who died in
infancy; Machteld; Cornelis;
Willem, a baker; and, after
Rembrandt, Lijsbeth. It appears
that Rembrandt's name was
given him in memory of his
mother's grandmother,
Reijmptje Cornelisdochter van
Banchem, who belonged to
one of the foremost families in
Leiden which had also gone
over to calvinism.

The family name, van Rijn,
had been adopted by
Rembrandt's father because his
windmill was on the bank of
the Oude Rijn.

1613–20 Rembrandt attends
the Latijnse School of Leiden.

1620 20 May He enrols at
the university of Leiden
("Rembrandus Hermanni
leydensis an. 14 stud[iosus]
Litt[erarum] apud parentes"),
but gives it up after a few
months.

Fifteen etched self-portraits. A: 70 × 58 mm., c. 1628.
B: 67 × 54 mm., c. 1628. C: 51 × 46 mm., 1630, first state.
D: 146 - 130 mm., 1631, second state. E: 146 × 118 mm., 1633,
first state. F: 124 × 108 mm., 1634, first state. G: 197 × 162 mm.,
1634, first state (this, like the following, is also held to be a
portrait of Philips van Dorp). H: 130 × 108 mm., same etching as
the preceding, second state. I: 104 × 96 mm., 1636, first state
(self-portrait combined with a portrait of Saskia). J: 134 × 103
mm., 1638. K: 207 × 164 mm., 1639, first state (self-portrait
modelled on Raphael's Portrait of Baldassare Castiglione *and*
Titian's Portrait of Ludovico Ariosto)*. L: 95 × 61 mm., c. 1642–3,*
first state. M: 157 × 128 mm., 1648, second state. N: 111 × 92 mm.,
c. 1651 (self-portrait with other figures). O: 118 × 64 mm., 1658.

1621–3 He is a pupil and
apprentice of the painter Jacob
Isaczoon van Swanenburch
(1571–1638) who had come
back to Leiden in 1617 after a
sojourn of several years in Italy
where he acquired a Neapolitan
wife, Margherita Cordona.
Perhaps soon after this
Rembrandt becomes a friend
of another "Italianate" painter,
Jacob Symonszoon Pynas
(c. 1585–post 1648).
1624 Rembrandt attends, in
Amsterdam and for about six
months, the studio of Pieter
Pieterszoon Lastman (1583–
1633), the best known Dutch
"History" painter of the time,
who had come back in 1610
from a long sojourn in Italy
where he had probably come
into contact with Caravaggio
and his circle.

That same year Rembrandt
returns to Leiden where he
probably completes his
apprenticeship with Joris van
Schooten (1587–1651) and
opens his own studio in his
parents' house in the
Weddesteeg.

1625 Rembrandt's first dated
work, *The Stoning of St
Stephen* (no. 1).

1626 He is joined in his studio
by his near contemporary Jan
Lievens (1607–74), also a
native of Leiden and also a
former pupil of Lastman's.
Lievens, in 1629 or 1631 goes
to England until 1632.

1628 Arnoldus Buchelius (the
Utrecht jurist and art expert,
Arent van Buchell) is, as far as
we know, the first to mention

Rembrandt. He says in his
Res Pictoriae "molitoris . . .
leidensis filius magni fit, sed
ante tempus" (much notice is
given to a miller's son, but it is
too early [to judge]).

1628 14 February Gerrit
(Gerard) Dou (1613–75), the
first of Rembrandt's pupils,
joins his studio.

1628 The first two dated
etchings, two small portraits of
Rembrandt's mother.

83

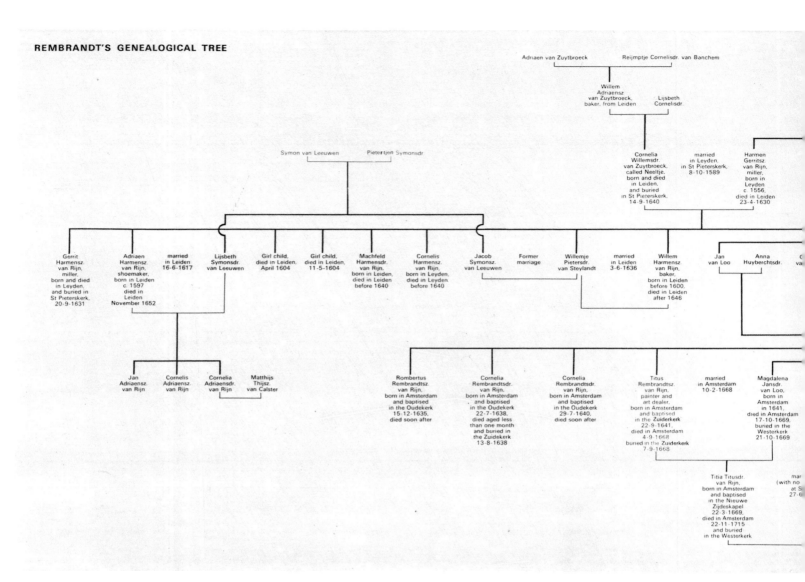

1630 23 April Death of Rembrandt's father.

c. 1630 Constantijn Huygens (see also c. 1634) mentions Rembrandt and Lievens in his diary, stating that "the miller's son and the embroiderer's son" are already "equal to the most famous painters and will soon be superior to them"; a statement which belies the hitherto traditional belief that noble blood had more talent than humble blood. The two young painters' parents' modest means allowed them to have only modest teachers; these, "if they could see today their pupils' works would feel the same sense of shame as the teachers of Virgil, Cicero and Archimedes once did"; the young painters owe nothing to their teachers, for they would have made the same progress without any formal teaching at all. Huygens adds that Lievens has more freshness of invention and spontaneity, whilst Rembrandt is superior in his judgment and the expression of feelings; his small pictures, which are very carefully painted, show a power of expression which cannot be found in his companion. For example, Rembrandt has painted a picture representing *Judas Returning the Thirty Pieces of Silver* (no. 32) which can be equalled to "anything that has been produced in Antiquity and in Italy: here a young boy, the beardless son of a Batavian miller, has proved superior to Protogenes, Appelles and Parrhasius".

1631 First engravings after paintings by Rembrandt, made by Jan Joris van Vliet and Willem van der Leeuw. Soon after this other engravers start reproducing his works; among these are Pieter de Bailiu, Salomon Savery and Hendrick de Thier.

1631 20 June Rembrandt becomes the partner of the Amsterdam art dealer Hendrick van Uylenburch; his contribution to the partnership is of 1000 florins. Soon after this he moves to Amsterdam, a livelier city than Leiden, with its 110,000 inhabitants. He opens his own studio in Uylenburch's house at the corner of the Zwanenburgwal and St Anthonie Breerstraat.

1632 Date of the *Anatomy Lesson of Dr Tulp* (no. 81).

1632 26 July Because of a bet between two men the preceding year (to the effect that one hundred important citizens would or would not be alive the following year — among them Rembrandt, although he had only just become a resident of that city), the painter receives the visit of a solicitor who states that he found him alive and well.

c. 1633 Drawing in red chalk (365 × 475 mm., New York, Lehman Collection), from a simple engraving by Fra Antonio da Monza (230 × 450 mm., London, British Museum), of Leonardo da Vinci's *Last Supper.*

1634 June The German merchant Burchard Grossman visits Hendrick van Uylenburch's shop and Rembrandt writes a few words in the album the German carries with him: "Een vroom gemoet// Acht eer voor goet".

1634 22 July Rembrandt marries his partner's wealthy niece, Saskia van Uylenburch (who brings him a dowry of over 40,000 florins), born in 1612, whose father, Rombertus, died in 1624 after a lifetime of public appointments including those of burgomaster of Leeuwarden and member of the High Court of Justice in Friesland, the region from which this powerful family originated. Saskia's elder sister, Titia, is married to the very wealthy Gerrit van Loo. Rembrandt and Saskia – whom the painter met when she came to visit her uncle in Amsterdam

Drawings by Rembrandt of his father, his mother and Saskia. A: His father shortly before his death; 240 × 189 mm., c. 1630, charcoal, red chalk and watercolour; Oxford, Ashmolean Museum. B: His mother; 240 × 162 mm., c. 1638, red chalk; Paris, Louvre. C: Saskia; 184 × 107 mm., 8 June 1633, silverpoint; Berlin, Kupferstichkabinett; autograph writing by Rembrandt: "This is a drawing of my wife at the age of twenty-one, on the third day after our engagement."

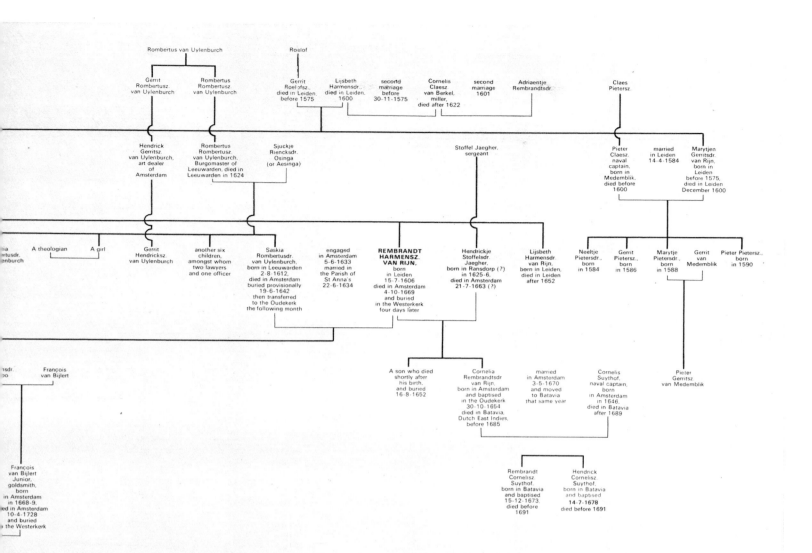

Rombertus van Uylenburch — Roelof

Gerrit Rombertusz. van Uylenburch — Rombertus Rombertusz. van Uylenburch — Gerrit Roelofsz., died in Leiden before 1575 — Lijsbeth Harmensdr., died in Leiden 1600 — second marriage before 30-11-1575 — Cornelis Claesz. van Berkel, miller, died after 1622 — second marriage 1601 — Adriaentje Rembrandtsdr. — Claes Pietersz.

Hendrick Gerritsz. van Uylenburch, art dealer of Amsterdam — Rombertus Rombertusz. van Uylenburch, Burgomaster of Leeuwarden, died in Leeuwarden in 1624 — Sjuckje Rienscksdr. Osinga (or Aesinga) — Stoffel Jaegher, sergeant — Pieter Claesz. naval captain, born in Medemblik, died before 1600 — married in Leiden 14-4-1584 — Marytjen Gerritsdr. van Rijn, born in Leiden before 1575, died in Leiden December 1600

...tia ...rtusdr. ...nburch — A theologian — A girl — Gerrit Hendricksz. van Uylenburch — another six children, amongst whom two lawyers and one officer — Saskia Rombertusdr. van Uylenburch, born in Leeuwarden 2-8-1612, died in Amsterdam buried provisionally 19-6-1642 then transferred to the Oudekerk the following month — engaged in Amsterdam 5-6-1633 married in the Parish of St Anna's 22-6-1634 — **REMBRANDT HARMENSZ. VAN RIJN,** born in Leiden 15-7-1606 died in Amsterdam 4-10-1669 and buried in the Westerkerk four days later — Hendrickje Stoffelsdr. Jaegher, born in Ransdorp (?) in 1625-6, died in Amsterdam 21-7-1663 (?) — Lijsbeth Harmensdr. van Rijn, born in Leiden, died in Leiden after 1652 — Neeltje Pietersdr. born in 1584 — Gerrit Pietersz. born in 1586 — Marytje Pietersdr. born in 1588 — Gerrit van Medemblik — Pieter Pietersz., born in Leiden in 1590

...sdr. ...o — François van Bijlert — A son who died shortly after his birth, and buried 16-8-1652 — Cornelia Rembrandtsdr. van Rijn, born in Amsterdam and baptised in the Oudekerk 30-10-1654 died in Batavia, Dutch East Indies, before 1685 — married in Amsterdam 3-5-1670 and moved to Batavia that same year — Cornelis Suythof, naval captain, born in Amsterdam in 1646, died in Batavia after 1689 — Pieter Gerritsz. van Medemblik

François van Bijlert Junior, goldsmith, born in Amsterdam in 1668-9, ...ed in Amsterdam 10-4-1728 and buried ...the Westerkerk

Rembrandt Cornelisz. Suythof, born in Batavia and baptised 15-12-1673, died before 1691 — Hendrick Cornelisz. Suythof, born in Batavia and baptised 14-7-1678 died before 1691

---

from her native Leeuwarden — had become engaged on 5 June of the preceding year.

Rembrandt and his wife live temporarily in the house of Hendrick van Uylenburch.

c. 1634 Through the intervention of the Stadtholder's secretary, Constantijn Huygens (1596–1687), the lawyer and poet, father of the famous physicist and the mathematician, Christian Huygens, Rembrandt obtains from the

Portrait of Geertje Dircks;
pen and watercolour drawing,
130 × 77 mm., c. 1642,
London, British Museum.

Stadtholder, Prince Frederick Henry, a commission for three pictures representing scenes of the Passion of Christ: the *Ascension* (no. 185), the *Entombment* (no. 224) and the *Resurrection* (no. 225), as a complement to two pictures he had already executed: the *Raising of the Cross* (no. 144) and the *Descent from the Cross* (no. 145), which had been acquired by the prince.

1635 The couple move to a house in the Nieuwe Doelenstraat "next door to that of the pensioner Boereel", writes Rembrandt in his first letter to Constantijn Huygens (see p. 89); today the house bears the numbers 16–18.

1635 December Birth of the painter's first son, Rombertus, who does not live.

c. 1635 Rembrandt's artistic activity is so enormous, and so great is the number of his pupils that he is compelled to move his studio out of Uylenburch's house into vast premises which had been formerly used as a commercial warehouse, in the Bloemgracht. There he both houses and teaches his pupils, even after his own move to a larger house (see 1 May 1639).

1636 February In his first letter to Constantijn Huygens Rembrandt says that he is busy finishing the three Passion paintings commissioned by the Stadtholder (see p. 89).

1638 July Birth of a daughter, Cornelia, who dies before the age of one month.

1638 Saskia's relatives accuse Rembrandt of having squandered his wife's dowry through his own prodigality. The painter's reply is that, quite to the contrary, their joint fortune is considerable, and the quarrel eventually dies out.

1639 January Rembrandt and Saskia go to live in the house of Jan van Veldestijn, owner of the pâtisserie "De Vier Suykerbrooden" in the Binnenamstel (see Rembrandt's third and seventh letters to Huygens, p. 89), which now corresponds to no. 41 Zwanenburgerstraat.

1639 12 January In his third letter to Constantijn Huygens Rembrandt states that he has now finished the last two Passion scenes for the Stadtholder (nos. 224 and 225) and adds that he would like to make Huygens a gift of a painting (no. 184, q.v.). A few days later, he writes again,

saying that he has sent the present (see p. 89).

1639 4 April The art dealer Lucas van Uffelen holds an auction sale of Italian paintings. The wealthy art dealer Alfonso Lopez, a Sephardi Jew, who has had dealings with Rembrandt, buys there, for his own collection, Raphael's *Portrait of Baldassare Castiglione* (now in the Louvre) as a companion piece to Titian's *Portrait of Ludovico Ariosto* (now in the National Gallery), which he had acquired previously. Rembrandt has the opportunity of studying these two paintings; from both he derives a certain formal influence which can be detected in the works of that period, as for example, in his *Self-Portrait in a Frilled Shirt* (no. 233) and in the etched self-portrait of 1639 (see p. 83).

1639 1 May Rembrandt and Saskia (and possibly also the painter's sister, Lijsbeth) move to a large house (eight rooms, two cellars and a vast attic) which they have bought in Sint Anthonies Breerstraat — today nos. 4–6 Jodenbreestraat — next door to Uylenburch's house, near the artists' quarter and on the threshold of the Jewish quarter.

It is a superb and costly house, built in 1607, which Rembrandt has bought from one Christoffel Thijssens for 13,000 florins, a sum which he does not possess, and on which he pays an advance on the understanding that he will pay the remaining three quarters within five or six years.

He is now at the beginning of the richest and happiest period in his life, a period which is to last until Saskia's death. He fills his house with countless works of art — paintings, engravings, sculptures, casts — and curios (ancient or exotic costumes, ancient weapons, helmets, musical instruments, textiles, various strange objects and theatrical props and knick-knacks with which he adorns and disguises his models) which he buys compulsively in public auctions, often paying far beyond their actual value (see the Inventory, pp. 89–90).

The house itself which, since 1911, has been the seat of the Het Rembrandthuis Foundation, a public museum of Rembrandt's works, containing mainly his etchings, is not structurally the same as it was in Rembrandt's lifetime. After the painter was forced to leave the house, the attic was made

Rembrandt and his studio. A: 175 × 232 mm., c. 1648, pen and watercolour drawing; Paris, Louvre. B: 200 × 189 mm., c. 1650, pen and watercolour; Oxford University Museum. C: 121 × 207 mm., c. 1650, pen, Weimar, Staatliche Kunstsammlungen. D: Self-portrait in his working smock; 198 × 133 mm., c. 1654, pen and bistre; Amsterdam, Rembrandtshuis. E: 180 × 266 mm., charcoal and white lead, c. 1650; Darmstadt, Hessisches Landesmuseum. F: The painter and his model; 188 × 161 mm., c. 1647; London, British Museum. Drawings C and E are by pupils of Rembrandt's.

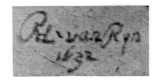
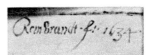

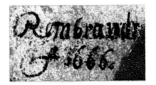

Evolution of Rembrandt's signature from the early monograms to the style he adopted in 1633 and kept up to his last paintings.

habitable and four large windows and two smaller ones pierced in the roof on the sides of the triangular pediment which replaced the original stepped gable.

1640 July Birth of a second daughter, also named after her paternal grandmother, but once again, the child does not live.

1640 September Death of Rembrandt's mother at Leiden. The painter inherits a large portion of her wealth which is valued at 9,960 florins.

1640 Peter Mundy, the English traveller, author of *The Travels of Peter Mundy in Europe and Asia: 1608–1667*, reports in his diary the fame attained in Holland by Rembrandt who is in fact the only Dutch painter he mentions.

1641 The second edition of *Beschrijvinge der Stadt Leyden (Description of the City of Leiden)* by Johanners Orlers,

former burgomaster of that city, contains a piece which constitutes the first biographical datum on Rembrandt. It was probably compiled on information obtained from Rembrandt's mother and for a long time it formed the base of all succeeding biographies of Rembrandt.

1641 In the German edition of Tommaso Garzoni's *Piazza universale*, published by Matthäus Merian of Basle, Rembrandt is listed as one of the greatest engravers of the time, together with Jacques Callot and Abraham Bosse, but he is not mentioned in the chapter dedicated to painters.

1641 After giving birth to three children who died in infancy, Saskia gives birth to a healthy son. On 22 September the child is baptised in the Zuiderkerk and given the name of Titus.

1641 18 October The painter Philips Angel (1616–post

1683) praises Rembrandt's *Samson's Wedding Feast* (no. 209), in a session of the Guild of St Luke, at Leiden.

1642 5 June Saskia, gravely ill with consumption, makes a will in which she leaves her fortune which amounts to over 40,000 florins, to her son Titus and to any other children whom she might bear. To Rembrandt she leaves the entire income of her possessions until the day he remarries in which case half the interest is to go to Saskia's sister, Titia.

1642 14 June Death of Saskia at the age of thirty. She is buried five days later in a provisional grave.

1642 9 July Rembrandt buys a vault in the Oudekerk and has Saskia's remains transferred there.

1642 Date of the *Night Watch* (no. 246).

1642 Rembrandt hires Geertje Dircks, widow of the trumpeter Abraham Claeszoon to look after his young son Titus.

1642–5 Rembrandt works on the etching *Christ the Healer*, the so-called "Hundred Guilder Print" (see p. 136, no. 18).

1645 Date of *Tobit, Anna and the Kid* (no. 268); of the *Dream of Joseph at Bethlehem* (no. 269) and of the two paintings of the *Holy Family* (nos. 270 and 271).

1646 26 November The Stadtholder Frederick Henry buys Rembrandt's *Adoration of the Shepherds* (no. 273) and now lost *Circumcision*, for a sum of 2,400 florins. The paintings were both approximately of the same format as the Passion series which the prince already owned.

1647 The inventory of Saskia's possessions is now finished and the whole amount is assessed at 47,750 florins.

1648 24 January Geertje Dircks makes a will in which she leaves Titus everything she owns, including several pieces of jewellery which had belonged to Saskia and which had been given to Geertje by Rembrandt.

Later, however, she quarrels with the artist, leaves his house and sues him for breach of promise, for he had apparently promised to marry her. The magistrate rejects her plea, but compels Rembrandt — who had offered to pay Geertje a pension of 160 florins a year on condition that she put off revoking her will — to raise the annuity to 200 florins.

Some time after this, Rembrandt hears that Geertje has pawned the pieces of jewellery that he had given her in order to repay some debts, and after her attempt at redeeming them from the pawnbroker has failed, he sues her in court for dissolute conduct; on 23 October 1649 Geertje is condemned to twelve years' imprisonment in the reformatory at Gouda. Rembrandt continues to send her her annuity, but after obtaining a remission of sentence after five years, Geertje dies.

1648 Date of the *Risen Christ at Emmaus* (no. 287)

1649 During Rembrandt's litigations against Geertje Dircks one of the witnesses in his favour was a young woman who had probably been in his service since before Geertje's departure from his house. The girl was country-bred, being born at Ransdorp in 1625 or 1626, the daughter of a sergeant; her name was Hendrickje Stoffelsdochter Jaegher, but she is generally known as Hendrickje Stoffels.

It is probably during this same year that a long relationship starts between Rembrandt and Hendrickje which the

painter does not attempt to keep secret. He does not marry her, however, probably in order not to diminish his income as stipulated in Saskia's will of 1642.

1650 In a poem praising the art collection of Maerten Kretzer where, next to several of Rembrandt's works, are paintings by Rubens and Titian, Lambert van den Bos writes: "I shall not try to extol your fame with my scrawly pen, Rembrandt, as the admiration everyone has for you becomes evident as soon as I mention your name."

1650 Two experts sent by Rembrandt's creditors value his movable possessions (paintings and collection) to 17,000 florins, 6,400 of which are assessed to paintings by his own hand.

1652 Rembrandt receives a commission to paint a picture representing Aristotle from a nobleman from Messina, Don

Antonio Ruffo, through the latter's Amsterdam agent. The painting is executed and sent to Ruffo two years later (see no. 316 for further details). This meets with Ruffo's approval and he orders from Rembrandt two other paintings, *Homer* (no. 425) and *Alexander the Great* (see nos. 411 and 426), as well as a series of etchings (see below, 1661 and 1662).

1652 Death of Rembrandt's brother Adriaen at Leiden.

1653 Having squandered his considerable earnings in thousands of questionable acquisitions in order to appease his feverish collector's instincts, Rembrandt finds himself in a dire financial situation which is made even more precarious by the general economic crisis which has been affecting the Dutch for some time. Rembrandt borrows money from several people, among them his friend Jan Six (see no. 320), Cornelis Witsen, the former burgomaster of Amsterdam and the dealer Isaac van Hertsbeeck who lends him 4,200 florins. To all these (as well as to Christoffel Thijssens who had sold him his house in 1639 and to whom he still owes over half the sum they had agreed upon), he pledges himself to repay them within one year and gives them as his guarantee all his estates and possessions.

1654 Rembrandt and Hendrickje are summoned to the Ecclesiastical Court on a charge of concubinage. They refuse to appear in court and at the beginning of July the Consistory of the Calvinist church summons them in turn, but this time Hendrickje alone is to appear: it may be deduced from this that the artist had perhaps stopped belonging to the church; or perhaps, as suggested by Baldinucci (see pp. 9–10), he now belongs to the Mennonite sect.

Other summons follow and finally Hendrickje appears before the ecclesiastical judges to whom she readily admits her situation and who advise her to put an end to her illicit relationship and make penance; in addition she is forbidden to receive Holy Communion.

1654 Unable to honour his promise vis-à-vis his creditors, Rembrandt makes another agreement with Thijssens whereby he promises to pay him about 50 florins a year, and he renews the guarantee of his possessions to his other numerous creditors. The artist's financial situation grows worse every day, aggravated by the fact that his paintings sell less and less because of his very personal and ever growing conception and technique which do not appeal to all clients.

1654 October Hendrickje gives birth to a girl child who is baptized in the Oudekerk and given the name Cornelia,

(Left) Drawing in red chalk by Rembrandt of Leonardo's Last Supper *(365 × 475 mm., c. 1633, New York, Lehman Collection), made after a sixteenth-century engraving by Fra*

after Rembrandt's mother(and like the two little girls born to Saskia and who died in infancy).

c. 1655 Quarrel with a Portuguese dealer, Diego Andrade who, having commissioned Rembrandt to paint the portrait of a young woman and given him an advance of 75 florins with the guarantee that the rest of the money would be paid on completion of the picture, refused to do so at the agreed time, saying that the portrait did not resemble the sitter and demanding that the artist should alter it. Rembrandt is violent in his rejection of this suggestion; he declares that he will take the painting before the Guild of St Luke and will retouch it only if the members deem it necessary; he adds that if Andrade refuses to comply with this he will simply not give him the painting but will sell it on his own account.

1656 Rembrandt, anxious to recover his reputation in order to start repaying his debts, asks Geertje Dircks' brother to return 140 florins which he

lent his sister in addition had lent his sister in addition to the money which he had agreed to give her regularly at the time of his quarrel with her. As Geertje's brother refuses to comply, Rembrandt sues him and wins the case.

1656 17 May Rembrandt tries to persuade the Orphans' Court to put the ownership of his house in Titus' name so as to save it from his creditors, although he has used it as a guarantee. Not only does he fail in this enterprise, but his move also causes the court to appoint a guardian for Titus, so as to make sure that the child's possessions are kept separate from his father's.

1656 June Rembrandt, constantly besieged by creditors, asks the High Court for a *cessio bonorum (boedelafstand)*, a declaration of bankruptcy which he justifies by pretending that he has suffered severe losses in trade and "at sea".

1656 20 July The High Court names Frans Janszoon Bruyningh (see no. 315) as the administrator in charge of the

Poster for the auction sale of Rembrandt's possessions (see Outline biography 1657–8), Amsterdam, Rembrandtshuis.

liquidation and sale of the artist's possessions.

1656 25 and 26 July The inventory of Rembrandt's possessions is drawn up (see pp. 89–90).

1656 Date of *Jacob Blessing Joseph's Children* (no. 344) and of the *Anatomy Lesson of Dr Deyman* (no. 345).

1657 Titus makes a will in favour of Hendrickje and little Cornelia, nominating his father as usufructuary.

1657–8 In the tavern "De Keysers Kroon" (the building still stands today, no. 71 Kalverstraat) three public sales are held, in which all of Rembrandt's possessions are disposed of. In December 1657, the paintings are sold, among which are about seventy of his own hand, and the objets d'art; on 13 February 1658, the house, the furniture, etc.; on the following 24 September, the drawings and etchings. A printed facsimile of one of the proclamations for the auctions (19,5 × 17 cm.) hangs in the Rembrandthuis and states that "The Administrator of the possessions of Insolvents [in charge of those of] Rembrandt van Rijn, artist painter, with the authority granted by the local commissioners in charge of possessions abandoned [to creditors], will hold a judiciary sale of the works of art which are still among these possessions and which consist of works by several of the most excellent Italian, French, German and Dutch masters, collected with the utmost care by the self-same Rembrandt van Rijn, as well as a large quantity of drawings and sketches by the self-same Rembrandt van Rijn. The sale will take place on the day, hour and year indicated, in the property of Barent Janszoon Schuurman, innkeeper and owners of the Keysers Kroon, in the Kalverstraat, where the preceding sale took place."

The house, with its furniture and general contents, is sold for 11,218 florins to the

Antonio da Monza (230 × 450 mm., London, British Museum). (Right) Another drawing by Rembrandt of Raphael's Portrait of Baldassare Castiglione *(163 × 207 mm., 1639, pen and watercolour, Vienna, Albertina).*

shoemaker Lieven Symons; altogether the proceeds of the house and of all the other possessions do not even reach the figure of 20,000 florins, which represents more or less the extent of Rembrandt's debts, and which the artist is never to succeed in repaying completely. Only four of the numerous creditors are remunerated in full; the others, unsatisfied, or at any rate not wholly satisfied, attempt, but to no avail, to fall back on Titus' patrimony, pretending that Saskia's legacy had been cunningly overvalued in 1647 in order to defraud them.

The ludicrous amount for which Rembrandt's works were sold at the auction can be gathered through a comparison with an assessment made in June 1657 of the value of eleven paintings by the same artist which were in the collection of the art dealer Johannes de Renialme. These eleven paintings were valued collectively at 2560 florins and a twelfth, *Christ and the Woman Taken in Adultery* (no. 256), was valued at 1500 florins.

1658 Date of the *Self-Portrait with a Stick* (no. 266), of *Jupiter and Mercury Visiting Philemon and Baucis* (no. 370) and of *Tobit and Anna Waiting* (no. 371).

1660 In the collection of poems *De Hollantsche Parnas*, there is a poem by Jeremias de Decker which contains numerous words of praise about Rembrandt; another poem by H. F. Waterloos, in the same collection, concerns a portrait of the same de Decker made by Rembrandt before 1660 and now lost.

1660 Date of the *Apostle Peter Denying Christ* (no. 392).

1660 13 June The Emilian painter Guercino, in a letter to Don Antonio Ruffo (who had commissioned him to paint a picture which would serve as a companion to Rembrandt's *Aristotle Contemplating a Bust of Homer*), says this of Rembrandt: "As far as the half-length figure by Reimbrant which Your Excellency owns is concerned, it can only be absolutely perfect, for I have seen several etchings of his which have come to our part of the country and which are indeed extremely beautiful, wonderfully cut and well executed; we can but guess from this that his colours themselves will be equally exquisite and perfect and I sincerely hold him to be a man of genius."

1660 15 December Elaboration (by means of a formal contract signed and endorsed by all concerned — Hendrickje even adds a sign of the cross —) of an agreement between Rembrandt, Titus and Hendrickje to the effect that the artist's property and the exclusive right to sell his paintings, etchings and drawings up to six years after his death are granted to Titus and Hendrickje who have become partners in a modest art business. In return they engage themselves to lodge, feed him and generally look after him for the whole of his natural life. This agreement which makes Rembrandt his son's and his servant's dependent (he also recognises his debt to them of 800 and 950 florins respectively) means however that his remaining creditors are kept at bay and that he is able from now on to work without any material worries.

1660 18 December The new owner having paid the whole sum of purchase, Rembrandt now leaves his house and after a brief stay in the inn "De Keysers Kroon" where the sale has taken place, he goes to stay with Hendrickje, Titus and the baby Cornelia, in a modest house on Rozengracht (today no. 184), in front of the Nieuwe Doolhof, in the popular quarter of Jordaan, at the south-western end of the old city. The building today bears the following inscription: "Hier / stond / Rembrandts / laatste /

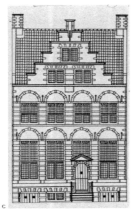

Rembrandt's houses. A: The mill (the lower of the two) and the house (first row, second from left, between the two mills) of the Rembrandts in Leyden; detail of an engraving by Pieter Bast, 375 × 44 mm 1600, Leyden University. B: Location of the house in Sint Anthonies Breestraat, Amsterdam. C, D, E: Rembrandt's house as it was in his time, as it is today (Rembrandtshuis Museum) and in a painting by Cornelis Springer, 1852 (Private collection).

woning / †4.10.1669."

1661 In Cornelius de Bie's *Het Gulden Cabinet*, published in Antwerp, Rembrandt's paintings are described in most praiseworthy terms.

1661 Possible date of the *Oath of the Batavians* (no. 415).

1661 July A painting of

The Westerkerk at Amsterdam, where Rembrandt was buried on 8 October 1669; engraving by F. de Wit, 130 × 130 mm., c. 1650, London, British Museum.

Alexander the Great (perhaps no. 411) is sent to Don Antonio Ruffo, to be exchanged two years later for another one on the same subject (perhaps no. 426?).

1661 7 August Hendrickje who has been ill for some time makes a will in which her daughter Cornelia is the only heir. In the event of her lacking natural heirs she is to nominate her brother Titus as her own heir. Rembrandt himself becomes the guardian of the child and the income of her estate is to be his until his death, after which it goes to Titus. In the will Hendrickje is described in the same terms as Saskia: "Juffrouw [Mrs] Hendrickje Stoffels, huisvrouw [wife and housewife] van Rembrandt".

1662 In spite of the declining interest of the general public, Rembrandt's work is still greatly admired by the experts. Jan Vos, in a poem celebrating the re-establishment of the Guild of St Luke, places Rembrandt amongst the most famous painters of Amsterdam. There appears another poem in praise of *Ahasuerus, Esther and Haman at the Table* (no. 390), and a third on the portrait of Lieven van Coppenol, made by Rembrandt perhaps as a sketch for a portrait etched in 1658.

1662 Date of the *Sampling Officials of the Drapers' Guild* (no. 424).

1662 On 27 October Rembrandt sells Saskia's tomb in the Oudekerk and buys a new one in the Westerkerk which is much nearer to his new house on Rozengracht.

1662 November The painting of *Homer* (no. 425) is sent to

Monument to Rembrandt in the Rembrandtsplein, Amsterdam (L. Royer, 1847).

Don Antonio Ruffo who judges it to be incomplete and sends it back to the painter. Rembrandt completes it according to his patron's wishes and sends it back to him the following year.

1663 21 July Probable date of Hendrickje's death.

1664 Spring The collector Harmen Becker who had commissioned Rembrandt to paint a *Juno* (probably no. 432), complains that the painting is not yet finished.

1665 At the beginning of the year, after legal proceedings Titus receives the sum of 4200 florins which the creditor Isaac van Hertsbeeck had received after the sale; the following November Titus receives a further 7000 florins which was roughly the sum he had been promised on the sale of his father's possessions.

1665 Probable date of the *Jewish Bride* (no. 434) and the *Self-Portrait* (no. 436)

1666 15 October Rembrandt's collecting passion is not yet spent and he gives 1000 florins for a painting by Holbein the Younger.

1667 A posthumous essay by the poet Jeremias de Decker (1610–66), who had already expressed his admiration for Rembrandt (see 1660), especially for his portrait of him (see no. 440), appears in the *Lof der Geldsuch Vervolg der Rijmoeffeningen*.

1667 29 December Filippo Corsini who was in the retinue of Grand Duke Cosimo III de Medici during his travels in Europe in 1667–9, wrote in his diary: "Thursday 29 the weather at first was good though very cold but grew worse towards five o'clock; according to this particular climate the mists grow thicker and last until the night which is usually clear. After mass His Highness went with Blaeu and Ferroni to see the works of various painters such as Wan Welde, Reinbrent, a famous painter, Scamus, a painter of seascapes, and others who did not have perfect examples of their work with them and indicated in which houses these could be found; whereupon His Highness went to visit them and was greeted everywhere with every display of esteem and graciousness."

1668 10 February Titus marries Magdalena van Loo, niece of Saskia's sister Titia.

1668 Probable date of the *Return of the Prodigal Son* (no. 447).

1668 4 September Death of Titus. He is buried on 7 September in the Zuiderkerk.

1668–9 Probable date of the *Family Portrait* (no. 448).

1669 March Birth of Titus's posthumous daughter, who is

given the name of Titia in the Nieuwe Zijdeskapel, on the 22. Her uncle François Biljert (husband of Magdalena's sister Sara, and whose son is to marry Titia in 1686) is appointed as her guardian.

1669 September The painter Allaert van Everdingen and his son Cornelis visit Rembrandt in whose house they see an unfinished painting representing *Simeon Holding the Infant Jesus* (no. 451) which may be Rembrandt's last work.

1669 4 October Death of Rembrandt. He is buried four days later in the Westerkerk in whose register the following words are inscribed: "8 October 1669, Rembrandt van Rijn, painter, who lived in the Rozengracht, in front of the Doolhof, borne by sixteen bearers; leaving two girl children. Receipt: twenty florins."

1669 17 October Two weeks after Rembrandt's death Magdalena van Loo, Titus's widow dies. Only two girls remain of the painter's direct family: his daughter Cornelia, aged fifteen (whose guardians are Abraham Fransen — see no. 35, p. 138 — and Christiaan Dusart) and his granddaughter Titia not yet one year old.

1675–9 Joachim von Sandrart's *Teutsche Academie der Edelen Bau-, Bild- und Mahlerey-Kunste* is published in Nuremberg and contains a biography of Rembrandt (see pp. 8–9).

1678 Samuel van Hoogstraten, once a pupil of Rembrandt's, publishes his treatise on painting, *Inleyding tot de Hooge Schoole der Schilder-Konst: anders de Zichtbaere Werelt. Verdeelt in negen Leerwinkels yder bestiert door eene der zang-godinnen* in which are many and frequent passages of praise about Rembrandt and an analysis of his technical and aesthetic theories (see no. 246).

1681 In the poem *Gebruik en misbruik des tooneels* of Andries Pels, there is a long passage dedicated to Rembrandt. A few lines of it are quoted in Houbraken's biography (see p. 13).

1681–1728 Filippo Baldinucci's *Notizie de' professori del disegno da Cimabue in qua* is published posthumously in Florence. (see pp. 9–10).

1685 In his *Entretiens sur les vies et sur les ouvrages des plus excellens peintres anciens et modernes*, André Félibien has a dialogue which describes the existing knowledge of Rembrandt's life (see p. 10).

1699 A biography of Rembrandt and a critical analysis of his work appear in Roger de Piles' *Abrégé de la vie des peintres avec des réflexions sur leurs ouvrages*, published in Paris (see pp. 10–11).

Reproduced below are:

1) Seven letters (all that has been discovered so far in terms of documents in Rembrandt's own hand), sent by the artist to Constantijn Huygens, secretary to the Stadtholder Frederick Henry. The first two are dated February 1636; the third, 12 January 1639; the fourth, a few days later; the fifth, 27 January 1639; the sixth, 13 February 1639; and the seventh a few days later. The letters concern the series of paintings on the theme of the Passion of Christ, commissioned by the prince: *The Raising of the Cross* (no. 144), *The Descent from the Cross* (no. 145), *The Ascension* (no. 185), *The Entombment* (no. 224) and *The Resurrection* (no. 225). In the third and fifth letters there is a mention of a picture sent by the artist as a gift to Huygens (probably the *Samson Blinded by the Philistines* (no. 184), to whom, as is obvious from the first letter, Rembrandt had already sent some etchings). The first of these letters is now at Harvard University, the second and seventh in the British Museum, the third in the archives at The Hague, the fourth and fifth in the Custodia Foundation, Paris, and the sixth in the museum of Mariemont Castle Belgium.

2) The inventory of Rembrandt's possessions, drawn up in 1656 and kept in the Amsterdam archives.

Letters

1

My dear and gracious Mr Huygens,

I hope that you will inform His Excellency that I have been finishing, with great diligence and as quickly as possible, the three Passion paintings commissioned by His Excellency himself, namely an Entombment, a Resurrection and an Ascension of Christ, which are to be followed by a Raising of the Cross and a Descent from the Cross. Of the first three paintings the one representing Christ ascending to heaven is already finished, and the other two are more than half-finished. I should be grateful, dear Sir, if you could let me know whether His Excellency would like me to send him the finished picture immediately, or whether he would prefer to receive the three together. I shall endeavour to do my utmost to please His Excellency. As for yourself, I should like to send you some specimens of my latest works, as a token of my humble friendship, and I hope you will look kindly upon them.

I send you my most respectful greetings and wish you the very best of health.

Your humble and devoted servant,

Rembrandt

I live in Niuwe Doelstraat, next door to the pensioner Boereel's.

2

Dear Sir,

I send you my respectful greetings and write to say that

I agree to come and see how my painting goes with the other two. As far as the price of the picture is concerned, I could have sold it for at least twelve hundred florins, but I shall be content with what His Excellency will be kind enough to pay me. I should like to say, without risking offending you, that I shall not fail to recompense you.

Your humble and devoted servant,

Rembrandt

The painting will look best in His Excellency's gallery where the light is strong.

3

Dear Sir,

Owing to my hard work and devotion I have now finished the two paintings commissioned by His Highness

Rembrandt's fourth letter, dated January 1639; 306 × 203 mm.; Paris, Fondation Custodia.

and representing the entombment and the resurrection of Christ from the dead, to the great terror of the guards. I am now ready to send them to His Highness and hope they will meet with his approval, for I have put in them my strongest and most sincere feelings, which is the reason why they have taken me so long. I should, therefore, be grateful if you would kindly inform His Highness of this and tell me whether you would like the two paintings sent to your own house first, as we did last time. Since these matters have given you much trouble, I should like to send you as a token of my esteem, a picture measuring ten feet by eight, which is good enough to hang in your house.

I wish you every happiness and the blessing of heaven upon you, Amen.

Your humble and devoted servant,

Rembrandt

I live in Binnen Amstel, in the

pastry-maker's house.

4

Dear Sir,

Upon your authorization I send you these two paintings, and I think that His Highness will find their quality such that he will pay me not less than a thousand florins for each of them. Should, however, His Highness not think that they are worth so much, he can give me less, according to what he thinks they are worth. I know the reputation and discretion of His Highness and shall be content and grateful to receive what he thinks fit to give me.

I send you my greetings,

Your humble and devoted servant,

Rembrandt

The frames and packing came to forty-four florins altogether.

5

Dear Sir,

I have read your letter of the 14th with the utmost pleasure and you have shown me such kindness and benevolence that I should like to offer my services to you and also my friendship, with all my heart. I am therefore sending you with this letter, and against your wish, a painting which I hope you will kindly accept, for it is the first sign of gratitude I have shown you.

The receiver-general Uytenbogaert who came to see me as I was packing the two paintings, wanted to see them, and he told me that if His Highness agreed he could pay me himself straight from his Amsterdam office. I should therefore be grateful if you could let me know how much His Highness has decided to pay me as it would be particularly useful for me to have this money at the present moment.

I respectfully expect an

answer to this letter and wish you and your family every happiness and blessing. With all my best wishes.

Your humble and loving servant,

Rembrandt

Dear Sir, please hang this painting in strong sunlight and where it can be viewed from a distance, as this is how it looks most effective.

6

Most honoured Sir,

I have faith in your benevolence in every way and, in particular, where my fee for the last two paintings is concerned; I think that if everything is to your satisfaction you will not argue on the agreed price. As far as the earlier paintings are concerned, I received only six hundred florins for each of them; but if His Highness cannot be persuaded to pay a higher price, although it is obvious that they are worth it, I shall be content to receive six hundred florins for each of them again, as long as the cost of the two ebony frames I ordered and the packing — forty-four florins altogether — is reimbursed. I shall be grateful, however, if you could very kindly send me what I am owed here in Amsterdam, and I hope to receive the money very soon. I am extremely obliged to you for all your kindness.

I send you and your closest friends my greetings and hope that God may keep you all in good health for years to come.

Your humble and loving servant,

Rembrandt

7

Noble Sir,

I hesitate to send you this letter for fear of bothering you: I do it only because the receiver-general Uytenbogaert has told me to, as I was complaining to him about not having been paid for the last two paintings. The treasurer Volbergen says that it is not true that the taxes are collected once a year only. Uytenbogaert told me last Thursday that until now Volbergen has collected his taxes twice a year and that he has more than four thousand florins at his disposal at the moment in his office. As things stand, I beg you, kind Sir, to put my payment through so that I may finally receive my well-earned twelve hundred and forty-four florins; I shall be forever grateful to you for this and shall always show you every devotion and friendship.

I send you my greetings and hope that God may keep you in good health for years to come, and bestow his blessing upon you.

Your humble and loving servant,

Rembrandt

I live in Binnen Amstel, in the pastry-maker's house.

Inventory of paintings, furniture and other objects found in the house of Rembrandt van Rijn, resident of the Breestraat, near the lock of Sint Anthonies.

1. Small painting by Adriaen Brouwer representing a pastry-maker. 2. Small painting with figures of players, by the same Brouwer. 3. Small painting by Rembrandt van Rijn representing a woman and child. 4. Small painting with a painter's studio by the same Brouwer. 5. Well-appointed table by Brouwer. 6. Plaster head. 7. Two naked children, plaster. 8. Sleeping child, plaster. 9. Painting representing [. . .] shoe. 10. Small landscape by Rembrandt. 11. Another landscape by Rembrandt. 12. Small standing figure by Rembrandt. 13. Nativity by Jan Lievens. 14. St Jerome by Rembrandt. 15. Small painting of hares by Rembrandt. 16. Small painting of a hog by Rembrandt. 17. Small landscape by Hercules Seghers. 18. Landscape by Jan Lievens. 19. Another landscape by Jan Lievens. 20. Small landscape by Rembrandt. 21. Lion hunt by Rembrandt. 22. Moonlight scene by Jan Lievens. 23. Head by Rembrandt. 24. Another head by Rembrandt. 25. Still-life, retouched by Rembrandt. 26. Soldier in a suit of armour by Rembrandt. 27. *Vanitas*, retouched by Rembrandt. 28. *Ibid.* with a sceptre, retouched by Rembrandt. 29. Seascape completed by Hendrick van Anthonissen. 30. Four Spanish chairs covered in red leather. 31. Two Spanish chairs with black seats. 32. Pine folding stools.
In the antechamber:
33. Painting representing the Good Samaritan, retouched by Rembrandt. 34. The Wealthy Feaster by Palma Vecchio which is half-owned by Pieter de la Tombe. 35. Rustic courtyard by Rembrandt. 36. Two greyhounds painted from life by Rembrandt. 37. Large Descent from the Cross by Rembrandt, with fine gilded frame. 38. The Raising of Lazarus by Rembrandt. 39. Courtesan dressing her hair by Rembrandt. 40. Wooded landscape by Hercules Seghers. 41. Tobias by Lastman. 42. The Raising of Lazarus by Jan Lievens. 43. Small mountain landscape by Rembrandt. 44. Landscape by Govaert Jansz. 45. Two heads by Rembrandt. 46. Monochrome painting by Jan Lievens. 47. Two monochrome paintings by Porcellis. 48. Head by Rembrandt. 49. Head by Brouwer. 50. View of the sand dunes by Porcellis. 51. *Ibid.*, smaller. 52. Small painting representing a hermit by Jan Lievens. 53. Two small heads by Lucas van Walckenburgh. 54. Burning camp by Bassano the Elder. 55. Charlatan, copy of a painting by Brouwer. 56. Two heads by Jan Pynas. 57. Perspective by Lucas of Leiden. 58. Priest, copy of a painting by Jan Lievens. 59. Small study of a model by Rembrandt. 60. Small painting with a shepherd and his flock by Rembrandt. 61. Drawing by Rembrandt. 62. The Flagellation of Christ by Rembrandt. 63. Monochrome painting by Porcellis. 64. Monochrome painting by Simon de Vlieger. 65. Small landscape by Rembrandt. 66. Head painted from life by Rembrandt. 67. Head by Raphael of Urbino. 68. Several horses painted from life by Rembrandt. 69. Landscape painted from life by Rembrandt. 70. Group of houses by Hercules Seghers. 71. Juno by Pynas. 72. Mirror with an ebony frame. 73. Ebony frame. 74. Marble wine-cooler. 75. Walnut table with Tournai tapestry cover. 76. Seven Spanish chairs with green velvet seats.
In the room behind the antechamber: 77. Painting of Jephtah. 78. Virgin and Child by Rembrandt. 79. Sketch for a Crucifixion by Rembrandt. 80. Female nude by Rembrandt. 81. Copy of a painting by Annibale Carracci. 82. Two half-bust figures by Brouwer. 83. Another copy of a painting by Carracci. 84. Small seascape by Porcellis. 85. Head of an old man by Van Eyck. 86. Portrait of a dead man by Abraham Vinck. 87. The Last Judgement by Aert van Leyden. 88. Sketch by Rembrandt. 89. Copy of a sketch by Rembrandt. 90. Two heads painted from life by Rembrandt. 91. The Consecration of the Temple of Solomon by Rembrandt. 92. The Circumcision, copy of a painting by Rembrandt. 93. Two small landscapes by Hercules Seghers. 94. Gilded frame. 95. Small oak table. 96. Four cardboard moulds. 97. Oak chest. 98. Four ordinary chairs. 99. Four green cushions for chairs. 100. Copper kettle. 101. Cupboard.
In the room behind the living room. 102. Small wooded landscape by an unknown painter. 103. Head of an old man by Rembrandt. 104. Large landscape by Hercules Seghers. 105. Head of a woman by Rembrandt. 106. The Unification of the Netherlands by Rembrandt. 107. View of a village by Govaert Jansz. 108. Small painting of an ox, painted from life by Rembrandt. 109. Large painting representing the woman from Samara by Giorgione, which is half-owned by Pieter de la Tombe. 110. Three antique statues. 111. Sketch by Rembrandt of the Burial of Christ. 112. St Peter's Boat by Aert van Leyden. 113. Christ Risen from the Tomb by Rembrandt. 114. Painting of the Virgin by Raphael of Urbino. 115. Head of Christ by Rembrandt. 116. Small wintery landscape by Grimmer. 117. The Crucifixion by Lelio da Novellara. 118. Head of Christ by Rembrandt. 119. Oxen by Lastman. 120. *Vanitas*, retouched by Rembrandt. 121. Ecce Homo, monochrome painting by Rembrandt. 122. The Sacrifice of Abraham by Lievens. 123. *Vanitas*, retouched by Rembrandt. 124. Monochrome landscape by Hercules Seghers. 125. Night scene by Rembrandt. 126. Large mirror. 127. Six chairs with blue seats. 128. Oak table. 129. Embroidered tablecloth. 130. Cedar wood chest. 131. Cedarwood blanket chest. 132. Bed with eiderdown. 133. Two pillows. 134. Two bedspreads. 135. Blue curtain for the bed. 136. Wicker chair. 137. Warming-pan.
In the curiosity cabinet:
138. Two terrestrial globes. 139. Box full of minerals. 140. Small column. 141. Small pewter vase. 142. Urinating child. 143. Two East-Indian cups. 144. An East-Indian cup and a Chinese cup. 145. Statue of an empress. 146. Gunpowder horn from the East Indies. 147. Statue of the emperor Augustus. 148. Indian cup. 149. Statue of Tiberius. 150. East-Indian sewing box. 151. Head of Caius. 152. Caligula. 153. Two grotesque porcelain figures. 154. Heraclitus. 155. Two small porcelain figures. 156. Nero. 157. Two iron helmets. 158. Japanese helmet. 159. Buffalo-skin helmet(?). 160. Roman emperor. 161. Cast of a moor's head, taken from life. 162. Socrates. 163. Homer. 164. Aristotle. 165. Antique head. 166. Faustina. 167. Iron armour and helmet. 168. The emperor Galba. 169. The emperor Otho. 170. The emperor Vitellius. 171. The emperor Vespasian. 172. The emperor Titus Vespasian. 173. The emperor Domitian. 174. The emperor Silius Brutus (?). 175. Forty-seven examples of land or sea creatures, and other objects of the same kind. 176. Twenty-three examples of land or sea animals. A hammock and two flasks, one of them copper. 178. Eight large plaster models, taken from life.
In the bookcase at the end: 179. Large quantity of shells, marine animals, objects in plaster taken from life and other curios in that vein. 180. Figure representing an antique Cupid. 181. A small trombone and a pistol. 182. Iron shield decorated with figures by Quintino; a rare object. 183. Old-fashioned gunpowder horn. 184. Turkish gunpowder horn. 185. Small cabinet containing medals. 186. Engraved shield. 187. Two completely nude figures. 188. Death mask of Prince Maurits. 189. Lion and bull modelled from life. 190. Various walking sticks. 191. Cross-bow. Series of art books. 192. Book containing sketches by Rembrandt. 193. Book with wood-engravings by Lucas of Leiden. 194. *Ibid.*, with wood-engravings by Was . . . . 195. *Ibid.*, with wood-engravings by Vanni and Baroccio. 196. *Ibid.* with engravings by (or from?) Raphael of Urbino. 197. Gilded, boxed book modelled from Verhulst. 198. *Ibid.*, with engravings by Lucas of Leiden. 199. *Ibid.*, containing drawings by the greatest masters in the world. 200. The precious book [of engravings] by Andrea Mantegna. 201. Large book as above, containing drawings and prints by many artists. 202. Another, larger book, of the same kind. 203. *Ibid.*, containing curious drawings in miniature, wood-engravings and engravings of various subjects. 204. *Ibid.*, with prints by Bruegel the Elder. 205. *Ibid.*, with prints by Raphael of Urbino. 206. *Ibid.*, with very precious prints by the same master. 207. *Ibid.*, with prints by Antonio Tempesta. 208. *Ibid.*, with prints by Lucas Cranach. 209. *Ibid.*, with prints by Annibale, Agostino and Ludovico Carracci, Guido Reni and Spagnoletto. 210 *Ibid.*, with etchings and engravings by Antonio Tempesta. 211. Another large book as above. 212. Another book as above. 213. *Ibid.*, with copper engravings of portraits by Goltzius and Muller. 214. *Ibid.*, with copies after Raphael of Urbino. 215. *Ibid.*, with drawings by Adriaen Brouwer. 216. Another very large book containing almost all of Titian's works. 217. Several rare cups of Venetian glass. 218. Book with a collection of sketches by Rembrandt. 219. Old book. 220. Large book containing sketches by Rembrandt. 221. Another old book, but blank. 222. Small table for backgammon. 223. Very old chair. 224. Chinese bowl containing minerals. 225. Large piece of white coral. 226. Book with engravings of statues. 227. *Ibid.*, with the complete engravings of Van Heemskerk. 228. *Ibid.*, with portraits by Van Dijk, Rubens and others. 229. *Ibid.*, with landscapes by various masters. 230. *Ibid.*, with the complete works of Michelangelo Buonarrotti. 231. Two small woven wicker baskets. 232. Book containing erotic pictures by Raphael, Rosso, Annibale Carracci and Giulio Bonasone. 233. *Ibid.*, with landscapes by various famous masters. 234. *Ibid.*, containing scenes of Turkish life and Turkish buildings by Melchior Lorch, Hendrick van Aelst and others. 235. Small East-Indian chest containing various prints by Rembrandt, Hollar, Cock and others. 236. Book bound in black leather containing Rembrandt's best sketches. 237. Folder containing engravings by Martin Schongauer, Holbein, Hans Brosmar, and Israel van Mecken. 238. Another book with all Rembrandt's works. 239. Book with drawings by Rembrandt of male and female nudes. 240. *Ibid.*, with drawings of Roman buildings and views by famous artists. 241. East-Indian basket full of casts and plaster heads. 242. Blank album. 243. *Ibid.* 244. Album with landscapes by Rembrandt drawn from life. 245. *Ibid.*, with proofs of prints by Rubens and Jordaens. 246. *Ibid.*, with portraits by Van Mierevelt, Titian and others. 247. Small Chinese basket. 248. Album with prints of architectural subjects. 249. *Ibid.*, with prints by Frans Floris, Buyteweg, Goltzius and Abraham Bloemaert. 250. *Ibid.*, with drawings by Rembrandt of animals taken from life. 251. Collection of drawings from the antique by Rembrandt. 252. Five quarto books with drawings by Rembrandt. 253. *Ibid.*, with architectural prints. 254. *Medea*, tragedy by Jan Six. 255. The journey to Jerusalem by Jacques Callot. 256. Book bound in parchment containing landscapes drawn from life. 257. *Ibid.*, full of sketches of figures by Rembrandt. 257a. *Ibid.*, as above. 258. Small book bound in wood containing drawings of plates. 259. Small book with views drawn by Rembrandt. 260. *Ibid.*, with samples of calligraphy. 261. Book with drawings of statues by Rembrandt. 262. *Ibid.* 263. *Ibid.*, with pen sketches by Pieter Lastman. 264. *Ibid.*, with sketches by Lastman in red chalk. 265. *Ibid.*, with pen sketches by Rembrandt. 266. *Ibid.* 267. *Ibid.* 268. *Ibid.* 269. *Ibid.* 270 Large album with drawings of Tyrol, drawn from life by Roelant Savery. 271. *Ibid.*, with drawings of various famous masters. 272. *Ibid.*, in quarto, with sketches by Rembrandt. 273. The book of proportions by Albrecht Dürer, with wood engravings. 274. Another book of engravings, including some works by Jan Lievens and Ferdinand Bol. 275. Several collections of sketches by Rembrandt and others. 276. A large quantity of large sheets of drawing paper. 277. Box containing engravings by Van Vliet copied from paintings by Rembrandt. 278. Spanish screen covered in cloth. 279. Iron breast-plate. 280. Small chest containing a bird of paradise and six fans. 281. Fifteen books of various sizes. 282. Book on military matters, written in German. 283. *Ibid.*, with wood-engravings. 284. A Giuseppe Flavio book in German, with figures by Tobias Stimmer. 285. An old Bible. 286. Small marble ink-stand. 287. Plaster mask of Prince Maurits.
Antechamber before the curiosity cabinet: 288. Joseph by Aert van Leyden. 289. Three framed prints. 290. Annunciation. 291. Small landscape painted from life by Rembrandt. 292. Head, from landscape by Hercules Seghers. 293. Entombment by Rembrandt. 294. Head, from life. 295. Head of a dead man repainted by Rembrandt. 296. Plaster of Diana bathing by Adam van Vianne. 297. Study of a model, from life. 298. Two puppies, from life, by Titus van Rijn. 299. Illustrated book by Titus van Rijn. 300. Head of the Virgin by Titus van Rijn. 301. Small moonlit landscape repainted by Rembrandt. 302. Copy of the Flagellation of Christ by Rembrandt.

303. Small study of female nude by Rembrandt. 304. Small unfinished landscape by Rembrandt. 305. Horse, from life, by Rembrandt. 306. Small painting by Hals the Younger. 307. Small fish, from life. 308. Plaster cup with nude figure by Adam van Vianne. 309. Old coffer. 310. Four chairs with black leather seats. 311. Fir wood table.

Small studio, first shelf:
312. Thirty-three ancient weapons and wind instruments. Second shelf: 313. Thirty-three ancient weapons, arrows, sticks, spears and bows. Third shelf: 314. Thirteen wind instruments and bamboo pipes. Fourth shelf: 315. Thirteen arrows, bows, shields, etc. Fifth shelf: 316. Large number of plaster casts of hands and heads, a harp and a Turkish bow. Sixth shelf: 317 Seventeen plaster casts of hands and arms. 318. Group of antlers. 319. Four bows and cross-bows. 320. Five old helmets and shields. 321. Nine flasks and bottles. 322. Two carved heads of Barthel Beham and his wife. 323. Plaster cast of a Greek sculpture. 324. Statue of the emperor Agrippa. 325. Statue of the emperor Aurelius. 326. Head of Christ, study from life. 327. Head of a satyr, with a horn. 328. Antique Sybil. 329. Antique Laocoon. 330. Large marine plant. 331. Vitellius. 332. Seneca. 333. Three or four antique heads of women. 334. Another four heads. 335. Small metal cannon. 336. Series of ancient textiles of various colours. 337. Seven string instruments. 338. Two small paintings by Rembrandt.

Large studio: 339. Twenty halberds, swords and Indian fans. 340. Two Indian costumes, male and female. 341. Giant helmet. 342. Five breast-plates. 343. Wooden horn. 344. Painting of two moors by Rembrandt. 345. Small child by Michelangelo. On the hat-stand: 346. Lion and lioness skins and two brightly coloured jackets. 347. Large figure of Danae. 348. Peacock, from life, by Rembrandt. 349. Ten paintings, large and small, by Rembrandt. 350. Bed frame.

Small kitchen: Pewter kettle for water. 352. Various pots and pans. 353. Small table. 354. Sideboard. 355. Various old chairs. 356. Two cushions for chairs.

Corridor: 357. Nine white cups. 358. Two earthenware plates. Linen cupboard: 359. Three man's shirts. 360. Six handkerchiefs. 361. Twelve napkins. 362. Three tablecloths. 363. Various collars and cuffs.

Drawn up on 25 and 26 July 1656.

Catalogue of works

A first attempt at cataloguing Rembrandt's works was made by Edmé-François Gersaint in Paris in 1751; then in London in 1836 by John Smith — who, like Gersaint, was an art dealer; in the present century the task was taken up mainly by Hofstede de Groot, Valentiner, Bredius, Bauch and finally Gerson (for details, see the *Bibliography*, p. 82).

As research into both Rembrandt's work and Dutch painting in general progressed, many paintings which had previously been attributed to Rembrandt were re-examined and their attribution questioned. Yet those previous attributions, though inconsistent, were sometimes credible: such is the case, for instance, with *The Good Samaritan*, in the Louvre, which caused Eugène Fromentin to write some of the best passages in *Maîtres d'autrefois* and one of the most perceptive interpretations of Rembrandt's art; nevertheless this work is nowadays thought to be of the school of Rembrandt (probably by Barent Fabritius).

So, as research progressed, the catalogue of Rembrandt's works became thinner, in spite of the addition of newly authenticated works: from the thousand-odd paintings it comprised originally, it was reduced to 620 by Bredius in 1935; to little over 560 by Bauch in 1966 and finally to 421 by Gerson in 1968. Even so these critics do not necessarily consider their attributions definite, for many of the paintings included in their catalogues may be autograph only in part.

The present catalogue is also based on a similar proviso. It gives only 451 works which the author considers autograph (or partly autograph); autograph copies and other versions are also mentioned in the catalogue. Each catalogue entry is preceded by a number of symbols (see p. 82 for their significance) which specify the degree to which each work is autograph, not only in the present author's opinion, but also in the opinion of the majority of modern critics. The reader is thus made aware of the degree of doubts or uncertainty surrounding each work.

There are only 348 paintings which can be said to be wholly and undoubtedly autograph. The remaining 103 are questionable in part, and more research is needed as far as they are concerned in order to prove to what extent Rembrandt worked on them.

A supplementary catalogue given in topographical order (from p. 127 to p. 133) includes paintings which were formerly attributed to Rembrandt, especially some in public collections and which the reader may find still attributed to the master in books and museum catalogues, although they cannot be included by the present author in his own catalogue of autograph works. This supplementary catalogue comprises another 207 paintings, bringing the works illustrated in this book to 758 altogether. It is unlikely that any other works should also be included, unless, of course, future research brings out some new facts. The author has omitted those works which, though still ascribed to Rembrandt in public collections, are nevertheless now thought (by the curators themselves) to be by some other artist.

According to the usual style of this series of books, the main catalogue is given in chronological order, and not divided into subjects, as are most of the other catalogues of Rembrandt's works. But so that the reader may see whether the works described here are included or excluded in the other catalogues (the entries in the present catalogue do not, on the whole, provide this information), a table of concordance is given on pages 125–6 and each entry is given with its corresponding numbers in the catalogues of Hofstede de Groot, Bredius, Bauch and Gerson.

Most of Rembrandt's paintings are signed; quite often also Rembrandt signed his pupil's works, thus further confusing the issue. Many paintings were given a date by the master, so that there are few problems of chronology. It is interesting to see how, in some periods of Rembrandt's life, the number of portraits was far greater than the number of general compositions, whilst the contrary situation happened in other periods, depending on whether the artist was more inclined to give in to popular demand than follow his own bend. Other years show fewer paintings altogether, but a much greater number of etchings.

In the entries the transcription of the dates and signatures (and in some, of further writing in the painting itself or on the back of the canvas) is given as it is: thus if a letter or a digit is missing, it is shown by a full point. The same applies to Rembrandt's letters and to the inventory of his possessions (see pp. 89–90).

The author has tried wherever possible, to give information regarding the subject-matter or the identification of the model portrayed; one must point out, however, that in practically none of the paint-ings traditionally thought to represent Rembrandt's father, mother, sister or brothers, the information is substantiated. The paintings representing a Biblical scene are given the corresponding Biblical reference.

The dimensions given are to the nearest half-centimetre. Several paintings were mutilated in the past and details of their original state and dimensions are given; also, wherever possible, there is some illustration (a copy or an engraving) showing their original appearance (see nos. 19, 119, 179, 183, 246, 345, 415, and 425).

All symbols and abbreviations given in the catalogue are described in detail on p. 82.

The ancient texts given from p. 8 to p. 14 are often full of factual errors. The reader will find an up-to-date biography of Rembrandt in *Outline biography* starting on p. 83.

The genealogical tree on pp. 84–5 is the fullest that has ever been compiled in any catalogues of Rembrandt's works; it was expanded so as to show the many links between Rembrandt and people whom he painted or who are described in *Outline biography* and in the catalogue itself.

The price at which some of Rembrandt's paintings have been sold is given in the relevant entries. It is unfortunately difficult to transcribe in modern currency the value of certain sums given in the text in florins (see also *Outline biography*), especially since the seventeenth-century florin did not have a stable value. There is, nevertheless, some indication of the relative value of things, especially in 1650–60: for instance it is known that the annual salary of a university rector was of about 1500 florins, that of a special-ised workman 500 florins, that a middle-class couple, without children, would spend about 500 florins a year on household expenses, food and clothes. It may, therefore, be gathered from this that the very approximate value of a florin was perhaps a little over £3 or $10.50.

Finally although this book is primarily concerned with Rembrandt's painted *opus*, it has been thought essential to include some example of his drawing and etching, both of which have made him perhaps as famous as his paintings. These are given in two appendices at the back of the book and include some of the best-known examples of Rembrandt's graphic work. A further appendix describes some of Rembrandt's pupils and followers.

1 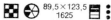 89,5×123,5
1625

The Stoning of St Stephen
Lyons, Musée des Beaux-Arts
Signed and dated: "Rf 1625".
Published first by HG in
BMML 1962 no. 4; it is the
first known dated painting by
Rembrandt; its attribution to
the painter, however, has not
been confirmed by many critics.
It has been said that the face
above the saint's head and the
one beneath his left hand are
portraits of Rembrandt and
Lievens respectively. See also
no. 3.

2 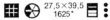 27,5×39,5
1625*

**David Presenting the Head
of Goliath to Saul**
Basle, Oeffentliche Kunstsammlung, Kunstmuseum
Signature and date possibly
apocryphal: "RH 162.".
Bible reference: I Kings, 17, 57.

3 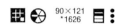 90×121
*1626

The Clemency of Titus
Leiden, Stedelijk Museum
"De Lakenhal"
Signed and dated: "Rf 16.6";
the third digit is illegible.
Published first by HdG in
BM 1924 no. 44. Some critics
think it may be a picture
reworked by Rembrandt
himself; others see it as a
collaboration between
Rembrandt and Lievens, or,
finally, as a Rembrandt
reworking of a painting by
Lastman. The subject-matter
itself has caused much
speculation: "The Judgment of
Brutus", "The Condemnation of
Manlius Torquatus's Son", "The
Capitulation of the German
Rebels to Consul Cerialis",
"The Absolution of Jonathan"
(I Kings, 14, 38 ff.). The face
showing behind the sceptre
may be a self-portrait.

4   39,5×30
1626

Tobit, Anna and the Kid
Amsterdam, Rijksmuseum
(Thyssen Loan)
Signed and dated: "RH 1626".
Published first by WB in AiA
1913 no. 1. Bible reference:
Tobit, 2, 19 ff, See no. 268.

5   63×46,5
1626

The Ass of Balaam
Paris, Musée Cognac-Jay
Signed and dated: "RL 1626".
Bible reference: Numbers 22, 27.

6 134,5×165
1626*

The Wrath of Ahasuerus
Raleigh (N.C.), North Carolina
Museum of Art
Bible reference: Esther, 7, 1.
Painting by Jan Lievens with
reworking by Rembrandt.

7 43×33
1626

**Christ Driving the Money-
Changers from the Temple**
Moscow, Pushkin Museum
Apocryphal signature and date:
"Rf 1626". Published as School

4 [Plate I]

5

7

15

16

17 [Plate II]

of Rembrandt, it was attributed to Rembrandt himself by KB in JPK 1924 no. 45; VB supports this statement in OH 1933 no. 50 and so does G 1968.

8   23,5×17 *1626*

Self-Portrait with Dishevelled Hair
Cassel, Staatliche Kunst-sammlungen, Gemäldegalerie
Known through other versions. According to G 1968 and other critics, this is the original.

9 39,5×29,5 *1626*

Soldier with a Sword
Lugano, Batthyany Collection
The signature may possibly be apocryphal: "RH van Rijn". First attributed to Rembrandt by B 1935, but this is disputed by many. A copy was sold in London, at Christie's, in 1952.

10 48×37 *1626*

Portrait of a Bald Man
Cassel, Staatliche Kunst-sammlungen, Gemäldegalerie
Some critics see in this a portrait of the artist's father, or of one of his brothers, possibly Gerrit or Adriaen.

11 24×20,5 *1626*

Portrait of an Old Man with a White Beard
Wassenaar (Holland), Van den Bergh Collection
This may be a portrait of the artist's father.

12   63×48 1626

The Concert
Whereabouts unknown
Signed and dated: "RHL 1626".

18
Formerly in the F. Cripps sale, London (Christie's), 16 November 1936, and in the N. Katz sale, Paris, 25 April 1951, it was on loan at the Stedelijk Museum "De Lakenhal" in Leiden. It was first published by VB in OH 1937 no. 50. It is almost unanimously considered autograph. B 1960 thinks that the models were Rembrandt's relatives.

13  32×42 1627

The Money-Changer
Berlin, Staatliche Museen, Gemäldegalerie
Signed and dated: "RH 1627".

21 [Plate V]

14 26,5×24 1627

The Flight into Egypt
Tours, Musée des Beaux-Arts
Signed and dated: "RH 1627".
First published by OB in BM 1954 no. 96.

15 55,5×44 1627*

The Presentation of Christ in the Temple
Hamburg, Kunsthalle
Signed: "Rembrandt f".

16 73×60,5 1627

St Paul in Prison
Stuttgart, Staatsgalerie

22 [Plate III]

Signed and dated: "Rf 1627". The words "Rembrandt fecit" are written on the book.

17 72,5×60 1628

Two Scholars Disputing
Melbourne, National Gallery of Victoria
Signed and dated: "RHL 1628". The painting was found in 1934 in Amsterdam. The subject-matter has been interpreted variedly as "Democritus and Heraclitus" (see also no. 436), "St Peter and St Paul", "Elijah Predicting his Own Death", etc.

18 55×46,5 *1628*

A Scholar in a Lofty Room
London, National Gallery
The signature is apocryphal: "Rem.randt". Oil sketch in grisaille, first published by CJH in BM 1917 no. 31.

19 25×31,5 *1628*

An Artist in the Studio (The Easel)
Boston (Mass.), Museum of Fine Arts
Formerly known through a copy (AiA 1918 no. 6), with the title *The Easel*, and representing Rembrandt himself or Gerrit Dou (who was his pupil from 1628), it was rediscovered in the Churston sale, at Christie's, London, 26 June 1925 and published by HdG in BM 1925 no. 47. It is almost unanimously recognised as autograph. Two strips were removed from the panel which measured originally about 35 × 31,5. Also reproduced here is a photograph of the painting (kindly lent by the Frick Art Reference Library, New York, by courtesy of the Boston Museum of Fine Arts) showing its original appearance.

20 59,5×49,5 1628

Samson Betrayed by Delilah
Berlin, Staatliche Museen, Gemäldegalerie

Signed and dated: "RHL van Rijn 1628". Bible reference: Judges, 16, 19.

21 21,5×16,5 1628

The Apostle Peter Denying Christ
Tokyo, Bridgestone Museum of Art, Ishibashi Foundation
Signed and dated: "RH 1628". The title was suggested by KB in SZK 1967. See also no. 392.

22 39×42 1628-29

The Risen Christ at Emmaus
Paris, Musée Jacquemart-André
Signed: "RHL".

13

14

12

19

Photograph of no. 19 in its original proportions.

20

27

28

29 [Plate IV]

26

30

31

36

37

38

28 ⊞ ⊗ 61×47 *1629* ▤ ○○

Self-Portrait with a Gold Chain
Whereabouts unknown
Exhibited at the N. Katz sale (Paris, 7 December 1950), this was also known through a small copy (London, Sotheby's, 21 June 1950).

29 ⊞ ⊗ 37,5×29 *1629* ▤ ○•

Self-Portrait with a Gorget
The Hague, Mauritshuis

30 ⊞ ⊗ 89×73,5 *1629* ▤ ○•

Self-Portrait in a Plumed Cap Boston (Mass.), Isabella Stewart Gardner Museum
This painting is in a bad state of preservation. It seems that the artist's monogram and the date 1629 were legible at one time but not today.

31 ⊞ ⊗ 22×16,5 *1629* ▤ ○•

Self-Portrait with Cap Pulled Forward
New York, Metropolitan Museum of Art
Signed: "RHL".

32 ⊞ ⊗ 80×102 1629 ▤ ○•

Judas Returning the Thirty Pieces of Silver
Mulgrave Castle (Yorkshire), Normanby Collection
Signed and dated: "RHL 1629". Highly praised by Constantijn Huygens (see *Outline biography*, 1630); known through various copies, it was rediscovered by Isherwood Kay and published by CHCB in BM 1939 no. 75.

33 ⊞ ⊗ 41,5×32,5 1629 ▤ ○•

The Tribute Money
Ottawa, National Gallery of Canada
Signed: "RH 1629".

34 ⊞ ⊗ 52×41 1629 ▤ ○•

Tobit Asleep
Turin, Galleria Sabauda
Signed and dated: "RHL 1629".
Bible reference: Tobit, 2, 10.

35 ⊞ ⊗ 65,5×48,5 1629-30 ▤ ○•

The Waiting of Tobit and Anna

32

33

52

London, National Gallery
Bible reference: Tobit, 10, 1 ff.
Painting by Gerrit Dou with patches by Rembrandt.

36 ⊞ ⊗ 15,5×12 1629-30 ▤ ○•

Laughing Soldier
The Hague, Mauritshuis
Some critics have seen in this painting a portrait of one of Rembrandt's brothers.

23 ⊞ ⊗ 15,5×12 1628-29 ▤ ○•

Rembrandt's Mother Praying
Salzburg, Residenzgalerie
In this painting, as in other presumed portraits of the artist's mother (nos. 40 and 54), the model is represented as the prophetess Hannah (Luke, 2, 36 ff.)

24 ⊞ ⊗ 74×62 *1629* ▤ ○○

Rembrandt's Mother Reading
Wilton House, Salisbury, Earl of Pembroke and Montgomery Collection
Long attributed to Rembrandt, this is now questioned by several scholars.

25 ⊞ ⊗ 60×45,5 *1629* ▤ ○○

Old Woman with a Shawl on her Head
Windsor Castle, Royal Collection
This is possibly a portrait of Rembrandt's mother. On the back of the painting a label states that the picture was presented by Sir Robert Kerr (who was in Holland in 1629) to King Charles I.

26 ⊞ ⊗ 72,5×58 *1629* ▤ ○•

Self-Portrait with a Scarf
Liverpool, Walker Art Gallery
The signature may be possibly apocryphal: "Rembrandt f". Formerly in the De L'Isle and Dudley Collection, it was sold at Sotheby's, London, 14 April 1948.

27 ⊞ ⊗ 15,5×12,5 1629 ▤ ○•

Self-Portrait with a White Collar
Munich, Alte Pinakothek
Signed and dated: "RHL 1629"
To the original dimensions (given above) were added two thin strips, less than a centimetre wide.

34

35

48

37 ⊞ ⊕ 41×34 *1630 ⊟ ⦂

Self-Portrait
Amsterdam, Rijksmuseum
Signed: "RL". The title given
to the painting by the museum
is *Study of His Own Face*.

38 ⊞ ⊕ 15×12 *1630* ⊟ ⦂

Self-Portrait in a Small
Cap
Stockholm, Nationalmuseum
The signature and date are
illegible.

39 ⊞ ⊕ 49×30 1630 ⊟ ⦂

Self-Portrait Bareheaded
Aerdenhout, Loudon Collection
Signed and dated: "RL 1630".

40 ⊞ ⊕ 35×29 *1630* ⊟ ○

Rembrandt's Mother as a
Prophetess
Essen, von Bohlen und Halbach
Collection
Critics are almost unanimous
in identifying the sitter with the
artist's mother, dressed in the
garb of the prophetess Anna
(see nos. 23 and 54).

41 ⊞ ⊕ 47×39 *1630* ⊟ ⦂

Portrait of a Man with a
Fur Collar
The Hague, Mauritshuis
This painting is also thought to
be a portrait of the artist's
father; the cap (G 1968) seems
to have been added later by
Rembrandt himself.

42 ⊞ ⊕ 22×17,5 1630 ⊟ ⦂

Portrait of an Old Man in a
Fur Hat
Innsbruck, Tiroler Landes-
museum Ferdinandeum
Signed and dated: "RHL 1630"
Another supposed portrait of
his father. Its attribution to
Rembrandt was made more
certain by the recent restoring.
A copy, dated 1633, is known.

43 ⊞ ⊕ 67,5×56 1630 ⊟ ⦂

Old Man with Gold Chains
and Cross
Cassel, Staatliche Kunstsammlungen, Gemäldegalerie
Signed and dated: "RHL 1630".

44 ⊞ ⊕ 36×26 1630 ⊟ ⦂

Old Soldier with an Earring
Leningrad, Hermitage
Signed: "RHL".

45 ⊞ ⊕ 82,5×74,5 *1630* ⊟ ⦂

Soldier in a Great Cloak
Chicago (Ill.), Art Institute
Signed: "RL". A copy is known
to exist.

46 ⊞ ⊕ 64,5×51 *1630* ⊟ ○

Soldier in a Plumed Hat
London, Mountain Collection
There is a modern signature:
"Rembrandt f.", covering a
former, autograph signature.

47 ⊞ ⊕ 83×78 *1630* ⊟ ⦂

The Abduction of Proserpina
Berlin, Staatliche Museen,
Gemäldegalerie

48 ⊞ ⊕ 62×50 *1630* ⊟ ⦂

David Playing the Harp
before Saul
Frankfurt, Städelsches
Kunstinstitut

49 ⊞ ⊕ 75×60 *1630* ⊟ ⦂

The Repentant St Peter
Boston (Mass.), Museum of
Fine Arts
This may be a study.

The painting is attributed to
Salomon Koninck by J. C. van
Dyke (*Rembrandt and his
School*, London 1923). Two
copies are known.

50 ⊞ ⊕ 47×39 *1630* ⊟ ⦂

St Paul in Meditation
Nuremberg, Germanisches
Nationalmuseum
It is possible that the sitter may
have been Rembrandt's father.

51 ⊞ ⊕ 58,5×45 1630 ⊟ ⦂

A Hermit Reading
Paris, Musée du Louvre

The signature and the date are
apocryphal: "RHL 1630".

52 ⊞ ⊕ 93,5×81 *1630* ⊟ ○

The Raising of Lazarus
Los Angeles (Calif.),
Ahmanson Collection
Formerly in the Dübi-Müller
Collection at Solothurn, it was
lent to the Rijksmuseum of
Amsterdam and exhibited in
the Rembrandt exhibition at
Amsterdam in 1956.

23

24

25

40 [Plate VI]

39

41

42

43

44

45

46

49

47

50

51

53 [Plate VII]   54   55

56 [Plate X]   57 [Plate XI]

60   61   62

63   64   65

66   74   67

53   58×46 1630

Jeremiah Foreseeing the Destruction of Jerusalem
Amsterdam, Rijksmuseum
Signed and dated: "RHL 1630"
Bible reference: Jeremiah, 6, 21. The sitter for the prophet may have been Rembrandt's father.

54   60×48 1631

The Prophetess Anna
Amsterdam, Rijksmuseum
Signed and dated: "RHL 1631"
Bible reference: Luke, 2, 36 ff. The sitter may have been Rembrandt's mother.

55   58×48 1631

St Peter in Prison
Brussels, Mérode-Westerloo Collection
Signed and dated: "RHL 1631".

56   60×48 1631

Scholar Reading
Stockholm, Nationalmuseum
The signature and date may be apocryphal: "Rembrandt fc 1631". It is thought to represent St Anastasius.

57   29×33 1631*

Scholar in Meditation
Paris, Musée du Louvre
Signed and dated: "RHL van Rijn 163."; the last digit is illegible.

58   61×48 1631

The Presentation of Christ in the Temple
The Hague, Mauritshuis
The signature and date have been repainted: "RHL 1631". The top corners were later cut to make an arch.

59   100×73 1631

Christ on the Cross
Le Mas d'Agenais (Lot-et-Garonne), Parish Church
Signed and dated: "RHL 1631". First published by KB in P 1962 no. 20. See no. 144.

60   109×101 *1631*

St Paul
Bremen, Kunsthalle
Remains of a signature. Work by Jan Lievens with retouchings by Rembrandt.

61   63,5×49,5 *1631*

Young Man with a Broad Collar
New York, Fleitman Collection
Work of uncertain attribution which may possibly be ascribed to Jan Lievens.

62   65×51 1631

Young Man in a Turban
Windsor Castle, Royal Collection
Signed and dated: "RHL 1631". Various copies are known.

63   56×45,5 1631

Young Soldier in a Small Cap
San Diego (Calif.), Fine Arts Gallery
Signed and dated: "RHL 1631".

58

59

68

71

64 ⊞ ⊕ 80,5×66 1631 ▤ ⦂
Young Man with a Gold Chain
Toledo (Ohio), Museum of Art
Signed and dated "RHL 1631".

65 ⊞ ⊕ 60,5×51,5 1631 ▤ ⦂
Old Man in a Cap, with a Gold Chain
Birmingham, City Museum and Art Gallery
Signed and dated: "RHL 1631". The sitter may be the same as in no. 10, though somewhat older. One cannot, it seems, identify him with the artist's father (who died in 1630), nor with any of his brothers.

66 ⊞ ⊕ 117×87,5 1631 ▤ ⦂
Portrait of Nicolaes Ruts
New York, Frick Collection
The signature is illegible, but it is dated "1631". Nicolaes Ruts (1573–1638) was a wealthy merchant of Amsterdam. There is an eighteenth-century copy.

67 ⊞ ⊕ 113×92 1631 ▤ ⦂
Writer at his Desk
Leningrad, Hermitage
Signed and dated: "RHL 1631".

68 ⊞ ⊕ 34,5×25 *1631* ▤ ⦂
Andromeda
The Hague, Mauritshuis

69 ⊞ ⊕ 61×47 1632 ▤ ○
The Abduction of Europa
New York, Klotz Collection
Signed and dated: "RHL van Rijn 1632".

70 ⊞ ⊕ 73,5×93,5 *1632* ▤ ○
Stories of Diana
Rhede (near Bocholt, Westphalia), Zu Salm-Salm Collection
Signed and dated: "Rembrandt fe 1635". The last digit which gives the painting an arguable date, seems to have been repainted. The picture shows, apart from Diana and the nymphs bathing, the stories of the hunter Actaeon and the nymph Callisto.

71 ⊞ ⊕ 25×21 *1632* ▤ ⦂
The Good Samaritan
London, Wallace Collection

72 ⊞ ⊕ 64×47 1632 ▤ ○
Bust of a Young Man
Vanås, Skåne (Sweden), Wachtmeister Collection
Signed and dated: "RHL van Rijn f 1632".

73 ⊞ ⊕ 58×44 1632 ▤ ⦂
Portrait of a Young Man with a Gold Chain
Cleveland (Ohio), Museum of Art
Signed and dated: "RHL van Rijn 1632". Formerly believed to have been a self-portrait painted as a pendant to Saskia (no. 163). B 1966 sees in it a portrait of Ferdinand Bol.

69

74 ⊞ ⊕ 101,5×81,5 *1632* ▤ ⦂
Portrait of a Man Sharpening a Quill
Cassel, Kunstsammlungen, Gemäldegalerie
Signed on the sheet of parchment: "RHL van Rijn". Some critics see in the sitter the master calligrapher Lieven Willemszoon van Coppenol.

75 ⊞ ⊕ 102,5×84 1632 ▤ ⦂
Portrait of Joris de Caullery
San Francisco (Calif.), M. H. de Young Memorial Museum
Signed and dated: "RHL van Rijn 1632". The sitter, formerly a naval captain, became subsequently a wine-merchant.

76 ⊞ ⊕ 63,5×48 1632 ▤ ⦂
Man with a Goatee Beard
Brunswick, Staatliche Herzog Anton Ulrich-Museum
Signed and dated: "RHL van Rijn . . . 2". The signature and date are covered by an apocryphal "Rembrandt f 1632". In the same museum is another painting, *Portrait of a Lady*, ascribed to Rembrandt, which may be a pendant to this work.

77 ⊞ ⊕ 31×24,5 1632 ▤ ⦂
Portrait of Maurits Huygens
Hamburg, Kunsthalle
Signed and dated: "RHL van Rijn 1632". On the back of the canvas is written: "Huygens, secretaris van den Raad van Staten in den Hage". The sitter, who was Constantijn Huygens' elder brother, was secretary to the Dutch Council of State. The painting is a pendant to the portrait of Jacob de Gheyn III (see no. 78).

78 ⊞ ⊕ 30×25 1632 ▤ ⦂
Portrait of Jacob de Gheyn III
London, Dulwich College Picture Gallery
Signed and dated: "RHL van Rijn 1632". On the back of the canvas is written: "Jacobus Geinius iunr H[uyge]ni ipsius effigie[m] extrememum munus morientis" (HEG in OH 1943 no. 60). When he died, the painter and engraver Jacob de Gheyn III left his close friend Maurits Huygens this portrait of himself which Rembrandt had made as a pendant to that of Huygens (see no. 78). Huygens' brother Constantijn, however, an old admirer of Rembrandt, did not much like the portrait, as can be gathered from a couplet which he dedicated to him: "Rembrandtis est manus ista, Gheinij vultus: // Mirare lectore, es ista, Gheinius non est."

79 ⊞ ⊕ 63,5×47 1632 ▤ ⦂
Self-Portrait in a Large Hat
Glasgow, Art Gallery and Museum
Signed and dated: "RHL van Rijn 1632". Copies exist.

80 ⊞ ⊕ 91,5×75 1632 ▤ ⦂
Portrait of Maerten Looten
Los Angeles (Calif.), County Museum of Art
Signed: "RHL". On the first line of the sheet of paper which the sitter (a wealthy merchant of Leiden and Amsterdam) is holding are the words: "Marten Looten XL January 1632". The other lines have been interpreted in a variety of ways.

81 ⊞ ⊕ 169,5×216,5 1632 ▤ ⦂
The Anatomy Lesson of Dr Tulp
The Hague, Mauritshuis
The signature and date have been repainted: "Rembrandt fe 1632". Dr Nicolaes Pieterszoon Tulp (1593–1674), major anatomist (*Praelector Anatomiae*) of the Surgeons Guild of Amsterdam, held, in January 1632, a public lecture on the physiology of the arm, demonstrated upon the cadaver of a man who had been condemned to death. The guild wanted to commemorate the event with a painting of it and the young Rembrandt, who had only just moved from Leiden to Amsterdam, was commissioned to paint it. The seven characters (none of whom was a doctor) around Dr Tulp are identified in the painting itself by means of ciphers above their heads which correspond to numbers given in a list which one of the characters (the one nearest to Dr Tulp) holds in his hand. The seven characters are "Jac. Blok, Hartman Hartmansz., Adr. Slabran, Jac. de Witt, Math.

70

72

73

76

79

75

77

78

80

97

Kalkoen, Jac. Koolvelt, Fr. v. Loenen''. Several critics hold that the figure on the extreme left and the one most in the background are not by Rembrandt himself; G 1968 thinks the former to be a later addition by Rembrandt or by Jacob Adriaensz. Backer.

82 🔲 ⊕ 152,5×112 / 1632 📇 ⋮
The Noble Slav
New York, Metropolitan Museum of Art
Signed and dated: ''RHL van Rijn 1632''.

83 🔲 ⊕ 112×89 / 1632 📇 ⋮
Portrait of a Man with his Hand at his Breast
New York, Metropolitan Museum of Art
Signed and dated: ''RHL van Rijn 1632''. It is believed to be a portrait of Cornelis van Berestijn-Vucht. See also the following entry.

84 🔲 ⊕ 112×89 / 1632 📇 ⋮
Portrait of a Lady with a Trinket in her Hand
New York, Metropolitan Museum of Art
Signed and dated: ''RHL van

Rijn 1632''. G 1968 remarks that the signature seems to have been copied from that on the preceding portrait and that the painting itself (which may represent Cornelis van Berestijn-Vucht's wife) is totally dissimilar to the male portrait in technique; Burroughs (*Art Criticism from a Laboratory*, Boston, 1938) suggests that it was Jacob Adriaensz. Backer who painted both portraits.

85 🔲 ⊕ 68,5×53,5 / 1632 📇 ⋮ ○
Portrait of a Young Girl in a Beret
Zurich, Wiederkehr Collection
Signed and dated: ''RHL van Rijn 1632''. For this painting as well as for four other female portraits of 1632 given below (nos. 86–9), it is suggested that Saskia may have been the sitter or perhaps Lijsbeth, Rembrandt's younger sister.

86 🔲 ⊕ 64×49 / 1632 📇 ⋮
Portrait of a Young Girl with a Gold Necklace
Allentown (Pa.), Art Museum, Kress Collection
Signed and dated: ''RHL van Rijn 1632''. See no. 85.

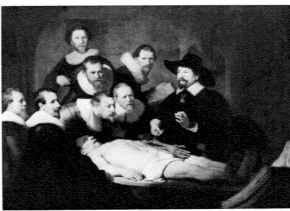

81 [Plates VIII–IX]

87 🔲 ⊕ 58×43 / 1632 📇 ⋮
Portrait of a Young Girl with Earrings and an Embroidered Robe
Boston (Mass.), Museum of Fine Arts
Signed and dated: ''RHL van Rijn 1632''. See no. 85.

88 🔲 ⊕ 55×48 / 1632 📇 ⋮
Portrait of a Young Girl in an Embroidered Robe
Milan, Pinacoteca di Brera
Signed and dated: ''RHL van Rijn 1632''. See no. 85.

89 🔲 ⊕ 72×54 / 1632 📇 ⋮
Portrait of a Young Lady with a Fan
Stockholm, Nationalmuseum
Signed and dated: ''RHL van Rijn 1632''. See no. 85.

90 🔲 ⊕ 68,5×55,5 / 1632 📇 ⋮
Portrait of Amalia van Solms
Paris, Musée Jacquemart-André
Signed and dated: ''RHL van Rijn 1632''. The countess Amalia van Solms-Braunfeld was the wife of Prince Frederick Henry (see no. 144). For a long time this painting was thought to have been a portrait of Saskia or Lijsbeth.

91 🔲 ⊕ 109×94 / 1632* 📇 ⋮
Young Woman Having her Hair Dressed
Ottawa, National Gallery of Canada
The signature and date may be apocryphal and the last digit is illegible: ''Rembrandt f 163 .''. Some critics, in an effort to exclude this painting from amongst the *genre* pictures, have interpreted it variously as ''Bathsheba Getting Ready for David'', ''Esther Getting Ready for Ahasuerus'', or also an episode from the story of the shepherdess Bocena, a character in the Dutch writer Jacob Cats's (1577–1660) *Trouringh*, which, however, was published in 1637.

92 🔲 ⊕ 75×55,5 / 1632 📇 ⋮ ○
Old Woman in a Cap
Paris, Private collection
Signed and dated: ''RHL van Rijn 1632''.

93 🔲 ⊕ 66×48,5 / 1632 📇 ⋮
St John the Baptist
Los Angeles (Calif.), County Museum of Art
The signature and date seem to have been repainted: ''Rembrandt ft 1632''. The oval panel was reduced.

94 🔲 ⊕ 72×54 / 1632 📇 ⋮
St Peter
Stockholm, Nationalmuseum
Signed and dated: ''RHL van Rijn 1632''. Painting on panel transferred onto canvas.

95 🔲 ⊕ 50×40,5 / 1632 📇 ⋮
Bald-headed Old Man
Cassel, Staatliche Kunstsammlungen, Gemäldegalerie
The signature and date may be apocryphal: ''RHL 1632''.

96 🔲 ⊕ 67×51 / 1632 📇 ⋮
Old Man with a White Beard
Cambridge (Mass.), Fogg Art Museum
Signed and dated: ''RHL van Rijn 1632''. This painting, however, is by Jacob Adriaensz. Backer with assistance by Rembrandt.

97 🔲 ⊕ 59,5×49,5 / 1632 📇 ⋮
Bearded Old Man with a Gold Chain
Cassel, Staatliche Kunstsammlungen, Gemäldegalerie
Signed and dated: ''RHL van Rijn 1632''.

98 🔲 ⊕ 75,5×52 / 1632 📇 ⋮
Portrait of a Forty-Year-Old Man
New York, Metropolitan Museum of Art, Loan of Mrs Lincoln Ellesworth
Signed and dated: ''RHL van Rijn 1632''. On the left is written ''AET 40''.

82

83

84

85

86

87

88

89 [Plate XIII]   90

91

102

103

99 ⊞ ◔ 60×47 1632 ▤ ⋮

Portrait of Aelbert Cuyper
Paris, Musée du Louvre
The signature and date may have been repainted: "Rembrandt ft 1632". Also inscribed "AE 47". The sitter was a Roman Catholic merchant of Danzig, born in Holland. See no. 100.

100 ⊞ ◔ 60×47 1633 ▤ ⋮

Portrait of Cornelia Pronck
Paris, Musée du Louvre
Signed and dated: "Rembrandt ft 1633". Also inscribed "AET 33". The sitter was the wife of Aelbert Cuyper. Although its attribution to Rembrandt is doubtful, it is a pendant to no. 99.

101 ⊞ ◔ 68×50 1633 ▤ ⋮

Portrait of a Middle-Aged Woman
New York, Metropolitan Museum of Art
Signed and dated: "Rembrandt f 1633". It seems possible that it may have been a pendant to no. 98 but its attribution to Rembrandt is doubtful.

102 ⊞ ◔ 160×127 1633 ▤ ⋮

Christ and his Disciples in the Storm
Boston (Mass.), Isabella Stewart Gardner Museum
Signed and dated: "Rembrandt f. 1633".

103 ⊞ ◔ 22.5×28,5 1633 ▤ ○

Daniel and Cyrus before the Idol of Bel
Great Britain, Private collection
Signed and dated: "Rembrandt 1633". Bible reference: Daniel, 14.

104 ⊞ ◔ 44×33 1633 ▤ ○

Boy in a Cap, with an Earring
France, Private collection
Signed and dated: "Rembrandt 1633". See no. 150.

105 ⊞ ◔ 21,5×14,5 1633 ▤ ⋮

Boy in a Cap and Embroidered Cape
London, Wallace Collection
Signed and dated: "Rembrandt f 1633".

106 ⊞ ◔ 59×48 *1633* ▤ ⋮

Female Figure in a Cape, with Musical Instruments
Berlin, Staatliche Museen, Gemäldegalerie
The presence of weapons, books and musical instruments in this painting has caused the figure to be interpreted as that of Minerva.

107 ⊞ ◔ 92×71 *1633* ▤ ⋮

Young Woman Seated
Vienna, Akademie der bildenden Künste, Gemäldegalerie
Signed and dated: "RHL van Rijn 163".

108 ⊞ ◔ 63,5×48,5 1633 ▤ ⋮

Woman with a Lace Collar
Santa Barbara (Calif.), Converse Collection

94

95

96

97

92

93

98

101

99

100

104

105

106

107

108

109

110

111 [Plate XIX]

112

113

Signed and dated: "Rembrandt f 1633".

109 ⊞ ◔ 62×55,5 1633 ▤ ⋮

Portrait of a Lady with a Gold Chain
South America, Private collection
Signed and dated: "Rembrandt f 1633".

110 ⊞ ◔ 66,5×49,5 1633 ▤ ⋮

Portrait of Saskia with a Pearl Necklace
Amsterdam, Rijksmuseum
Signed and dated: "Rembrandt ft 1633".

111 ⊞ ◔ 52,5×44,5 1633 ▤ ⋮

Portrait of Saskia Laughing

Dresden, Staatliche Kunstsammlungen, Gemäldegalerie
Signed and dated: "Rembrandt ft 1633".

112 ⊞ ◔ 58×45 1633 ▤ ⋮

Self-Portrait with a Moustache
Paris, Musée du Louvre
Signed and dated: "Rembrandt f 1633".

113 ⊞ ◔ 132×102 1633 ▤ ○

Portrait of Jan Uytenbogaert
Mentmore (Bucks), Rosebery Collection
Signed and dated: "Rembrandt f 1633". Also inscribed "AET 76". The sitter, a theologian from The Hague, was one of the leaders of the Dutch

114

115

116

117

Remonstrants. Rembrandt also made an etching of him in 1635. (In another etching made four years later, *The Weigher of Gold*, he depicted another Uytenbogaert, the powerful Receiver General whom he mentions in his fifth and seventh letters (see p. 89).

114 ⊞ ⊕ 9,5×6,5 1633 ▤ ⦂

Study of a Bareheaded Old Man
New York, Houghton Collection
The signature and date are apocryphal: "Rembrandt 1633". This is a grisaille study.

115 ⊞ ⊕ 72×56 *1633* ▤ ⦂

Old Man with his Hand on his Breast
Paris, Musée du Louvre
Signed and dated: "Rembrandt f 163". It is excluded in G 1968, but there appears, nevertheless, to be some traces of Rembrandt's hand. Copies are known.

116 ⊞ ⊕ 65×42 1633 ▤ ⦂

Bearded Old Man in a Cap
Metz, Musée Central
The signature and date are now illegible: "Rembrandt f 1633". G 1968 is of the opinion that it is the work of a follower of Rembrandt.

117 ⊞ ⊕ 86×64 1633 ▤ ⦂

Bust of a Man in Oriental Costume
Munich, Alte Pinakothek
Signed and dated: "Rembrandt f 1633".

118 ⊞ ⊕ 128,5×100,5 1633 ▤ ⦂

Portrait of Jan Krul
Cassel, Staatliche Kunst-sammlungen, Gemäldegalerie
Signed and dated: "Rembrandt f 1633". Jan Hermanszoon Krul (1602–1644), a craftsman and poet, was the founder of the Amsterdam Muziekkamer.

119 ⊞ ⊕ 114,5×169 1633 ▤ ⦂

Portrait of a Shipbuilder and his Wife
London, Buckingham Palace, Royal Collection
Signed and dated: "Rembrandt f 1633". The painting must have been cut; an engraving by Pieter de Frey reveals its original aspect.

120 ⊞ ⊕ 131×107 1633 ▤ ⦂

Portrait of a Couple in Black
Boston (Mass.), Isabella Stewart Gardner Museum
Signed and dated: "Rembrandt ft 1633".

121 ⊞ ⊕ 67,5×52 1633 ▤ ⦂

Portrait of Willem Burchgraeff
Dresden, Staatliche Kunst-sammlungen, Gemäldegalerie
Signed and dated: "Rembrandt f 1633". It is the portrait of a master baker and wheat merchant of Amsterdam. See also the following entry.

122 ⊞ ⊕ 68×55 1633 ▤ ⦂

Portrait of Margaretha Bilderbeeck
Frankfurt, Städelsches Kunstinstitut
Signed and dated: "Rembrandt f 1633". This painting represents the wife of the merchant Willem Burchgraeff (see no. 121).

123 ⊞ ⊕ 90×68,5 1633* ▤ ⦂

Portrait of a Seated Man with Gloves in his Hand
Vienna, Kunsthistorisches Museum, Gemäldegalerie
This is a pendant to the female portrait given in the following entry.

124 ⊞ ⊕ 90×67,5 1633* ▤ ⦂

Portrait of a Seated Lady with Gloves in her Hand
Vienna, Kunsthistorisches Museum, Gemäldegalerie
Pendant to the male portrait given in no. 123.

125 ⊞ ⊕ 124,5×99,5 1633 ▤ ⦂

Portrait of a Man Rising from a Chair
Cincinnati (Ohio), Taft Museum
Signed and dated: "Rembrandt f 1633". It has been suggested, but without much success, that this might be a portrait of Constantijn Huygens. See also no. 126.

126 ⊞ ⊕ 126×101 1633 ▤ ⦂

Portrait of a Young Woman with a Fan
New York, Metropolitan Museum of Art
Signed and dated: "Rembrandt ft 1633". This is a pendant to the male portrait no. 125. If the male portrait were that of Huygens, this would then represent his wife, Susanna van Baerle.

127 ⊞ ⊕ 63,5×50,5 1633 ▤ ⦂

Portrait of a Man with a Flat White Collar
Beverly Hill (Calif.), Loew Collection
Signed and dated: "Rembrandt fec 1633". B 1966 thinks it is a portrait of the painter Jacob Adriaensz. Backer and that it is a pendant to the female portrait given in the following entry.

128 ⊞ ⊕ 61×50 1633 ▤ ⦂

Portrait of a Lady in a Lace Cap
New York, Private collection (formerly at Piqua (Ohio), in the Flesh Collection)
Signed and dated: "Rembrandt f 1633". See no. 127.

129 ⊞ ⊕ 69,5×55 1633 ▤ ⦂

Portrait of a Man in a Wide-Brimmed Hat
Lugano Castagnola, Thyssen Collection
Signed and dated: "Rembrandt f 1633". See no. 130.

130 ⊞ ⊕ 66×52,5 1634 ▤ ⦂

Portrait of a Lady in a Large Ruff
London, Private collection
Signed and dated: "Rembrandt f 1634". It is a pendant to no. 129.

131 ⊞ ⊕ 210×135 1634 ▤ ⦂

Portrait of Maerten Soolmans
Paris, Rothschild Collection
Signed and dated: "Rembrandt f 1634". Traditionally believed to be a portrait of the soldier Maerten Daey; IHE in MA 1956 no. 43 identified the sitter as Maerten Soolmans, aged twenty-one, son of a refugee from Antwerp.

132 ⊞ ⊕ 209,5×134,5 1634* ▤ ⦂

Portrait of Oopjen Coppit
Paris, Rothschild Collection
The sitter was the wife of

119

Etching by J. P. de Frey (Amsterdam, Prints and Drawings Department of the Rijksmuseum), showing no. 119 in its original proportions.

120

140

118

139

121

122

123

124

125

126

127

128

129

130

131

132

133

134

135

136

137

138

Maerten Soolmans and the portrait is a pendant to his own. At one point it was thought to be a portrait of Machteld van Doorn, wife of Maerten Daey (see no. 131).

133 ⊞ ◓ 173×124 / 1634 ▤ ⋮
Portrait of John Elison
Boston (Mass.), Museum of Fine Arts
Signed and dated: "Rembrandt f 1634". The sitter was an English preacher.

134 ⊞ ◓ 174,5×124 / 1634 ▤ ⋮
Portrait of Mary Bockenolle
Boston (Mass.), Museum of Fine Arts
Signed and dated: "Rembrandt f 1634". The sitter was the wife of the English preacher John Elison, and her portrait is a pendant to his. See no. 133.

135 ⊞ ◓ 70×52 / 1634 ▤ ⋮
Portrait of a Man with a Wide-Brimmed Hat and a Lace Ruff
Boston (Mass.), Museum of Fine Arts
Signed and dated: "Rembrandt f 1634". See no. 136.

136 ⊞ ◓ 70×52,5 / 1634 ▤ ⋮
Portrait of a Lady with a Gold Chain and a Lace Collar
Boston (Mass.), Museum of Fine Arts
The signature and date are written in an unusual way, but the painting is a pendant to the male portrait no. 135.

137 ⊞ ◓ 70×52 / 1634 ▤ ⋮
Portrait of a Man with a Tasselled Hat
Leningrad, Hermitage
Signed and dated: "Rembrandt f 1634". See also the following entry.

138 ⊞ ◓ 71×53,5 / 1634 ▤ ⋮
Portrait of a Lady with a Tassel in her Hair
Edinburgh, National Gallery of Scotland (on loan from the Duke of Sutherland)
Signed and dated: "Rembrandt f 1634". It is possibly a pendant to no. 137.

139 ⊞ ◓ 67×52 / 1634 ▤ ⋮
Portrait of a Bearded Man in a Large Hat
Wassenaar, Kohn Collection
Signed and dated: "Rembrandt ft 1634". It is also inscribed "AET 47". It is thought that the sitter was a member of the Raman family. See also no. 193.

140 ⊞ ◓ 62×80 / 1634* ▤ ⋮
St John the Baptist Preaching
Berlin, Staatliche Museen, Gemäldegalerie
Grisaille on canvas (with additional strips of about ten centimetres on each side) transferred onto a panel. At the foot of the Baptist are the portraits of Rembrandt and his mother. This is one of the paintings mentioned by Houbraken (see p. 13).

101

141 ⊞ ⊕ 183,5×123 *1634* ▤ ⋮

The Holy Family
Munich, Alte Pinakothek
Signed and dated:
"Rembrandt f 1631"; the last
digit is painted on a strip of
canvas pasted over the painting.
Originally the picture had a
higher central part squared off.

142 ⊞ ⊕ 52×41 1634* ▤ ⋮

The Flight into Egypt
London, Wharton Collection
Signed and dated: "Rembrandt
f 1634", but the date is not
very legible. Discovered at the
Clinton sale (London,
Sotheby's, 19 July 1950), it is
accepted as an autograph
painting by nearly all scholars.

143 ⊞ ⊕ 54,5×44,5 1634 ▤ ⋮

**Ecce Homo (Christ before
Pilate and the People)**
London, National Gallery
Signed and dated: "Rembrandt
f 1634". Brown monochrome.

144 ⊞ ⊕ 96×72 *1634* ▤ ⋮

The Raising of the Cross
Munich, Alte Pinakothek
Executed by Rembrandt
probably on his own account
and intended as part of a
triptych, together with the
Christ on the Cross (no. 59)
and the *Descent from the Cross*
(see the following entry) it was
subsequently intended as part
of a series of five paintings on
the theme of the Passion
ordered around the year 1634
by the Prince of Orange-
Nassau, Frederick Henry,
Stadtholder of the United
Provinces (see nos. 145, 185,
224 and 225). Relating to these
five paintings are Rembrandt's
seven letters published on
p. 89. The figure in a beret, in
the centre of the painting,
seems to be a self-portrait.

145 ⊞ ⊕ 89,5×65 *1634* ▤ ⋮

The Descent from the Cross
Munich, Alte Pinakothek
The signature is apocryphal:
"C. Rhmbrant f". See no. 144.
The figure on the ladder seems
to be a self-portrait.

146 ⊞ ⊕ 158×117 1634 ▤ ⋮

The Descent from the Cross
Leningrad, Hermitage
Signed and dated: "Rembrandt
1634". See also no. 306.

147 ⊞ ⊕ 53×51 1634 ▤ ⋮

**The Incredulity of St
Thomas**
Moscow, Pushkin Museum
Signed and dated:
"Rembrandt f 1634".

148 ⊞ ⊕ 141×135 1634 ▤ ⋮

A Scholar in his Study
Prague, Národni Galerie
Signed and dated:
"Rembrandt f 1634". This may
be a Biblical figure.

149 ⊞ ⊕ 68,5×54 1634 ▤ ⋮

**Portrait of an 83-Year-Old
Woman**
London, National Gallery

Signed and dated:
"Rembrandt f 1634". It is also
inscribed "AE SUE 83". The
sitter has been identified as
Françoise van Wassenhoven.

150 ⊞ ⊕ 67×47,5 *1634 ▤ ⋮

**Portrait of a Richly Dressed
Boy**
Leningrad, Hermitage
HFW, in MA 1956 no. 43, sees
in the sitter (the same as in
no. 104?) the young son of
Hendrick van Uylenburch,
Gerrit. Various scholars
question its attribution.

151 ⊞ ⊕ 47×37 1634 ▤ ○

Bareheaded Boy
Welbeck Abbey

(Nottinghamshire), Portland
Collection
Signed and dated:
"Rembrandt f 1634".

152 ⊞ ⊕ 67×54 *1634* ▤ ⋮

**Self-Portrait with a Gorget
and a Beret**
Florence, Galleria degli Uffizi
The picture has been cut
at the bottom and a strip
has been added.

153 ⊞ ⊕ 68×53 1634 ▤ ⋮

**Self-Portrait with a
Moustache and a Cap**
Paris, Musée du Louvre
Signed and dated:
"Rembrandt f 1634"; the last
digit is not clearly legible.

154 ⊞ ⊕ 57×46 1634 ▤ ⋮

Self-Portrait in a Fur Collar
Berlin, Staatliche Museen,
Gemäldegalerie
Signed and dated:
"Rembrandt f 1634"; the last
digit is not clearly legible.

155 ⊞ ⊕ 80,5×66 1634 ▤ ⋮

Self-Portrait in a Helmet
Cassel, Staatliche Kunst-
sammlungen, Gemäldegalerie
Signed and dated:
"Rembrandt f 1634". The
painting is of doubtful
attribution; the name of the
painter of this portrait of
Rembrandt has been suggested
as Govaert Flinck.

156 ⊞ ⊕ 55×46 *1634* ▤ ⋮

**Self-Portrait in a Gorget
and Plumed Cap**
Berlin, Staatliche Museen,
Gemäldegalerie

157 ⊞ ⊕ 62×46 *1634* ▤ ⋮

**Young Soldier in a Plumed
Cap**
Detroit (Mich.), Wilson
Collection
Thought by Valentiner (V 1921,
p. 32, and V 1931, pl. 45) to be
autograph.

158 ⊞ ⊕ 99,5×79 *1634* ▤ ⋮

Portrait of Saskia in a Hat

141

142

143

147

148

165

144

145 [Plate XII]

146

149
150
151
152

Cassel, Staatliche Kunst-
sammlungen, Gemäldegalerie

159 ⊞ ◐ 125×101 1634
Portrait of Saskia as Flora
Leningrad, Hermitage
Signed and dated:
"Rembrandt f 1634".
Traditionally interpreted and
accepted (as here) as Saskia
dressed in the costume of the
goddess Flora. However ZFK
1941–2 no. 10 and G 1968
see her rather as a shepherdess.

160 ⊞ ◐ 142×153 1634
Artemisia
Madrid, Museo del Prado
Signed and dated:
"Rembrandt f 1634". The
subject-matter is not
unanimously agreed upon:
apart from Artemisia receiving
the cup containing the ashes of
Mausolos, the character has
been interpreted as Sophonisba
being handed the cup of poison
sent to her by Massinissa: in
either case the painting
illustrates an example of
conjugal love.

161 ⊞ ◐ 137×116 1635
**Female Figure with a
Laurel Crown**
London, Weitzner Collection
Signed and dated:
"Rembrandt f 1635". First
published by WRV in ZBK
1925–6 no. 59, and considered
to represent Minerva (see
no. 106). Its attribution to
Rembrandt is doubted by
several scholars, whilst others
consider it to be a work of the
master in collaboration with
Ferdinand Bol. B 1966 sees
Saskia as the sitter.

162 ⊞ ◐ 123,5×97,5 1635
**Portrait of Saskia in
Arcadian Costume**
London, National Gallery
The signature and date are
apocryphal: "Rem..a... 1635".
Traditionally interpreted as
"Flora" (see no. 159).

163 ⊞ ◐ 59×45,5 *1635*
**Portrait of Saskia with a
Veil**
Washington, D.C., National
Gallery of Art
See no. 73

164 ⊞ ◐ 92×72 1635
Self-Portrait in a Cloak
Whereabouts unknown
Signed and dated:
"Rembrandt f 1635". A copy,
dated 1638, is known.

165 ⊞ ◐ 161×131 *1635*
The Happy Couple
Dresden, Staatliche Kunstsammlungen, Gemäldegalerie
Signed: "Rembrandt f". It is
traditionally regarded as a self
portrait with his young wife,
painted in the early, carefree
days of their marriage. There is,
however, a recent tendency (IB
in NKJ 1966 no. 17; T 1968;
G 1968) to see in it the
"Prodigal Son in a Tavern".

153
154
155
156

158 [Plate XXI]
159
162
163

157
164
160
161

166
167
168
169

166 ⊞ ◐ 79,5×59 1635
Portrait of Philips Lucasz.
London, National Gallery
Signed and dated:
"Rembrandt 1635". Lucasz, who
had been born in Middelburg,
was a merchant and councillor
of the East India Company; in
1633 he had commanded the
mercantile fleet on its voyage
back from Batavia to Holland.
It seems that the painting has
been cut down. See also the
following entry.

167 ⊞ ◐ 76×60 1635
Portrait of Petronella Buys
New York, Meyer Collection
Signed and dated:
"Rembrandt f 1635". The sitter,
whose name is inscribed on
the back of the painting, was
the wife of Philips Lucasz.
See no. 166 to which this may
be a pendant.

168 ⊞ ◐ 76×65 1635
**Portrait of a Man with a
Ribbon on his Sleeve**
Indianapolis (Ind.), Townsend
Collection
Signed and dated:

"Rembrandt fec 1635". See
also the following entry.

169 ⊞ ◐ 77,5×66 1635
**Portrait of a Lady with a
Brooch on her Collar**
Cleveland (Ohio), Museum of
Art
Signed and dated:
"Rembrandt f 1635". This is
perhaps the pendant to no. 168.

170　171　172　173　174

175　176 [Plate XIV]　177 [Plate XVII]　186　187

188　190　191　192

193

170 ▦ ◑ 124×95 1635* ▤ ⁝
Portrait of an Old Man Seated
Washington, D.C., Corcoran Gallery of Art
The words "AET 69" can be made out and it seems that the date of 1637 was legible at one time. This may be a portrait of a member of the Mennonite sect. There is some controversy as to the attribution of the painting to Rembrandt.

171 ▦ ◑ 126×99 1635* ▤ ⁝
Portrait of an Old Woman Seated
New York, Metropolitan Museum of Art
Signed and dated: "Rembrandt fc 1635". The words "AET SUE 70" can also be made out. It may be the pendant to no. 170.

172 ▦ ◑ 83×67 1635 ▤ ⦂
Portrait of Anthonis Coopal
Greenwich (Conn.), Neumann de Végvár Collection
Signed and dated: "Rembrandt ft 1635." The diplomat Anthonis Coopal was a secret agent of the Stadholder Frederick Henry (his brother François — see no. 189 — was married to Saskia's sister Titia). On the back of the canvas are written the name and titles of the sitter.

173 ▦ ◑ 70×61 1635 ▤ ⦂
Old Man in the Costume of a Rabbi
Hampton Court Palace, Royal Collection
Signed and dated: "Rembrandt f 1635"; the last digit is not easily decipherable.

174 ▦ ◑ 66,5×52,5 1635 ▤ ⦂
Man with Dishevelled Hair
Pennsylvania, Private collection
Signed and dated: "Rembrandt 1635". It was sold in London (Sotheby's), 24 March 1965, thence to the Acquavella Galleries, New York and its present owner.

175 ▦ ◑ 99×76 *1635 ▤
Man in Oriental Costume
Washington, D.C., National Gallery of Art
Signed: "Rembrandt ft".

176 ▦ ◑ 72×54,5 1635 ▤ ⁝
Bust of a Man in Oriental Costume
Amsterdam, Rijksmuseum
Signed and dated: "Rembrandt f 1635".

177 ▦ ◑ 101,5×77 1635 ▤ ⦂
King Uzziah Stricken with Leprosy
Chatsworth, Duke of Devonshire Collection
Signed and dated: "Rembrandt f. 1635". Bible reference: 2 Chronicles, 26, 19.

178 ▦ ◑ 171×130 1635 ▤
The Abduction of Ganymede
Dresden, Staatliche Kunstsammlungen, Gemäldegalerie
Signed and dated: "Rembrandt ft. 1635".

179 ▦ ◑ 156×129 1635 ▤ ⁝
Samson Threatening his Father-in-Law
Berlin, Staatliche Museen, Gemäldegalerie
Signed and dated: "Rembrandt ft 163"; the last digit is indecipherable. Bible reference: Judges, 15, 1–3. The painting has been cut by about thirty centimetres on the left. We reproduce here a photograph of an old copy on canvas (160 × 170 cm.) which shows the original proportions.

180 ▦ ◑ 167,5×209 *1635* ▤ ⁝
Belshazzar's Feast
London, National Gallery
Signed and dated: "Rembrandt fecit 163."; the last digit is indecipherable. C 1966 dates it back to 1630. Bible reference: Daniel, 5, 5.

181 ▦ ◑ 193×133 1635 ▤ ⁝
The Sacrifice of Isaac
Leningrad, Hermitage
Signed and dated: "Rembrandt f 1635". Bible reference: Genesis, 22, 11 ff. Several copies are known of this painting. See also no. 182.

182 ▦ ◑ 195×132 1636 ▤ ⁝
The Sacrifice of Isaac
Munich, Alte Pinakothek
Work of Govaert Flinck which bears nevertheless the following words in Rembrandt's own hand: "Rembrandt verandert en overgeschildert 1636", which indicate modifications and reworking by Rembrandt.

178

183 [Plate XVIII]

Copy (Brunswick, Herzog Anton Ulrich-Museum) of no. 183 in its original proportions.

179

Copy (formerly at Goudstikker) of no. 179 in its original state.

181

182

183 47×39 / 1636

Tobit Healed by his Son
Stuttgart, Staatsgalerie
Signed and dated:
"Rembrandt f 1636". Bible
reference: Tobit, 11, 13. The
painting has been cut.
A copy in the Staatliches
Herzog Anton Ulrich-Museum
in Brunswick (oils on canvas,
48 × 65) shows the painting
in its original proportions.

184 236×302 / 1636

Samson Blinded by the Philistines
Frankfurt, Städelsches
Kunstinstitut
Signed and dated:
'Rembrandt f 1636". Bible
reference: Judges, 16, 21.
This is probably the painting
which Rembrandt gave as a
present to Constantijn Huygens
in 1639; see the third and fifth
letters of the artist, p. 89.

185 92,5×68,5 / 1636

The Ascension of Christ
Munich, Alte Pinakothek
Signed and dated:
"Rembrandt f 1636". This
painting is part of the "Passion"
group painted by Rembrandt
for Prince Frederick Henry.

186 126×109,5 / 1636

St Paul
Vienna, Kunsthistorisches
Museum, Gemäldegalerie
Dated: "1636", but the date
has now disappeared. It is the
work of a pupil with
interventions by Rembrandt.

187 57,5×44 / 1636*

Portrait of a Man with a Gold Chain
São Paulo, Museu de Arte
Signed: "Rembrandt". Formerly
thought to have been a self-
portrait. Some critics have expressed doubt as to its attribution.

188 125×105 / 1636

Portrait of a Standard-Bearer with a Moustache
Paris, Rothschild Collection
Signed and dated:
"Rembrandt f 1636". Scholars
consider this to be a self-portrait.

189 66×52 / 1636

Portrait of Frans Coopal
Zurich, Bührle Collection
Signed and dated:
"Rembrandt f 1636". This is a
supposed portrait (the
attribution to Rembrandt is
also disputed) of the brother of
Anthonis Coopal. The sitter has
also been identified as the
admiral Philips van Dorp, whose
portrait may have been painted
by Rembrandt but has since
been lost, the only remaining
clue to it being an engraving
(reproduced here), attributed
to Salomon Savery and dated
1634, which bears the words:
"Remb. van Ryn". See also
no. 190.

190 65×52 / 1636

Portrait of Titia van Uylenburch
Private collection
Signed and dated:
"Rembrandt f 1636". This may

180 [Plate XVI]

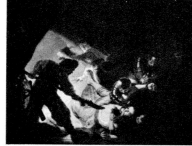

184 [Plate XV]

be the pendant to the preceding
portrait and may therefore
represent Saskia's sister Titia,
who was married to Frans
Coopal. The attribution to
Rembrandt is contested by
several critics.

191 155×122,5 / *1636*

Portrait of Jan Pellicorne with his Son Caspar
London, Wallace Collection
The signature and date are now
illegible: "Rembran..ft...".
The sitter was an Amsterdam
merchant. His son was born in
1628. See also the following
entry.

192 155×123 / *1636*

Portrait of Susanna van

189

Etching attributed to S. Savery (1634), possibly related to a painting mentioned in no. 189.

Collen with her Daughter
Eva Susanna
London, Wallace Collection
Signed and dated:
"Rembrandt ft 16.."; the last
two digits are illegible. The
sitter was the wife of the
merchant Jan Pellicorne, to
whose portrait (see the
preceding entry) this is a
pendant.

193 68,5×53,5 / 1636

Portrait of a Lady in a Ruff and a Cap
Rossie Priory (Perthshire),
Kinnaird Collection
Signed and dated:
"Rembrandt f 1636". This may
be a pendant to no. 139. A few

scholars reject its attribution to
Rembrandt.

194 85,5×108 / 1636

Landscape with a Baptism
Hanover, Niedersächsisches
Landesmuseum
Signed and dated:
"Rembrandt f 1636". This was
rediscovered at the
Ravensworth sale (London,
Christie's, 15 June 1920) and
first published in V 1921.

195 29,5×42,5 / 1637*

Landscape with a Stone Bridge
Amsterdam, Rijksmuseum
This may be a view of the
Oudekerk.

185

194

195

196 59×46,5 1637

St Francis at Prayer
Columbus (Ohio), Gallery of
Fine Arts
Signed and dated:
"Rembrandt f 1637". Several
copies are known.

197 68×52 1637

The Angel Leaving Tobias
Paris, Musée du Louvre
Signed and dated (both
repainted): "Rembrandt f 1637".
Several copies are known.
Bible reference: Tobit, 12, 21 ff.

198 31×42 1637

**The Parable of the Workers
in the Vineyard**
Leningrad, Hermitage
Signed and dated:
"Rembrandt f 1637".

199 51×39 *1637*

Joseph Relating his Dreams
Amsterdam, Rijksmuseum
Signed and dated:
"Rembrandt 163."; the last
digit is illegible. Bible reference:
Genesis, 37, 5 ff. Grisaille
sketch. An old copy is known.

200 47,5×39 1637

**Susanna Surprised by the
Elders**
The Hague, Mauritshuis
Signed and dated:
"Rembrandt f. 1637". The latter
part of the signature, from the
letter *a* onwards, is painted on a
strip which has been added later
to the painting; the date 1637,
nevertheless, is accurate. Bible
reference: Daniel, 13, 15 ff.

201 145×135,5 *1637*

Girl with Dead Peacocks
Amsterdam, Rijksmuseum
The signature – "Rembrandt" –
may be apocryphal. The dating
of this painting is controversial.

202 120,5×91 1637*

Girl with Still-Life
Zurich, Bührle Collection
Signed and dated:
"Rembrandt P 163"; the last
digit is illegible.

203 81,5×71 1637

Portrait of a Nobleman
New York, Metropolitan
Museum of Art
(Middendorf Collection Loan)
Signed and dated:
"Rembrandt 1637". This is a
supposed portrait of Prince
Frederick Henry of Orange-
Nassau.

204 134×103 1637

Old Man in Formal Dress
Mertoun (Scotland), Duke of
Sutherland Collection
Signed and dated:
"Rembrandt f 1637". G 1968
has doubts as to its attribution
to Rembrandt.

205 97×66,5 1637

**Portrait of a Man in Polish
Costume**
Washington, D.C., National

106

200

201

202

210

211

212

213

Gallery of Art
Signed and dated:
"Rembrandt f 1637". B 1966
and G 1968 suggest that this
may be a portrait of
Rembrandt's brother Adriaen.

206 62,5×47 *1637*

An Officer
The Hague, Mauritshuis
Signed: "Rembrandt f".
Traditionally taken to be a
self-portrait.

207 63,5×51 1638*

Self-Portrait with his Hand on his Breast
Formerly at Liverpool,
Walker Art Gallery (on loan
from the Heywood-Lonsdale
Collection)
Signed and dated:
"Rembrandt f 163."; one copy
is known. The painting was on
show at the Walker Art
Gallery, Liverpool then sold in
London (Christie's), 27 June
1969.

208 98×70 1638

Portrait of Saskia in a Beret
Switzerland, Private collection
Signed and dated:
"Rembrandt f 1638". G 1968
gathers from a restorer that
the last digit of the date was
once a 5; it appears, therefore,
that the painting covers an
earlier picture.

209 126×175 1638

Samson's Wedding Feast
Dresden, Staatliche Kunstsammlungen, Gemäldegalerie
Signed and dated:
"Rembrandt f 1638". Bible
reference: Judges, 14, 10–4
(Samson posing the riddle to
his thirty wedding guests).
The two characters in the
background on the right, one
with a flute, the other in a
beret, seem to be portraits;
HdG 1915 thought the second
to be a self-portrait; Scheidegg
*(Rembrandt und seine Werken
in der Dresdener Galerie*, 1958)
and E 1967 think the first
figure so.

210 61×49,5 1638

Christ Appearing to Mary Magdelene
London, Buckingham Palace,
Royal Collection
Signed and dated:
"Rembrandt f 1638". On the
back of the painting is stuck a
seventeenth-century handwritten
poem praising the painting.

211 46,5×66 1638

Landscape with the Good Samaritan
Cracow, Muzeum Czartoryski
Signed and dated:
"Rembrandt f 1638".

212 28×40 *1638*

Landscape with an Arched Bridge
Berlin, Staatliche Museen,
Gemäldegalerie

213 55×71,5 *1638*

Landscape with an Obelisk
Boston (Mass.), Isabella
Stewart Gardner Museum

The initial and date are
possibly apocryphal, with the
last digit almost illegible:
"R 1638".

214 30×46 *1639*

Landscape with Ruins
Wassenaar, Private collection
Signed and dated: "Remb.... f
163."; the signature and date
are almost totally obliterated.

215 52×72 *1639*

Landscape with Storm
Brunswick, Staatliches Herzog
Anton Ulrich-Museum
Signed: "Rembrandt f".

216 200×124 1639

Portrait of a Man Standing before a Doorway
Cassel, Staatliche Kunst-
sammlungen, Gemäldegalerie
Signed and dated:
"Rembrandt fc 1639". This life-
size portrait is supposed to
represent Captain Banningh
Cocq, the main character in the
Night Watch (see no. 246).

217 121×89 1639

Self-Portrait with a Dead Bittern
Dresden, Staatliche Kunst-
sammlungen, Gemäldegalerie
Signed and dated:
"Rembrandt fc 1639".

218 94×74,5 *1639*

Self-Portrait with a Gold Chain and Cross
Ottawa, National Gallery of
Canada
Signed: "Rembra...". A second
version (87,5×72,5) of this
painting is in the Duke of
Bedford's Collection at Woburn
Abbey (Bedfordshire): the
scholars are divided as far as
the attribution to Rembrandt of
either painting is concerned.

219 79,5×61,5 1639

Portrait of Rembrandt's Mother with a Stick
Vienna, Kunsthistorisches
Museum, Gemäldegalerie
Signed and dated:
"Rembrandt f 1639".

220 64,5×55,5 1639

Portrait of Alotte Adriaensdr. Trip
Rotterdam, Stichting W. van
der Vorm
Signed and dated:
"Rembrandt f 1639". The sitter
was the wife of Elias Trip,
brother of the merchant
portrayed in no. 416 (q.v.).
See also the following entry.

221 107×82 1639

Portrait of Maria Trip
Amsterdam, Rijksmuseum
Signed and dated:
"Rembrandt f 1639". G 1968
thinks that the painting has
been cut on all four sides. The
sitter was the daughter of the
merchant Elias Trip and Alotte
Adriaensdr. See no. 220.

214

215

222

224 [Plate XXII]

225

226

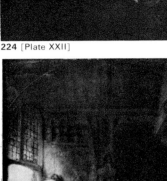

227 [Plate XXIII]

229

223

228

234

235

222 ⊞ ⊕ 32×26,5 *1639 ▤ ⋮

The Lamentation over the Dead Christ
London, National Gallery
Grisaille sketch on paper and canvas stuck onto a panel.

223 ⊞ ⊕ 32×40,5 *1639* ▤ ⋮

The Entombment of Christ
Glasgow, Hunterian Museum and University Art Collection
This monochrome sketch may have been made for an etching which was never executed.

224 ⊞ ⊕ 92,5×69 1639 ▤ ⋮

The Entombment of Christ
Munich, Alte Pinakothek
This painting is one of the Passion pictures commissioned by Prince Frederick Henry (see no. 144). The cost of the painting was 600 florins, like the *Resurrection* (see no. 225).

225 ⊞ ⊕ 92×67 1639 ▤ ⋮

The Resurrection of Christ
Munich, Alte Pinakothek
Signed and dated:
"Rembr...t 163.", but both signature and date are illegible in parts. The painting was transferred onto a panel which bears on the back the writing of an eighteenth-century restorer: "Rimbrand creavit me P H Brinckmann resuscitavit Te. 1755". This painting belongs to the "Passion" cycle commissioned by Prince Frederick Henry (see no. 144).

226 ⊞ ⊕ 57,5×48,5 1640 ▤ ⋮

The Visitation
Detroit (Mich.), Institute of Arts
Signed and dated:
"Rembrandt 1640".

227 ⊞ ⊕ 41×34 1640 ▤ ⋮

The Holy Family
Paris, Musée du Louvre
Signed and dated: "Rembrandt f 1640". Also known as *The Woodcutter's Family*.

228 ⊞ ⊕ 39×53 1640 ▤ ⋮

Biblical Scene with a Woman on a Donkey
London, Victoria and Albert Museum
Signed and dated: "Rembrandt f 1640". The panel was enlarged at the top by the addition of a strip of four centimetres. The subject-matter of this painting is traditionally taken to be "The Repudiation of Hagar".

229 ⊞ ⊕ 73,5×52 *1640* ▤ ⋮

Slaughtered Ox
Glasgow, Art Gallery and Museum
The signature and date may be apocryphal: "Rembrandt f 16..".

230 ⊞ ⊕ 75×55 1640 ▤ ⋮

Portrait of Herman Doomer
New York, Metropolitan Museum of Art
Signed and dated:
"Rembrandt f 1640". Doomer was a frame-maker and gilder of Amsterdam. His portrait is the pendant to his wife's

230

231

232

233

239 [Plate XXVII]

240

241

242

described in the following entry. Both the portraits were bequeathed to the sitters' son, Lambert Doomer, a pupil of Rembrandt's, under the condition that he should give a copy of the two paintings to each of his five remaining brothers; several copies, in fact, are known, amongst which are some signed by Doomer.

231 🔲 ⊘ 76×56 1640 🗔 ⦂
Portrait of Baartgen Martens
Leningrad, Hermitage
Signed: "Rembrandt f". The sitter was the wife of the frame-maker Herman Doomer. For details, see the preceding entry.

232 🔲 ⊘ 64×49 1640 🗔 ⦂
Self-Portrait with a Fur Collar and Gold Chains
London, Wallace Collection
The signature may be apocryphal: "Rembrandt". The top corners of the panel were rounded off at a later date.

233 🔲 ⊘ 100×80 1640 🗔 ⦂
Self-Portrait in a Frilled Shirt
London, National Gallery
Signed and dated: "Rembrandt f 1640"; the word "conterfeycel" (portrait) is written in a different hand. The painting is obviously and intentionally reminiscent of Raphael's *Portrait of Baldassare Castiglione* and, Titian's *Portrait of Ludovico Ariosto* (see *Outline biography*, **1639**). The top corners of the painting were rounded off.

234 🔲 ⊘ 42×60 *1640* 🗔 ⦂
Landscape with a Church
Madrid, Duchess of Alba Collection
This has been attributed by some to Hercules Seghers.

235 🔲 ⊘ 46×64 *1641* 🗔 ⦂
Landscape with a Coach
London, Wallace Collection

236 🔲 ⊘ 176×210 1641 🗔 ⦂
Portrait of Cornelis Claeszoon Anslo with a Woman
Berlin, Staatliche Museen, Gemäldegalerie
Signed and dated: "Rembrandt f 1641". Anslo was a very famous Mennonite minister to whom Rembrandt dedicated an etched portrait which the poet Joost van den Vondel thought unsuccessful because it did not give any impression of the sitter's exceptional oratory power; The painting must have been executed the same year as the etching. The woman portrayed on the right may be Anslo's wife, Aeltje Gerritse Schouten, or else a servant; in either case the female figure is there as a listener, introduced into the painting by the artist in order to emphasize Anslo's oratory talent. The attribution of this

236 [Plate XXIV]

figure to Rembrandt has, however, been questioned by several critics: G 1968 thinks it a later addition by Rembrandt

237 🔲 ⊘ 105,5×84 1641 🗔 ⦂
Portrait of Nicolaes van Bambeeck
Brussels, Musées Royaux des Beaux-Arts
Signed and dated: "Rembrandt f 1641"; the painting also bears the words: "AE 44". It was formerly thought to be a portrait of Frans Coopal (see no. 189), but the identity of the sitter was given as that of Nicolaes van Bambeeck, a rich merchant of Amsterdam, by I. H. van

First state of the etching (186 × 157 mm.) representing the preacher Cornelius Claeszoon Anslo, made by Rembrandt in 1641, probably before the painting discussed under no. 236.

Eeghen. See no. 238.

238 🔲 ⊘ 105.5×84 1641 🗔 ⦂
Portrait of Agatha Bas
London, Buckingham Palace, Royal Collection
Signed and dated: "Rembrandt f 1641"; the painting also bears the words "AET 29". Formerly thought to be a portrait of Saskia's sister, Titia; IHE (see the preceding entry) identified the sitter as the daughter of a burgomaster of Amsterdam and the wife of Nicolaes van Bambeeck whose portrait, to which this is a pendant, is described in the preceding entry.

239 🔲 ⊘ 98.5×82,5 1641 🗔 ⦂
Portrait of Saskia with a Pink
Dresden, Staatliche Kunstsammlungen, Gemäldegalerie
The signature and date are not very clear: "Rembrandt f 1641". This may be the last portrait of Saskia made during her lifetime.

240 🔲 ⊘ 104×76 1641 🗔 °⦂°
Young Girl at the Window-Sill
Whereabouts unknown
Signed and dated: "Rembrandt f 1641". This painting, together with the one described in no. 241 once belonged to the Lanckoronski Collection, in Vienna, now dispersed.

241 🔲 ⊘ 104×76 1641 🗔 °⦂°
Scholar at his Desk
Whereabouts unknown
Signed and dated: "Rembrandt f 1641". See the preceding entry for details.

242 🔲 ⊘ 96×80 1641 🗔 ⦂
Portrait of Anna Wijmer
Amsterdam, Six Collectie
Signed and dated: "Rembrandt f 1641". This portrait is traditionally thought to be that of Anna Wijmer, mother of Jan Six (see no. 320); but this identification and the attribution of the painting to Rembrandt are disputed.

243 🔲 ⊘ 74,5×101 1641 🗔 ⦂
Allegory of the Concord of the State
Rotterdam, Museum Boymans-van Beuningen
Signed and dated: "Rembrandt f 1641". Monochrome sketch in brown, except for some blue in the sky, intended as a study for an etching or for a larger painting which were never executed. Rembrandt probably intended to represent the unification of all the Netherlands forces (civil political, military and religious) against the common Spanish enemy.

237

238 [Plate XXVI]

243 [Plate XXX]

244

242×283 / **1641**

Manoah and the Angel
Dresden, Staatliche Kunstsammlungen, Gemäldegalerie
The signature and date may be
apocryphal: "Rembrandt f
1641". Bible reference: Judges,
13, 19 ff. This is probably the
work of Jan Victors with
retouchings by Rembrandt.

245

73×61,5 / **1642**

**Biblical Scene with Two
Figures Embracing**
Leningrad, Hermitage
Signed and dated:
"Rembrandt f 1642". The
subject-matter which is
traditionally interpreted as
"The Reconciliation of David
and Absalom" (2 Kings, 14, 33)
is also interpreted as "David
and Jonathan Embracing".
(1 Kings, 20, 41).

246

359×438 / **1642**

The Night Watch
Amsterdam, Rijksmuseum
Signed and dated:
"Rembrandt f 1642". This
painting, executed on three
horizontal strips of canvas,
was commissioned by the Civic
Guards Guild and intended to
be displayed — together with
other collective portraits
painted between 1639 and
1643 by Joachim von Sandrart
(*The Company of Captain
Cornelis Bicker*), Govaert
Flinck (*The Guild Syndics and
the Company of Captain Bas*),
Bartholomeus van der Helst
(*The Company of Captain
Roelof Bicker*), Nicolaes
Eliasz., known as Pickenoy
(*The Company of Captain Van
Vlooswijck*) and Jacob
Adriaensz. Backer (*The
Company of Captain De
Graeff*), and now in the
Rijksmuseum, Amsterdam — in
the great hall of the
Kloveniersdoelen (the
headquarters of the Civic
Guards, situation in the Nieuwe
Doelenstraat, Amsterdam). The
painting was transferred in
1715 to the small War Council
chamber, on the second floor
of the Nieuwe Stadhuis (now
the Royal Palace); in order for
it to be taken through two
doors, the painting was cut
by about 25 centimetres on the
vertical left hand side (and
more at the top, so that the
arch in the background is now
mutilated; slightly less at the
bottom, but enough to remove
the foreground, so that the
captain's foot now grazes the
very edge of the painting), and
about ten centimetres on the
right. The original dimensions
were about 3,88 × 4,79 metres.
At the beginning of 1808,
when Louis Napoleon declared
his intention of taking
possession of the Stadhuis in
order to transform it into a
royal palace, the painting was
removed to the Trippenhuis
(today the seat of the Royal
Academy of Sciences, Letters
and Arts), situated at no. 29
Kloveniersburgwal, in order to
avoid any further harm to it,
and put in the care of the art
dealer C. S. Roos. Louis
Napoleon, however, demanded

246 [Plates XXVIII–XXIX]

*Copies of no. 246 in its original proportions. (From top to
bottom) Seventeenth-century oil painting by Gerrit Lundens
(Amsterdam, Rijksmuseum). Watercolour (before 1655) which is
part of an album (Amsterdam, Rijksmuseum); see no. 246 for the
transcription of the text on its opposite page. Engraving by J. van
Meurs from a painting by F. von Zesen, showing the
Kloveniersdoelen*

its restitution, and, on 6 August
of the same year, the painting
was duly returned to the
Stadhuis where it stayed until
the fall of the French empire
in 1815, when the Stadhuis
did become a royal residence
and all the art collections in it
were transferred to the
Trippenhuis which then
became a museum. It was only
in 1885 that the painting was
definitively moved to the then
new building of the Rijksmuseum.
The mutilation of the
painting affected the figures of

two men and one child,
originally painted on the left,
and which have now
completely disappeared, and
was responsible for the cutting
in half of the drummer on the
right-hand side. The original
proportions of the *Night
Watch* can be seen in a
drawing made before
1655 which was part of an
album owned by the main
character in Rembrandt's
painting, Captain Frans
Banningh Cocq (this is now
displayed in a case in the same

room at the Rijksmuseum as
the larger painting), and which
bears the words: "Schets van
de Schilderije op de groote
Sael van de Cleveniers Doelen,
daerime de Jonge Heer van
Purmerlandt, als Capiteijn,
geeft last aen sijnen
Lieutenant de Heer van
Vlaerdingen, om sijn
Compaignie Bürgers te doen
marcheren". ("Sketch of the
painting in the great hall of the
Kloveniersdoelen, representing
the young squire of
Purmerland as Captain,
commanding his Lieutenant,
the squire of Vlaerdingen, to
march off with his civic guards
company"). The proportions
are also shown in a copy (oils
on panel, 67,5 × 86 cm.)
painted by Gerrit Lundens
(1622–post September 1683)
in 1649 and lent by the
National Gallery of London to
the Rijksmuseum where it is
displayed above the case
containing the watercolour of
the *Night Watch*. Another two
works show the original
proportions: a drawing
(watercolour, 333 × 425 mm.)
by Jacob Cats (1741–99),
painted in 1779 and also in
the Rijksmuseum; and an
etching (465 × 617 mm.) by
L. A. Claessens (1764–1834),
made in 1797; both of these
works must have been
executed after a copy.

The main character in the
scene — which, according to
the tradition of official
corporation group portraits,
should have been a simple and
more or less static series of
portraits, and, moreover, not be
distinguished by a proper title —
is Frans Banningh Cocq
(1605–55; see also no. 216),
an illustrious member of
Amsterdam society. Married to
the daughter of the
burgomaster Volckert
Overlander, he owned a
considerable fortune and
acquired the squireship of
Purmerland; he was later
ennobled by James II and
became in his turn
burgomaster of Amsterdam in
1650. At the time when the
painting was commissioned he
was captain of the company of
civic guards, painted by
Rembrandt as they were abou
to march on their night watch
along the edge of a canal
which can still be dimly seen
on the left of the painting.
The company was made up in
the painting of about thirty
men, but only twenty-eight of
them are intact today, plus
three children and a dog. It has
been suggested that the face
with one eye showing behind
the left shoulder of the
standard-bearer is a
self-portrait. The identity of
eighteen of the men is known
(although it is possible to
actually identify only very few of
them) through a list written on
the shield hung on the great
archway at the back and
painted after Rembrandt's death
(the shield does not figure in
Lunden's copy, but an X-ray
made in 1953 showed it to
exist).

The men are identified as:

244

245

250

251

in the centre, dressed in black,
Captain Frans Banningh Cocq;
next to him, in yellow, and
with the emblems of
Amsterdam embroidered on his
doublet, Lieutenant Willem van
Ruytenburch van Vlaerding;
at the back, towards the left,
holding the blue and orange
standard of the company, with
the city coat of arms
embroidered on it, the
standard-bearer Jan Visscher
Cornelissen; seated on the
parapet of the bridge on the
left, with a helmet and
halberd, Sergeant Reynier
Engelen; in black, on the
extreme right, with
outstretched arm,
Sergeant Rombout Kemp; at
the back, between Sergeant

Kemp and the Lieutenant, the guard Jacob Dircksen de Roy, in a tall dark hat; the other guards are identified as: Barent Hermansen, Jan Adriaensen Keyser, Elbert Willemsen, Jan Claesen Leydeckers, Jan Ockersen, Jan Pietersen Bronchorst, Herman Jacobsen Wormskerck, Jan van der Heede, Walich Schellingwou, Jan Brugman, Paulus Schoonhoven and Claes van Cruysbergen; the latter was perhaps one of the

Rembrandt must have collected altogether from the sixteen civic guards 1,600 florins, not to mention what he received from the two officers. All the other figures in the painting – the children, the supposed self-portrait and the figure of the dog – were added by him without commission in order to enliven the scene, fill in gaps and generally complete the composition.

The enigmatic, shimmering figures of the two little girls

255

two figures which were cut off when the painting was mutilated.

According to a statement made about fifteen years after Rembrandt's painting by one of the characters in it, the textile merchant Jan Pietersen Bronchorst – to the effect that "he had been painted by Rembrandt together with fifteen other members of the company, in a picture then hanging in the great hall of the Kloveniersdoelen, and that, as far as he could remember, they had each paid the artist about one hundred florins, some more and some rather less according to the prominence of their position in the painting' –

in the centre (the first of the two has a cock hanging from her belt) have baffled critics for centuries and given rise to all sorts of fanciful suppositions; it is possible also that the luminescent quality of the two little girls is just one of the light effects of the composition. The cleaning of the painting, made by H. H. Maertens in 1946, has removed the pervading atmosphere of night which had been responsible for the famous title traditionally given to the picture; it might be more appropriate to call the picture "The Marching of the Civic Guard", although this title may be less suggestive.

247 ▦ ✪ 70,5×58 *1642* ▤ ⦂
Self-Portrait with an Earring
Windsor Castle, Royal Collection
Signed and dated:
"Rembrandt f 164 .

248 ▦ ✪ 71×57 *1643* ▤ ⦂
Self-Portrait with Gold Chains
Boston (Mass.), Museum of Fine Arts
This may be the pendant to the painting given in no. 249, but its attribution to Rembrandt is not universally accepted.

249 ▦ ✪ 72×59 1643 ▤ ⦂
Posthumous Portrait of Saskia
Berlin, Staatliche Museen, Gemäldegalerie
Signed and dated:
"Rembrandt f 1643". See no. 248.

250 ▦ ✪ 57×76 1643 ▤ ⦂
Bathsheba at her Toilet
New York, Metropolitan Museum of Art
Signed and dated:
"Rembrandt ft 1643".

251 ▦ ✪ 70,5×53,5 1643 ▤ ⦂
Scholar in Meditation
Budapest, Szépművészeti Múzeum
Signed and dated:
"Rembrandt f 1643".

252 ▦ ✪ 102,5×75 *1643* ▤ ⦂
Man Standing in a Doorway
Tisbury (Wiltshire), Margadale Collection
Signed and dated:
"Rem.....f 164.".

253 ▦ ✪ 51×42 *1643* ▤ ⦂
Old Man in a Beret
Leningrad, Hermitage
The signature may be apocryphal: "R f". The panel seems to have been enlarged A copy is known, incorrectly signed and dated 1632.

256

254 ▦ ✪ 71×58 1643 ▤ ⦂
Old Man in a Sumptuous Costume
Woburn Abbey (Bedfordshire), Duke of Bedford Collection
Signed and dated:
"Rembrandt f 1643".

255 ▦ ✪ 44,5×70 *1643* ▤ ⦂
Landscape with a Castle
Paris, Musée du Louvre

256 ▦ ✪ 84×65,5 1644 ▤ ⦂
Christ and the Woman Taken in Adultery
London, National Gallery
Signed and dated:
"Rembrandt f 1644". This is one of the paintings mentioned by

Houbraken (see p. 13); in 1657 its value was estimated at 1,500 florins.

257 ▦ ✪ 103×86,5 1644 ▤ ⦂
Seated Young Man with a Sword
Brunswick (Maine), Bowdoin College Museum of Art
Signed and dated:
"Rembrandt ft 1644".

258 ▦ ✪ 92,5×73,5 *1644* ▤ ⦂
Portrait of a Fair Young Man
Buscot Park (Berkshire), Faringdon Collection
Signed: "Rembrandt f". taken as a portrait of Clement de Jonghe.

247

248

249

252

253

254

257

258

259

259 ▦ ✪ 91×72,5 1644 ▤ ⦂
Portrait of a Dark Young Woman
Buscot Park (Berkshire), Faringdon Collection
Signed and dated:
"Rembrandt f 1644". Formerly thought to be a portrait of Jan Six's wife (see no. 320), Margaretha Tulp. The painting is now supposed to represent Jacomintje Jacobs, wife of Clement de Jonghe.

III

260 ⊞◔ 127×105,5 1644* ▤⁝
Portrait of a Man Holding a Pair of Spectacles
Cologne, Wallraf-Richartz-Museum

268

269

274

Signed and dated:
"Rembrandt f 1644", but the last digit could also be a 5. The sitter has been identified by some as the theologian and preacher Jan Cornelis Sylvius to whom Rembrandt dedicated a posthumous etching made in 1646. Formerly thought not entirely autograph by several critics. See also no. 261.

261 ⊞◔ 124,5×100,5 1644 ▤⁝
Portrait of a Lady Holding a Handkerchief
Toronto, Art Gallery

Signed and dated:
"Rembrandt f 1644". This may be taken as the portrait of Sylvius's wife, Aaltje van Uylenburch, a cousin of Saskia's, and considered as the pendant to no. 260.

262 ⊞◔ 110×82 1645 ▤⁝
Old Man in a Fur-Lined Coat
Berlin, Staatliche Museen, Gemäldegalerie
The signature and date are apocryphal: "Rembrandt f 1645"

263 ⊞◔ 128×112 1645 ▤⁝
Old Man with a Walking-Stick
Lisbon, Fundação Calouste Gulbenkian
Signed (illegibly) and dated:
"......... f 1645".

264 ⊞◔ 80,5×67,5 1645* ▤⁝
Man Holding a Pair of Gloves
New York, Metropolitan Museum of Art
Signed and dated:
"Rembran.. f 164.".

265 ⊞◔ 69×56 1645 ▤⁝
Oval Self-Portrait
Karlsruhe, Staatliche Kunsthalle
There are traces of a signature and a date which, in a copy in the Ostra Collection, Amsterdam, read: "Rembrandt f 1645". Beneath the painting is a former painting of a bearded man which can be detected by the naked eye through the double ear on the left.

266 ⊞◔ 100×84 1645 ▤⁝
Portrait of a Young Woman at a Door
Chicago (Ill.), Art Institute
The signature and date are mostly apocryphal: "Rembrandt f 1645". There have been suggestions that the model was Geertje Dircks. G 1968 thinks it may be the work of a pupil, perhaps Jan Victors, after a drawing by the master.

267 ⊞◔ 77,5×62,5 1645 ▤⁝
Young Girl at a Window
London, Dulwich College Picture Gallery

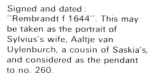

 260

 261

 262

 263

 264

 265

 266

 267 [Plate XXXI]

 279

Signed and dated:
"Rembrandt ft 1645". The top corners were rounded off at a later date.

268 ⊞◔ 20×27 1645 ▤⁝
Tobit, Anna and the Kid
Berlin, Staatliche Museen, Gemäldegalerie
Signed and dated:
"Rembrandt f 1645".
This painting has the same characteristics of style and composition as *The Dream of Joseph*, also in Berlin, described in no. 269

269 ⊞◔ 20×27 1645 ▤⁝
The Dream of Joseph at Bethlehem
Berlin, Staatliche Museen, Gemäldegalerie
Signed and dated: "Rembrandt f 1645". See no. 268.

270 ⊞◔ 117×91 1645 ▤⁝
The Holy Family
Leningrad, Hermitage
Signed and dated:
"Rembrandt f 1645". Fragonard made several copies of this painting.

271 ⊞◔ 46,5×69 1646 ▤⁝
The Holy Family
Cassel, Staatliche Kunstsammlungen, Gemäldegalerie
Signed and dated:
"Rembrandt fc 1646". The curtain, cornice and frame on the sides and at the bottom of the painting, are also painted; originally the picture was perhaps framed on the top as well.

272 ⊞◔ 65,5×55 1646 ▤⁝
The Adoration of the Shepherds
London, National Gallery
Signed and dated:
"Rembrandt f 1646".

273 ⊞◔ 97×71,5 1646 ▤⁝
The Adoration of the Shepherds
Munich, Alte Pinakothek
Signed and dated: ".....ndt f 1646". This was painted for Prince Frederick Henry, together with a *Circumcision* now lost, but known through an old copy on canvas (98 × 73 cm.) in the Herzog Anton Ulrich-Museum, Brunswick, a photograph of

Copy (Brunswick, Herzog Anton Ulrich-Museum) of the Circumcision (no. 273).

272 [Plate XXXII]

273

270

271

276

277

288

which is published here. Rembrandt was paid on 29 November 1646 a sum of 2,400 florins for both paintings. The sum is significant in view of the fact that seven years earlier he had in vain requested 1,000 florins for nos. 224 and 225, and had to accept 600 (see p. 89).

274 ⊞ ⊗ 16×21 1646 ▤ ○
Abraham and the Angels
Bennbrock, Haarlem, Von Pannwitz Collection
Signed and dated:
"Rembrandt f 1646". Bible reference: Genesis, 18.8.

275 ⊞ ⊗ 17×23 1646 ▤ ⦂
Winter Landscape
Cassel, Staatliche Kunst-sammlungen, Gemäldegalerie
Signed and dated:
"Rembrandt f 1646".

276 ⊞ ⊗ 185×203 1636-50 ▤ ⦂
Danae
Leningrad, Hermitage
Signed and dated:
"Rembrandt f 16. 6". Originally painted in 1636, the painting was reworked ten to fifteen years after. The subject-matter was identified by EP in OH 1933 no. 50 amongst several other suggestions: "Venus Awaiting Mars", "Rachel Awaiting Jacob", etc.

277 ⊞ ⊗ 76×91 1647 ▤ ⦂
Susanna Surprised by the Elders
Berlin, Staatliche Museen, Gemäldegalerie
The signature and date have been repainted: "Rembrandt f 1647". Bible reference: Daniel, 13, 15 ff. Beneath the painting there is another version on the same theme which must have been painted ten years before.

278 ⊞ ⊗ 34×48 1647 ▤ ⦂
Rest during the Flight into Egypt
Dublin, National Gallery of Ireland
Signed and dated:
"Rembrandt f 1647".

279 ⊞ ⊗ 108×90 1647 ▤ ⦂
Old Woman with a Book and Spectacles
Washington, D.C., National Gallery of Art
Signed and dated:
"Rembrandt f 164."; the last digit is illegible.

280 ⊞ ⊗ 24,5×20,5 1647* ▤ ⦂
Young Jew in a Waistcoat
Berlin, Staatliche Museen, Gemäldegalerie

281 ⊞ ⊗ 25×22,5 1647 ▤ ⦂
Old Man in a Fur Hat
Rotterdam, Museum Boymans-van Beuningen
The signature and date have been repainted: "Rembrandt f 1647".

282 ⊞ ⊗ 19×15 1647 ▤ ⦂
Portrait of Dr Bueno
Amsterdam, Rijksmuseum
Unfinished sketch for a well-known etching. Dr Ephraim Bueno was a famous Jewish physician and writer.

275

278

286

287 [Plate XXXIII]

283 ⊞ ⊗ 74×67 1647 ▤ ⦂
Portrait of Hendrick Maertenszoon Sorgh
London, Westminster Collection
Signed and dated:
"Rembrandt f 1647"; the last digit could also be read as a 4. Sorgh (1611–c. 1670) was a painter of Amsterdam. See also the following entry.

284 ⊞ ⊗ 74×67 1647 ▤ ○
Portrait of Ariaentje Hollaer
London, Westminster Collection
Signed and dated:
"Rembrandt f 1647"; as in the preceding portrait, the last digit of the date could be read as a 4. The sitter was the wife of the painter Sorgh and her portrait is the pendant to his. See no. 283.

285 ⊞ ⊗ 81×67 *1648* ▤ ⦂
Portrait of Hendrickje in Bed
Edinburgh, National Gallery of Scotland
Signed and dated; "R. m. ra... f 164.". Not all scholars agree on the identification of the sitter as the young Hendrickje. It is possible that the subject-matter of the painting was meant to be a Biblical one perhaps "Hagar Awaiting Abraham" (Genesis, 16, 4), or "Sarah Awaiting Tobias" (Tobit, 8).

286 ⊞ ⊗ 89,5×111,5 1648 ▤ ⦂
The Risen Christ at Emmaus
Copenhagen, Statens Museum for Kunst
Signed and dated:

"Rembrandt f 1648". Deleted in B 1966.

287 ⊞ ⊗ 68×65 1648 ▤ ⦂
The Risen Christ at Emmaus
Paris, Musée du Louvre
Signed and dated:
"Rembrandt f 1648".

288 ⊞ ⊗ 40,5×31,5 *1649* ▤ ⦂
Biblical Scene with an Old Woman and a Child
Edinburgh, National Gallery of Scotland (on loan from the Duke of Sutherland)
Signed and dated:
"Rembrandt f 16..."; the last two digits are practically illegible. It is perhaps the work of a pupil of Rembrandt's (Samuel van Hoogstraten who worked at Rembrandt's studio

280

281

282

283

284

285 [Plate XXXIV]

289

290

291

292

293

294

295

296

in 1640–2?), with reworkings by the master himself. As far as the subject-matter is concerned, several suggestions have been made: "Hannah in the Temple at Jerusalem" (1 Kings, 1–2), "Timothy and Lois" (second letter of St Paul's to Timothy, 1,5), etc.

289 ⊞ ✦ 25,5×21 *1650* ▤ ⦂
Christ
The Hague, Bredius Museum
This is part of a series of heads and busts of Christ which were all life studies of young Jews and can be dated to the late 1650s or the early 1660s. See the next seven entries.

290 ⊞ ✦ 25,5×23 *1650* ▤ ⦂
Christ
Detroit (Mich.), Institute of Arts
The signature may be apocryphal: "Rembrandt f".

291 ⊞ ✦ 25,5×20 *1650* ▤ ⦂
Christ
Whereabouts unknown
Published by WRV in DIAB 1930 no. 12. The painting was formerly in the possession of the Amsterdam art dealer P. de Boer.

292 ⊞ ✦ 24×19 *1650* ▤ ⦂
Christ
Tilburg (Holland), Weyers Collection
Excluded in G 1968.

293 ⊞ ✦ 24,5×20 *1650* ▤ ⦂
Christ
Philadelphia (Pa.), John G. Johnson Art Collection
The signature and date are apocryphal and written on a strip added to the original panel: "Rembrandt f 1656". First published by SS in ABu 1965 no. 47.

294 ⊞ ✦ 25,5×20 *1650* ▤ ⦂
Christ
Cambridge (Mass.), Fogg Art Museum

295 ⊞ ✦ 25×20 *1650* ▤ ⦂
Christ
Berlin, Staatliche Museen, Gemäldegalerie

296 ⊞ ✦ 47,5×37 *1650* ▤ ⦂
Christ
New York, Metropolitan Museum of Art
The canvas was made larger; the original dimensions were 42,5 × 34,5 cm.

297 ⊞ ✦ 96×116 *1650* ▤ ⦂
The Vision of Daniel
Berlin, Staatliche Museen, Gemäldegalerie
Bible reference: Daniel, 8, 1 ff.

298 ⊞ ✦ 80×67 1650 ▤ ⦂
Portrait of a Bareheaded Man
The Hague, Mauritshuis
Signed and dated: "Rembrandt f 1650". This is a supposed portrait of Rembrandt's brother Adriaen.

299 ⊞ ✦ 67×50 *1650* ▤ ⦂
The Man with the Golden Helmet
Berlin, Staatliche Museen, Gemäldegalerie
It has been suggested that the model for this painting had been Rembrandt's brother Adriaen.

300 ⊞ ✦ 81,5×68,5 1650 ▤ ⦂
Portrait of a Man at a Window
Cincinnati (Ohio), Taft Museum
Signed and dated: "Rembrandt f 1650". Some critics see in it a self-portrait. G 1968 has doubts as to its attribution to Rembrandt.

301 ⊞ ✦ 126×103 1650 ▤ ⦂
Man in a Fanciful Costume

Cambridge, Fitzwilliam Museum
Signed and dated: "Rembrandt f 1650". See the following entry.

302 ⊞✦ 134,5×101,5 1650 ▤ ⦂
Woman in a Fanciful Costume
Sarasota (Fla.), John and Mable Ringling Museum of Art
Also known as *The Duchess of Lorraine*. This is the pendant to no. 301. Doubts still exist as to its attribution.

303 ⊞ ✦ 62×52 1650 ▤ ⦂
Portrait of a Child
Fullerton (Calif.), Norton Simon Foundation
This may be a portrait of Rembrandt's son Titus, and could also be dated to 1653–4. It was bought by the present owner on 19 March 1965 for £798,000 at a memorable auction sale at Christie's, London. The former owner, heir to Sir Frederick Cook, had inherited it from the latter who had bought it in 1915 for £60,000.

304 ⊞ ✦ 66×86 *1650* ▤ ⦂
Landscape with Swans
Cassel, Staatliche Kunst-sammlungen, Gemäldegalerie
Signed "Rembrandt f".

305 ⊞ ✦ 65×79 1651 ▤ ⦂
"Noli Me Tangere"
Brunswick, Herzog Anton Ulrich-Museum
Signed and dated: "Rembrandt 165.". There are traces of former writing. The direct attribution to Rembrandt must be doubted.

306 ⊞ ✦ 143×111 *1651* ▤ ⦂
The Descent from the Cross
Washington, D.C., National Gallery of Art
Signed and dated: "Rembrandt f 165.". See also no. 146.

307 ⊞ ✦ 107×91 *1651* ▤ ⦂
Girl with a Broom
Washington, D.C., National Gallery of Art
Signed and dated: "Rembrandt f 1651"; the digits are not very clear. According to B 1966 the model is the same as in no. 308.

304

308 ⊞ ✦ 78×63 1651 ▤ ⦂
Girl at a Window
Stockholm, Nationalmuseum
Signed and dated: "Rembrandt f 1651". See also the preceding entry.

309 ⊞ ✦ 79×76 1651 ▤ ⦂
Old Man in Sumptuous Dress
Chatsworth (Derbyshire), Duke of Devonshire Collection
Signed and dated: "Rembrandt f 1651".

310 ⊞ ✦ 30×26 1651 ▤ ⦂
King David
New York, Kaplan Collection
Signed and dated: "Rembrandt f 1651".

311 ⊞ ✦ 77×66 1651 ▤ ⦂
Old Man with his Hand on his Breast
Vanås, Skåne (Sweden), Wachtmeister Collection
Signed and dated: "Rembrandt f 1651".

312 ⊞ ✦ 111×88 1652 ▤ ⦂
Old Man in an Armchair
London, National Gallery
Signed and dated: "Rembrandt f 1652".

313 ⊞ ✦ 51×37 *1652* ▤ ⦂
Jacob
Berlin, Staatliche Museen, Gemäldegalerie
The identification of the character was given in B 1966.

314 ⊞ ✦ 112×81,5 1652 ▤ ⦂
Self-Portrait with his Hands on his Hips
Vienna, Kunsthistorisches Museum, Gemäldegalerie
Signed and dated: "........dt f 1652". The painting was cut by about eight centimetres on the left. Several copies are known.

315 ⊞ ✦ 107,5×91,5 1652 ▤ ⦂
Portrait of Nicolaes Bruyningh
Cassel, Staatliche Kunst-sammlungen, Gemäldegalerie
Signed and dated: "Rembrandt f 1652". The sitter was a relative of Frans J. Bruyningh.

316 ⊞✦ 143,5×136,5 1653 ▤ ⦂
Aristotle Contemplating a Bust of Homer
New York, Metropolitan Museum of Art
Signed and dated: "Rembrandt f 1653". For the figure of Aristotle Rembrandt probably used the same model as in nos. 359, 360, 412 and 413. The bust of Homer was probably based on the one owned by Rembrandt himself (see the *Inventory*, no. 163, p. 90). The painting was probably reduced in size after some damage. It was originally painted for the Sicilian nobleman Don Antonio Ruffo and sent to Messina in 1654 (see *Outline biography*, **1652**).

298

299 [Plate XXXVI]

300

301

302

309 [Plate XXXVIII]

03

307

308 [Plate XXXV]

0

311

312

3

314

315 [Plate XXXIX]

297

305

306

316 [Plate XXXVII]

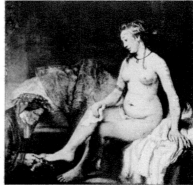

317 [Plate XLI]

One Cornelis Eysbert van Goor acted as intermediary between Ruffo and Rembrandt. The cost of the painting to Ruffo was 500 florins and the transportation cost 15,85 florins. The painting is described as follows in the inventory of the Ruffo Collection where it remained until 1760: "Aristotle with his hand on a statue, half-length figure, life-size." In 1660 Ruffo who wanted to add to his collection a series of paintings with relating themes, commissioned the painter Guercino to execute another half-length figure as a kind of pendant to Rembrandt's painting and on his request sent the painter a sketch of Rembrandt's work so that he could make his own painting similar in style (see *Outline biography*, **1660**). Guercino, in a letter dated 6 October, interpreted the subject-matter (which Ruffo must have neglected to describe) as a physiognomist studying in a statue the significance of human traits; the subject-matter he proposed to Ruffo for his own painting was that of a cosmographer contemplating a terrestrial globe. The next year Ruffo turned for a third painting to Mattia Preti who, in his turn, armed with sketches of the first two pictures, interpreted them as portraits of ancient rulers and promised to paint a portrait of Dionysius Seragosenus, a tyrant of Syracuse, whom he would paint wearing a turban "like the other two" (the sketches were obviously not very clear). Both Guercino's painting and Preti's have been lost; it is evident that Ruffo preferred Rembrandt's *Aristotle* to the other two, as can be seen from an excerpt of a letter sent to him on 24 January 1670 by the painter Abraham Bruegel: "I see from Your Excellency's letter of the 29th of last month, that Your Excellency has commissioned several half-length figures from the best painters in Italy and that none of them can compare for quality with that painted by Rymbrant: it is quite true and I agree with you." The painting eventually found its way into the hands of the great art dealer Sir Joseph Duveen who sold it in 1928 for $750,000 to the American collector Alfred Erickson from whom he re-bought it in 1933 for $500,000 and to whom he re-sold it in 1936 for $590,000. The painting was auctioned, at Parke-Bernet's, New York, 15 November 1961, and was bought by the Metropolitan Museum of Art.

317 ▦ ◷ 142×142 ▤ ⋮
1654

Bathsheba with David's Letter
Paris, Musée du Louvre
Signed and dated:
"Rembrandt ft 1654". Bible
reference: 2 Kings, 11, 4. The
model may be Hendrickje.

319

320

321

322

318 ⊞ ✇ 25,5×39,5 / 1654 ▤ ⦂
Landscape with Huts
Montreal, Museum of Fine Arts
Signed and dated:
"Rembrandt f 1654".

319 ⊞ ✇ 140,5×115 / 1654 ▤ ⦂
Portrait of a Standard-Bearer
New York, Metropolitan

Museum of Art
Signed and dated:
"Rembrandt fe 1654". The sitter was obviously the standard-bearer of one of the companies of Civic Guards in Amsterdam (for details about the Civic Guards, see no. 246).

320 ⊞ ✇ 112×102 / 1654 ▤ ⦂
Portrait of Jan Six
Amsterdam, Six Collectie

Jan Six was a poet, a writer and finally a burgomaster of Amsterdam; he was the friend and patron of Rembrandt until the time of Rembrandt's financial difficulties. He composed a distich on his portrait by Rembrandt on which can be read the date 1654. For further details on the relationship of Rembrandt and Jan Six, see *Outline biography*, **1653**.

321 ⊞ ✇ 73×60 / *1654* ▤ ⦂
Self-Portrait with a Beret and Gold Chains
Cassel, Staatliche Kunst-sammlungen, Gemäldegalerie
Signed and dated:
"Rembrandt f 165.". The present figure was painted over that of a woman which dates back to fifteen or twenty years previously. See also the following entry.

322 ⊞ ✇ 72×60 / *1654* ▤ ⦂
Portrait of Hendrickje in Sumptuous Dress
Paris, Musée du Louvre
This is possibly a pendant to the painting discussed in the preceding entry.

323 ⊞ ✇ 65,5×54 / *1654* ▤ ⦂
Portrait of Hendrickje in a Stole
Fullerton (Calif.), Norton Simon Foundation

324 ⊞ ✇ 39,5×32,5 / 1654 ▤ ⦂
Young Woman at her Mirror
Leningrad, Hermitage
Signed and dated:
"Rembrandt f 165.". The original panel has been enlarged by the addition of two small strips at the top and the bottom.

325 ⊞ ✇ 108×86 / *1654* ▤ ⦂
Old Man Seated
Leningrad, Hermitage
Signed: "Rembrandt f".

326 ⊞ ✇ 75×65 / *1654* ▤ ⦂
Old Woman with Folded Hands
Copenhagen, Statens Museum for Kunst
This painting was transferred onto a new canvas in 1890.

327 ⊞ ✇ 82×72 / *1654* ▤ ⦂
Old Woman Seated, with a Veil
Moscow, Pushkin Museum
Signed and dated:
"Rembrandt f 16..".

328 ⊞ ✇ 109×84 / 1654 ▤ ⦂
Portrait of an Old Lady with Folded Hands
Leningrad, Hermitage
Signed and dated:
"Rembrandt f 1654". This painting has been enlarged. G 1968 has doubts as to its attribution to Rembrandt. See no. 329.

329 ⊞ ✇ 109×85 / 1654 ▤ ⦂
Portrait of an Old Man with Folded Hands
Leningrad, Hermitage
Signed and dated:
"Rembrandt f 1654". This painting, like the preceding one to which it may be a pendant, has been enlarged. In this case also G 1968 doubts its attribution to Rembrandt.

330 ⊞ ✇ 74×63 / 1654 ▤ ⦂
Portrait of an Old Man in a Beret
Moscow, Pushkin Museum
Signed and dated:
"Rembrandt 1654". It has been suggested that the model for this painting, as for nos. 298 and 299, was Rembrandt's brother Adriaen. If this is indeed the case this would be a posthumous portrait, for Adriaen died in November 1652. See also no. 331.

331 ⊞ ✇ 74×63 / 1654 ▤ ⦂
Portrait of an Old Woman in a Veil
Moscow, Pushkin Museum

318

337

339

344 [Plate XLIII]

338

345

Drawing relating to no. 345 (Amsterdam, Rijksmuseum).

323

324

325

327

328

329

326

331

332

330

333

334 [Plate XL]

Signed and dated:
"Rembrandt f 1654". This is the
pendant to no. 330.

332 🔲 ⊕ ⁷⁹,⁵×⁶⁶,⁵ 🔳 :
1655
Old Woman Reading
Drumlanrig Castle, Thornhill
(Dumfrieshire), Duke of
Buccleuch Collection
Signed and dated:
"Rembrandt f 1655". This may
be an allegory of Faith.

333 🔲 ⊕ ⁶⁶×⁵³ 🔳 :
1655
**Self-Portrait with an
Earring and a Gold Chain**
Vienna, Kunsthistorisches
Museum, Gemäldegalerie
Signed and dated:
"Rembrandt f 1655".

334 🔲 ⊕ ⁶²×⁴⁷ 🔳 :
1655
**Young Woman Bathing in a
Stream**
London, National Gallery
Signed and dated:
"Rembrandt f 1655". Con-
sidered a portrait of Hendrickje.

335 [Plate XLII]

335 🔲 ⊕ ⁷⁷×⁶³ 🔳 :
1655
Portrait of Titus Studying
Rotterdam, Museum Boymans-
van Beuningen
Signed and dated:
"Rembrandt f 1655".

336 🔲 ⊕ ⁸⁹×⁶⁶,⁵ 🔳 :
1655*
Monk with Folded Hands
London, National Gallery
Signed and dated:

336

"Rembrandt f 165." Formerly
thought to represent a
Capuchin monk, this is now
taken to represent a Franciscan
monk, even possibly St
Francis. See also no. 384.

337 🔲 ⊕ ¹¹⁵×¹³⁵,⁵ 🔳 :
1655
**Riding Figure (The Polish
Rider)**
New York, Frick Collection
Originally signed and perhaps
dated, but most of the writing

has now disappeared because
the canvas was cut by about
ten centimetres at the bottom
and on the right. The figure of
the rider has been interpreted
as that of Gijsbrecht van
Amstel, the legendary founder
of Amsterdam, or that of a
Polish rider, a symbolic figure
representing Freedom.

338 🔲 ⊕ ⁹⁴×⁶⁷ 🔳 :
1655
Slaughtered Ox
Paris, Musée du Louvre
Signed and dated:
"Rembrandt f 1655". Several
copies were made by
Delacroix, Daumier, Soutine etc.

339 🔲 ⊕ ⁶³×⁸⁴ 🔳 :
1655
The Tribute Money
Bywell (Northumberland),
Allendale Collection
Signed and dated:
"Rembrandt f 1655". This
painting has also been
attributed to Gerbrandt van
Eeckhout.

340 🔲 ⊕ ⁶²×⁴⁹,⁵ 🔳 :
1655
**Christ and the Woman of
Samaria**
New York, Metropolitan
Museum of Art
Signed and dated:
"Rembrandt f 1655".

341 🔲 ⊕ ⁴⁶,⁵×³⁹ 🔳 :
1655
**Christ and the Woman of
Samaria**
Berlin, Staatliche Museen,
Gemäldegalerie
Signed and dated:
"Rembrandt f 1655".

342 🔲 ⊕ ¹⁰⁶×⁹⁸ 🔳 :
1655
**Joseph Accused by
Potiphar's Wife**
Washington, D.C.,
National Gallery of Art
Signed and dated:
"Rembrandt f 165." Bible
reference: Genesis, 39, 16 ff.
B 1966 and G 1968 think that
it is the work of a pupil with
additions by Rembrandt.

343 🔲 ⊕ ¹¹⁰×⁸⁷ 🔳 :
1655
**Joseph Accused by
Potiphar's Wife**
Berlin, Staatliche Museen,
Gemäldegalerie
Signed and dated:
"Rembran.. f 1655". A copy of
it was sold at Christie's in
London, 8 December 1961.

344 🔲 ⊕ ¹⁷⁷,⁵×²¹⁰,⁵ 🔳 :
1656
**Jacob Blessing Joseph's
Children**
Cassel, Staatliche Kunst-
sammlungen, Gemäldegalerie
The signature and date are
apocryphal: "Rembran.. f
1956". Bible reference:
Genesis, 48, 14 ff.

345 🔲 ⊕ ¹⁰⁰×¹³⁴ 🔳 :
1656
**The Anatomy Lesson of
Dr Deyman**
Amsterdam, Rijksmuseum
Signed and dated:
"Rembrandt f 1656". Dr Jan
Deyman was the successor of
Dr Tulp (see no. 81) as major
anatomist (*Praelector*

340

341

342

343

Anatomiae) of the Surgeons'
Guild of Amsterdam. Together
with his assistant Gysbrecht
Matthyszoon Calckoen
(shown on the left, holding the
cadaver's brain-case), Dr
Deyman gave, on 29 January
1656, a lesson on the
physiology of the cranium on
the corpse of a thief. The
painting was hung in the Hall of
Anatomy of the Guild, in the
Sint Anthoniesweg,

117

346

347

348

349

350 [Plate XLV]

351 [Plate XLIV]

352

353

354

355

Amsterdam; a fire there, on 8 November 1723, destroyed over three quarters of the painting. A drawing by Rembrandt in the same museum (109 × 132 mm.), made after the painting to show how the artist wanted it to be framed and placed in the small space which had been allocated for it, shows what the original composition was like, with seven spectators leaning out of the amphitheatre where the lecture took place.

346 ⊞ ◔ 76×62 1656 ▤ ⦂
Portrait of Dr Tholincx
Paris, Musée Jacquemart-André
Signed and dated: "Rembrandt f 1656". Dr Arnold Tholincx was a Health inspector of Amsterdam; he was followed in the same post by Dr Deyman no. 345).

347 ⊞ ◔ 76×62 *1656* ▤ ⦂
Portrait of a Young Man in a Large Beret
New York, Payson Collection
Signed: "Rembrandt f".
Formerly thought to be Titus.

348 ⊞ ◔ 77,5×66 *1656* ▤ ⦂
Portrait of a Young Man in a Pearl-Embroidered Beret
Copenhagen, Statens Museum for Kunst
Signed: "Rembrandt f".
This may be a pendant to the female portrait discussed in the following entry. There are doubts as to its attribution to Rembrandt. Absent in G 1968.

349 ⊞ ◔ 78×68,5 *1656* ▤ ⦂
Portrait of a Young Lady Holding a Carnation
Copenhagen, Statens Museum for Kunst
The signature and date are apocryphal: "Rembrandt f 1656". This may be a pendant to no. 348. There are doubts as to its attribution.

350 ⊞ ◔ 86×65 1656-57 ▤ ⦂
Portrait of Hendrickje at a Window
Berlin, Staatliche Museen, Gemäldegalerie

351 ⊞ ◔ 70,5×64 1656-57 ▤ ⦂
Portrait of Titus Reading
Vienna, Kunsthistorisches Museum, Gemäldegalerie

352 ⊞ ◔ 67×55 *1657* ▤ ⦂
Portrait of Titus with a Chain and a Pendant
London, Wallace Collection
Only the Initial "R" remains of the signature. According to B 1966 the dimensions of the painting have been reduced.

353 ⊞ ◔ 100×92 *1657* ▤ ⦂
Portrait of Hendrickje as Flora
New York, Metropolitan Museum of Art

354 ⊞ ◔ 125,5×98,5 1657 ▤ ⦂
Portrait of Catrina Hooghsaet
Penrhyn Castle (Wales), Douglas-Pennant Collection
Signed and dated: "Rembrandt f 1657"; there are

also the words: "Catrina Hooghsaet out 50 Jaer". The sitter was the wife of the dyer, Hendrick Jacobszoon Rooleeuw.

355 ⊞ ◔ 81,5×64,5 1657 ▤ ⦂
Old Man in a Large Beret
Kenosha (Wis.), Whitacker Collection

356 ⊞ ◔ 129×102 *1657* ▤ ⦂
St Paul
Washington, D.C., National Gallery of Art
Signed: "Rembrandt f".

357 ⊞ ◔ 123×99,5 1657 ▤ ⦂
St Bartholomew
San Diego (Calif.), Timken Gallery of Art, Putnam Foundation
Signed and dated: "Rembrandt f 1657". See no. 358.

358 ⊞ ◔ 71×58 *1657* ▤ ⦂
Man Frowning

Berlin, Staatliche Museen, Gemäldegalerie
According to B-1966 the model was the same as for painting no. 357.

359 ⊞ ◔ 78,5×65,5 1657 ▤ ⦂
Man with a Gold Chain
San Francisco (Calif.), California Palace of the Legion of Honor
Signed and dated: "Rembrandt f 1657". The model was probably the same as for *Aristotle Contemplating a Bust of Homer* (no. 316) and paintings nos. 360, 412 and 413. A copy is known; the painting was first published in JR in BCP 1948 no. 6.

360 ⊞ ◔ 78×66,5 *1657* ▤ ⦂
Portrait of a Rabbi
London, National Gallery
Signed and dated: "Rembrandt f 165."; the last digit is indecipherable. A copy of this painting, by Thomas Gainsborough, is in Hampton Court Palace. See also no. 359.

361 ⊞ ◔ 130,5×164 *1657* ▤ ⦂
David Playing the Harp before Saul
The Hague, Mauritshuis
Bible reference: 1 Kings, 18, 10

362 ⊞ ◔ 114×87 *1657* ▤ ⦂
Man in a Fur-Lined Coat
Boston (Mass.), Museum of Fine Arts
The signature and date are illegible: "Rembrandt f…".

363 ⊞ ◔ 53×43,5 *1657* ▤ ⦂
Self-Portrait in a Stand-Up Collar
Edinburgh, National Gallery of Scotland
Signed and dated: "Rembrandt f 1657".

364 ⊞ ◔ 49×41 *1657* ▤ ⦂
Self-Portrait in a Wide-Brimmed Beret
Vienna, Kunsthistorisches Museum, Gemäldegalerie
Signed: "Rembrandt f".

361

370 [Plate XLVII]

373

371 [Plate XLVI]

372

374

365 🔲⊘ 71,5×57,5 / 1657-58 🗒⋮
Self-Portrait in a Large Beret
Florence, Galleria degli Uffizi
Excluded in G 1968.

366 🔲⊘ 133,5×104 / 1658 🗒⋮
Self-Portrait with a Stick
New York, Frick Collection
The signature and date have been re-painted: "Rembrandt f 1658".

367 🔲⊘ 106,5×87,5 / 1658 🗒⋮
Man with Arms Akimbo
New York, Columbia University
Signed and dated: "Rembrandt f 1658".

368 🔲⊘ 108,5×86,5 / 1658 🗒⋮
Portrait of a Writer
New York, Metropolitan Museum of Art
Signed and dated: "Rembrandt f 1658". Formerly thought to be a portrait of the town-crier Thomas Jacobsz. Haring (see *Outline biography,* **1657–8**).

369 🔲⊘ 113×95,5 / 1658 🗒○
Man Holding a Letter
Switzerland, Private collection
Signed and dated: "Rembrandt f 1658"

370 🔲⊘ 54,5×68,5 / 1658 🗒⋮
Jupiter and Mercury Visiting Philemon and Baucis
Washington, D.C., National Gallery of Art
Signed and dated: "Rembrandt f 1658".

371 🔲⊘ 40,5×54 / 1659 🗒○
The Waiting of Tobit and Anna
Rotterdam, Stichting W. van der Vorm
Signed and dated: "Rembrandt f 1659". Bible reference: Tobit, 10, 1 ff.

372 🔲⊘ 60×75 / 1659 🗒⋮
Christ and the Woman of Samaria
Leningrad, Hermitage
Signed and dated: "Rembrandt f 1659".

373 🔲⊘ 137×116 / 1659 🗒⋮
Jacob Wrestling with the Angel
Berlin, Staatliche Museen, Gemäldegalerie
Signed: "Rembrandt f". Bible reference: Genesis, 33, 24 ff.

374 🔲⊘ 167×135 / 1659 🗒⋮
Moses with the Tables of the Law
Berlin, Staatliche Museen, Gemäldegalerie
Signed and dated: "Rembrandt f 1659". Bible reference: Exodus, 32, 15.

375 🔲⊘ 37,5×26,5 / 1659 🗒○
Old Man with White Hair
Birmingham, Cotton Collection
Signed and dated: "Rembrandt f 1659".

376 🔲⊘ 102×85,5 / 1659 🗒⋮
Portrait of an Old Man

356

357

358

359

360

362

366 [Plate XLVIII]

367

363

364

365

368

369

375

376

377

378

379

380 [Plate L]

381

with a Goatee Beard
London, National Gallery
Signed and dated: "Rembrandt 165.". In spite of the fact that the painting presents all the characteristics of a portrait, the character is identified as the Apostle Paul, because of the book and the sword. According to G 1968, the painting may be an old copy.

377 🔲⊘ 72×56 / *1659* 🗒⋮
Portrait of Titus in a Small Beret
Paris, Musée du Louvre

378 🔲⊘ 84,5×66 / 1659 🗒⋮
Self-Portrait Turned towards the Left
Washington, D.C., National Gallery of Art
Signed and dated: "Rembrandt f 1659".

379 🔲⊘ 114,5×94 / *1660* 🗒⋮
Self-Portrait with Palette and Brushes
London, Kenwood House, Iveagh Bequest
An old copy is in the museum at Aix-en-Provence (see p. 127).

380 🔲⊘ 111×85 / 1660 🗒⋮
Self-Portrait at the Easel
Paris, Musée du Louvre
The signature is repainted and incomplete and the date apocryphal: "Rem..... f 1660".

381 🔲⊘ 80,5×67,5 / 1660 🗒⋮
Self-Portrait in a Large Beret
New York, Metropolitan Museum of Art
Signed and dated: "Rembrandt f 1660". See also the following entry.

382

383

384 [Plate XLIX]

385

386

387

388

389

382 ⊞ ✪ 78,5×69 1660 ▤ ⁝

Portrait of Hendrickje with her Hand on her Breast
New York, Metropolitan
Museum of Art
Signed and dated:
"Rembrandt f 1660". See also
the self-portrait described in
the preceding entry, to which
this may be a pendant.

383 ⊞ ✪ 100×83,5 *1660 ▤ ○

Portrait of Hendrickje Seated
London, Morrison Collection
Signed and dated:
"Rembrandt f 166.".

414 [Plate LV]

384 ⊞ ✪ 79,5×67,5 1660 ▤ ⁝

Portrait of Titus Dressed as a Monk
Amsterdam, Rijksmuseum
Signed and dated:
"Rembrandt f 166."; the last
digit is not clearly legible. This
is also taken to be the portrait
of a Franciscan monk or a
"St Francis" for which the
model may have been Titus.

385 ⊞ ✪ 24,5×19 1660* ▤ ⁝

Study of an Old Man in a Beret
New York, Whitney Collection

386 ⊞✪ 103,5×86,5 *1660* ▤ ⁝

Portrait of Dirck van Os

Omaha (Nebr.), Joslyn Art
Museum
In the top right-hand side is
the coat of arms of the Os
family and the words: "D van
Os .... ef van d......".

387 ⊞ ✪ 82,5×64,5 *1660* ▤ ⁝

Man with Folded Arms
New York, Metropolitan
Museum of Art

388 ⊞ ✪ 48×41 1660* ▤ ⁝

Man Sitting in Front of a Stove
Winterthur, Sammlung Oskar
Reinhart
First published in V 1921.

389 ⊞ ✪ 93×87.5 1660 ▤ ⁝

Young Man Seated
Rochester (N.Y.), New York
University, George Eastman
Collection
Signed and dated:
"Rembrandt f 1660".

390 ⊞ ✪ 73×94 1660 ▤ ⁝

Ahasuerus, Esther and Haman at the Table
Moscow, Pushkin Museum
Signed and dated:
"Rembrandt f 1660". Bible
reference: Esther, 7, 1. This
may be one of the paintings
mentioned by Houbraken.

391 ⊞ ✪ 48×64 *1660* ▤ ⁝

The Risen Christ at Emmaus
Paris, Musée du Louvre
The complete attribution of this
painting to Rembrandt, which
has been contested by most
modern critics, has been re-
affirmed by G1968. It is
generally thought to be the
work of a pupil (Aert de
Gelder?) with reworkings by
the master.

392 ⊞ ✪ 154×169 1660 ▤ ⁝

The Apostle Peter Denying Christ

Amsterdam, Rijksmuseum
Signed and dated:
"Rembrandt 1660".

393 ⊞ ✪ 56,5×75 1661 ▤ ⁝

The Circumcision
Washington, D.C., National
Gallery of Art
Signed and dated:
"Rembrandt f 1661".

394 ⊞ ✪ 64×57 1661 ▤ ⁝

Young Jew with a Fastened Collar
Montreal, Van Horne Collection
Signed and dated:
"Rembrandt f 1661". Perhaps,
as suggested by G 1968, the

young man was used by
Rembrandt as the model for
his last heads of Christ.

395 ⊞ ✪ 62×49 *1661* ▤ ⁝

Christ
Milwaukee (Wis.), John
Collection
Published in HdG 1922.

396 ⊞ ✪ 109×90 1661* ▤ ⁝

Christ
Glens Falls (N.Y.), Hyde
Collection

397 ⊞ ✪ 95,5×81,5 1661 ▤ ⁝

Christ
New York, Metropolitan

Museum of Art
Signed and dated:
"Rembrandt f 1661". This is
also thought to represent an
apostle or a Jewish pilgrim.

398 ⊞ ✪ 78,5×63 1661 ▤ ⁝

The Risen Christ
Munich, Alte Pinakothek
Signed and dated:
"Rembrandt f 1661".

399 ⊞ ✪ 87,5×75 1661 ▤ ○

St Bartholomew
Sutton Place, New Guildford
(Surrey), Getty Collection
Signed and dated:
"Rembrandt f 1661". Sold in
London (Sotheby's), 27 July
1962, for £190,000.

400 ⊞ ✪ 98,5×79 1661 ▤ ⁝

St Simon
Zurich, Kunsthaus
Signed and dated:
"Rembrandt f 1661". First
published by LM in BM 1948
no. 90.

401 ⊞ ✪ 90×79 1661 ▤ ⁝

St James
New York, Metropolitan
Museum of Art
Signed and dated:
"Rembrandt f 1661".

402 ⊞ ✪ 82×66 1661 ▤ ⁝

Monk Reading
Helsinki, Ateneumin
Taidemuseo
Signed and dated:
"Rembrandt f 1661".

403 ⊞✪ 87,5×72,5 1661* ▤ ⁝

Apostle at Prayer
Cleveland (Ohio), Museum of
Art
The signature and date are

390

391

392 [Plate LI]

393

incomplete (and apocryphal?):
"Rembrand. f 166.". The
canvas had, on both its
vertical sides and bottom, a
strip just over two centimetres
wide (it is thought that
originally the top of the
painting had a strip as well,
which has since been removed)
which extended the painting
but which has been removed,
perhaps by Rembrandt himself,
in order to centre the figure
and achieve better proportions
(see Sherman E. Lee,
"Rembrandt, Old Man Praying",
in *The Bulletin of the
Cleveland Museum of Art*,
Vol. XIV, no. 10, December
1967). G 1968 had reservations
about its attribution to
Rembrandt.

404 ⊞ ◔ 104,5×84 / 1661* ▤ ⁝
Evangelist Writing
Boston (Mass.), Museum of
Fine Arts
Signed and dated:
"Rembrandt f 166."; the last
digit is illegible.

405 ⊞ ◔ 91×77 / 1661 ▤ ⁝
Self-Portrait as St Paul
Amsterdam, Rijksmuseum
Signed and dated:
"Rembrandt f 1661".

406 ⊞ ◔ 24,5×20 / *1661 ▤ ⁝
Head of an Old Man
Great Britain, Private collection
This may be a study for St
Matthew, discussed in the
following entry.

407 ⊞ ◔ 96×81 / 1661 ▤ ⁝
St Matthew and the Angel
Paris, Musée du Louvre
Signed and dated:
"Rembrandt f 1661". See also
the preceding entry.

408 ⊞ ◔ 107×81 / 1661 ▤ ⁝
The Virgin Mary
Épinal, Musée Départemental
des Vosges
Signed and dated:
"Rembrandt f 1661".

409 ⊞ ◔ 80×69 / 1661 ▤ ⁝
**Old Woman with Folded
Hands**
New York, Straus Collection
Signed and dated:
"Rembrandt f 1661".

410 ⊞ ◔ 104,5×86 / *1661 ▤ ⁝
Portrait of an Old Rabbi
Florence, Galleria degli Uffizi
Signed and dated:
"Rembrandt f 166."; the last
digit is illegible. It is thought
that the sitter may have been
the rabbi of the Portuguese
Synagogue, Haham Saul Levy
Monteyra (JZ in OH 1926
no. 43).

411 ⊞ ◔ 115,5×87,5 / 1655-61 ▤ ⁝
Alexander the Great
Glasgow, Art Gallery and
Museum
Signed and dated:
"Rembrandt f 1655". The canvas

395

396

397

398

394

399

400

401

402

403

404

405

406

407 [Plate LIV]

408

409

410

411

412

413

consists of several pieces sewn
together; some of them were
painted at the date indicated
above (they also comprised
a head of Titus which was
later transformed into the
head in the present painting)
and some five or six years later.
This is probably the first
Alexander the Great sent to
Don Antonio Ruffo (see no.
316) at Messina in July 1661,
for which Ruffo paid 500
florins, but which he

complained about a year later
because of the fact that it was
pieced together. Rembrandt
replied that he would paint
Ruffo another picture on the
same subject-matter, which
may possibly be the painting
described in no. 426.

412 ⊞ ◔ 71×61 / 1661 ▤ ⁝
Man with a Long Beard
Leningrad, Hermitage

Signed and dated:
"Rembrandt f 1661". See
no. 359.

413 ⊞ ◔ 98,5×79 / 1661* ▤ ⁝
Man with a Falcon
Göteborg, Konstmuseum
Some critics see in this painting
an imaginary portrait of
Floris V, Count of Holland
(1254–96), a popular figure in
poems and plays in
Rembrandt's time.

414 ⊞ ◔ 78×64,5 / 1661 ▤ ⁝
Two Negroes
The Hague, Mauritshuis
Signed and dated:
"Rembrandt f 1661". Some
scholars would date it back to
about 1654.

121

424 [Plate LII-LIII]

415 [Plate LVI]

Drawing by Rembrandt (Munich, Staatliche Graphische Sammlungen) relating to the composition of the painting discussed under no. 415, in its original proportions.

415 ⊞ ◐ 196×309 *1661* ▤ ⁝

The Oath of the Batavians
Stockholm, Nationalmuseum
The painting was executed for a particular wall in the Burgerzaal of the Nieuwe Stadhuis at Amsterdam which was to be decorated with examples of the age-long struggle for independence of the Dutch people. The artists commissioned included Govaert Flinck and others. Rembrandt's own painting in fact represents an episode of Roman history: the oath of Julius Civilis (see Tacitus, *Histories*, 4, 14–5). It is not known whether Rembrandt

was among the artists commissioned; nor is it known why the painting (which was displayed in the great hall in 1662) should have been removed barely a year after, and substituted with one by Jürgen Ovens which is still there today. The painting was returned to Rembrandt and, (almost certainly by him) retouched and reduced in size so as to find some other use for it. The original proportions and aspect can be seen in a drawing by Rembrandt (pen and watercolour, 196×180 mm.) in the Staatliche Graphische Sammlungen, Munich.

416 ⊞ ◐ 130,5×97 *1661* ▤ ⁝

Portrait of Jacob Trip
London, National Gallery
The signature is incomplete: "Rembr....". Jacob Jacobszoon Trip was a merchant of Dordrecht. See also no. 417.

417 ⊞ ◐ 130,5×97,5 *1661* ▤ ⁝

Portrait of Margaretha de Geer
London, National Gallery
The sitter was the wife of the merchant Jacob Trip to whose portrait this is a pendant. See both the preceding and the following entries.

418 ⊞ ◐ 75,5×64 1661 ▤ ⁝

Portrait of Margaretha de Geer
London, National Gallery
Signed and dated: "Rembrandt f 1661". See no. 417.

419 ⊞ ◐ 80,5×64 *1662* ▤ ⁝

Portrait of a Lady Holding a Puppy
Toronto, Art Gallery
Formerly thought to be a portrait of Magdalena van Loo.

420 ⊞ ◐ 90×71 1662 ▤ ⁝

Man in a Cloak and a Large Beret
St Louis (Mo.), City Art Museum
The signature and date are apocryphal.

421 ⊞ ◐ 82×71 *1662* ▤ ⁝

Profile of an Old Man in a Fanciful Costume
Dresden, Staatliche Kunstsammlungen, Gemäldegalerie
Several copies are known.

422 ⊞ ◐ 110×90 1662* ▤ ⁝

Young Man Seated with his Hand on his Hip
Washington, D.C, National Gallery of Art
Signed and dated: "Rembrandt f 1663".

423 ⊞ ◐ 121×94 *1662* ▤ ⁝

Man in a Tall Hat
Washington, D.C, National Gallery of Art

424 ⊞ ◐ 191,5×279 1662 ▤ ⁝

The Sampling Officials of the Drapers' Guild
Amsterdam, Rijksmuseum
The signature and date are inscribed on the cloth covering the table: "Rembrandt f 1662". The other signature and date, written on the wall on the top right-hand side, "Rembrandt f 1661", are later in date and apocryphal. The painting was commissioned by the Drapers' Guild of Amsterdam (just as the two *Anatomy Lessons* had been commissioned by the Surgeons' Guild and the *Night Watch* by the Civic Guards' Guild). The painting is a collective portrait of sampling officials of the guild, or else of

the officials in charge of the control of the material. The names of the officials who, that particular year, were responsible for these tasks are as follows: Officials in charge of the control of the material: Jan Bitter, Cornelis Egbertszoon Corver, Willem van Renevelt, Servaes del Court and Jan Janszoon Arentsburg. Officials in charge of sampling: Willem van Doyenburg, Volckert Janszoon, Jacob van Loon, Aernout van der Mye and Joachim de Neve. Towards the back, in the centre of the composition, and bareheaded is a servant or secretary of the guild. The painting was formerly housed in the guildhouse, the Saalhof, in the

Staalstraat, but transferred on 27 November 1771 to the Kunstkamer of the Stadhuis.

425 ⊞ ◐ 108×82,5 1662-63 ▤ ⁝

Homer
The Hague, Mauritshuis
Signed and dated: ".....andt f 1663". This painting was commissioned by Don Antonio Ruffo (see no. 316) It was partly destroyed in a fire in the eighteenth century; its original aspect can, however, be gathered from an autograph drawing (145×167 mm.) in the Stockholm Nationalmuseum; in this Homer can be seen to be dictating something to a scribe.

416

417

418

419

420

421

422

423

426 ⊞ ◑ 118×91 *1663* ⊟ ⁝

Alexander the Great
Lisbon, Fundação Calouste
Gulbenkian
This may be the second of the
two paintings with this title to
have been sent to Don Antonio
Ruffo (see no. 411). In the
Gulbenkian Foundation
catalogue it is listed as
Pallas Athene.

427 ⊞ ◑ 282×248 *1663* ⊟ ⁝

**Equestrian Portrait of
Frederick Rihel**
London, National Gallery
Signed and dated:
"R..brandt 1663"; the date is
not clearly legible. The sitter
was an Amsterdam merchant
who had been amongst
William III's escort when he
entered Amsterdam in 1660.

428 ⊞ ◑ 102×80 *1663* ⊟ ⁝

Writing Evangelist
Rotterdam, Museum Boymans-
van Beuningen

429 ⊞ ◑ 73×60 1663* ⊟ ⁝

Portrait of Titus in a Beret
London, Dulwich College
Picture Gallery
There are traces of a date
generally taken to be "1663".

430 ⊞ ◑ 71×57 *1664* ⊟ ⁝

**Self-Portrait with a Chain
and Pendant**
Florence, Galleria degli Uffizi
Formerly in the collection of
the Grand Dukes of Tuscany,
this is the self-portrait
mentioned by Baldinucci and

426

429 [Plate LVII]

430

436 [Plate LXIV]

431

432 [Plate LVIII]

433

Houbraken (see pp. 9 and 13).

431 ⊞ ◑ 120×101 1664 ⊟ ⁝

Lucretia
Washington, D.C., National
Gallery of Art
Signed and dated:
"Rembrandt f 1664".

432 ⊞ ◑ 127×123 1664-65 ⊟ ⁝

Juno
New York, Middendorf
Collection
This is probably the painting
commissioned by the collector
Harmen Becker, which, in the
spring of 1664 had not yet

been finished. See *Outline
biography*, **1664**.

433 ⊞ ◑ 56,5×47,5 *1665* ⊟ ⁝

**Portrait of a Richly
Dressed Young Woman**
Montreal, Museum of Fine Arts
Thought by many critics to be a
portrait of Hendrickje, this
painting is also taken to be
that of Magdalena van Loo,
Rembrandt's daughter-in-law.

434 ⊞ ◑ 121,5×166,5 *1665* ⊟ ⁝

The Jewish Bride
Amsterdam, Rijksmuseum
Signed and dated:
"Rembrandt f 16.."; the last
two digits are illegible. The
traditional title does not give
any indication as to the
subject-matter which may have
been inspired from the Bible
it may also be a double portrait:
amongst other names those of
Titus and Magdalena van Loo
have been put forward. See
also nos. 433, 446 and 448.

435 ⊞ ◑ 127×117 *1665* ⊟ ⁝

Biblical Character
Leningrad, Hermitage
The signature may be
apocryphal: "Rembrandt f".
Several critics think that only
the main figure is autograph.
The subject-matter has been
interpreted as: "Uriah's
Departure" or "Haman's
Disgrace".

436 ⊞ ◑ 82,5×65 1665* ⊟ ⁝

Self-Portrait Laughing
Cologne, Wallraf-Richartz-
Museum
On the left can be seen part of
a bust which has been
traditionally accepted as that
of Heraclitus, the sorrowful
philosopher (a bust of

Heraclitus did indeed figure
among Rembrandt's
possessions; see the *Inventory*,
no. 154, p. 90). Rembrandt's
own smile – or sneer – has
been interpreted as a reference
to Democritus, the philosopher
who laughed at human misery.

*Drawing (Stockholm,
Nationalmuseum) showing the
original aspect of no. 425.*

428

434 [Plate LIX]

427

435

425

437 ⊞ ◔ 112×87 / 1665 ▤ ⁝
Portrait of Gérard de Lairesse
New York, Lehman Collection
Signed and dated:
"Rembrandt f 1665". The painter
and engraver Gérard de
Lairesse, who was a native of
Liège, was active in
Amsterdam about 1664.

438 ⊞ ◔ 80,5×65 / 1666 ▤ ⁝
**Portrait of a Young Man
with a White Collar**
Kansas City (Mo.), William
Rockhill Nelson Gallery of Art,
Atkins Museum of Fine Arts
Signed and dated:
"Rembrandt f 1666". B 1966
thinks he detected in the sitter
the figure of the painter
Samuel van Hoogstraaten;
this identification is doubtful.

439 ⊞ ◔ 105×92,5 / 1666 ▤ ⁝
Lucretia
Minneapolis (Ind.), Institute
of Arts
Signed and dated:
"Rembrandt f 1666".

440 ⊞ ◔ 71×56 / 1666 ▤ ⁝
**Portrait of Jeremias de
Decker**
Leningrad, Hermitage
Signed and dated:
"Rembrandt f 1666". Six years
previously Rembrandt had
already made a portrait of de
Decker (1610—66) but the
painting has been lost (see
Outline biography, **1660**). The
present portrait was made the
year of the poet's death.

441. ⊞ ◔ 82×67,5 / 1667 ▤ ⁝⁝
**Portrait of a Paunchy Old
Man**
Cowdray Park (Sussex),
Cowdray Collection
Signed and dated:
"Rembrandt f 1667".

442 ⊞ ◔ 102×83 / 1667 ▤ ⁝
Portrait of a Seated Man
Melbourne, National Gallery of
Victoria
Signed and dated:
"Rembrandt f 1667".

443 ⊞ ◔ 99,5×83,5 / *1668* ▤ ⁝
Portrait of a Man in a Tall

437

438

439

440

441

442

443 [Plate LXII]

444 [Plate LXIII]

445

446

449

450

Hat, with Gloves
Washington, D.C., National
Gallery of Art
See also the following entry.

444 ⊞ ◔ 100×83 / *1668* ▤ ⁝
**Portrait of a Lady Holding
an Ostrich-Feather Fan**
Washington, D.C., National
Gallery of Art
This is the pendant to the male
portrait given in the preceding
entry.

445 ⊞ ◔ 91,5×74,5 / *1668* ▤ ⁝
**Portrait of a Man Holding a
Magnifying Glass**

446 ⊞ ◔ 92×74,5 / *1668* ▤ ⁝
**Portrait of a Lady Holding a
Carnation**
New York, Metropolitan

New York, Metropolitan
Museum of Art
There have been several
suggestions concerning the
identity of the sitter: among
them, Spinoza and Titus; in the
case of the latter the following
female portrait would then
represent Magdalena van Loo.
See also *The Jewish Bride*
(no. 434) for any resemblance
between them and the characters portrayed here and in no. 446.

Museum of Art
See the preceding entry.

447 ⊞ ◔ 262×206 / *1668* ▤ ⁝
**The Return of the Prodigal
Son**
Leningrad, Hermitage
The signature is unusual and
may be apocryphal: "R v Rijn f".

448 ⊞ ◔ 126×167 / 1668-69 ▤ ⁝
Family Portrait
Brunswick, Staatliches Herzog
Anton Ulrich-Museum
Signed: "Rembrandt f". It has
been suggested that this is a
portrait of Rembrandt's own
family: the painter's daughter-
in-law, Magdalena van Loo,
widow of Titus, with her
daughter Titia; Hendrickje's
daughter, Cornelia; and
Magdalena's brother-in-law,
François van Biljert with his
own son, François jr. (whom
Titia was later to marry).

449 ⊞ ◔ 86×70,5 / 1669 ▤ ⁝
**Self-Portrait with Folded
Hands**
London, National Gallery
There are traces of a signature
and dated: "1669". A small
strip has been cut on the left.

450 ⊞ ◔ 59×51 / 1669 ▤ ⁝
Last Self-Portrait
The Hague, Mauritshuis

Signed and dated:
"Rembrandt f 1669".

451 ⊞ ◔ 98×79 / *1669* ▤ ⁝
**Simeon Holding the Infant
Jesus**
Stockholm, Nationalmuseum
This is probably the painting
which Allaert and Cornelis van
Everdingen saw in its
unfinished state in the studio
just before the master's death
(see *Outline biography*, **1669**).
The attribution of the figure of
Mary to Rembrandt is rejected
by almost all critics.

447

448 [Plates LX—LXI]

451

Table of concordance

We present below and overleaf the concordance between the present catalogue of Rembrandt's paintings (CWA) and the four most recent catalogues: those of Hofstede de Groot, 1915 (HdG), Bredius, 1935 (B 1935), Bauch, 1966 (B 1966) and Gerson, 1968 (G 1968). See the Bibliography, p. 82.

CWA	HdG	B 1935	B 1966	G 1968	CWA	HdG	B 1935	B 1966	G 1968	CWA	HdG	B 1935	B 1966	G 1968
1	—	—	41	2	74	635	164	351	111	147	148	552	60	67
2	34	488	3	3	75	633	170	359	124	148	236	432	162	93
3	—	460	96	1	76	733	159	354	119	149	856	343	476	156
4	64 a	486	2	4	77	654	161	352	104	150	492	186	151	131
5	26	487	1	6	78	745	162	353	105	151	494	191	159	161
6	46 a	631	A 1	—	79	573	17	302	99	152	538	20	306	144
7	—	532	42	5	80	659	166	358	110	153	567	19	305	142
8	533	1	288	30	81	932	403	530	100	154	526	21	308	158
9	—	132	109	28	82	349	169	141	103	155	534	22	307	157
10	674	78	347	31	83	624	167	360	120	156	525	23	304	133
11	—	633	343	29	84	625	331	459	121	157	494	192	158	—
12	—	632	97	18	85	697	84	451	114	158	607	101	489	175
13	282	420	110	19	86	696	86	453	116	159	206	102	258	92
14	—	—	43	8	87	699	89	452	115	160	233	468	101	69
15	81	535	46	10	88	694	87	454	117	161	—	469	259	94
16	179	601	111	22	89	698	85	455	118	162	205	103	261	96
17	—	423	5	11	90	612	99	456	112	163	615	96	488	174
18	—	427	119	21	91	311	494	9	58	164	584	25	309	171
19	—	419	112	20	92	877	333	461	127	165	334	30	535	79
20	32	489	4	9	93	171	608	140	102	166	660	202	376	178
21	333	533	44	7	94	181	609	139	—	167	661	349	486	179
22	147	539	49	14	95	372	148	143	107	168	730	201	375	180
23	687	63	250	p. 504	96	417	147	A 8	—	169	846	350	485	181
24	320	68	—	34	97	373	152	146	109	170	738 / 794	212	382	—
25	688	70	251	37	98	761	160	357	122	171	868	348	491	185
26	552 a	12	297	41	99	668	165	356	125	172	634	203	377	183
27	542	2	290	32	100	669	336	471	126	173	387	207	166	172
28	552	7	294	40	101	867	335	462	123	174	415	205	167	173
29	544	6	295	39	102	103	547	58	60	175	351	180	170	182
30	529	8	292	38	103	50	491	11	59	176	353	206	163	170
31	564	10	293	—	104	490	190	150	145	177	346	179	164	70
32	—	—	47	12	105	491	188	149	—	178	207	471	102	73
33	117	536	48	15	106	209	466	253	90	179	31	499	14	78
34	293	428	121	—	107	884	330	460	128	180	52	497	21	77
35	66	—	A 6	—	108	873	340	475	146	181	9	498	13	74
36	543	134	113	—	109	691	95	468	143	182	8	—	A 10	—
37	531	5	298	33	110	606	94	473	132	183	69	502	16	75
38	570	11	299	44	111	608	97	474	134	184	33	501	15	76
39	530	9	300	45	112	566	18	303	129	185	149	557	64	80
40	685	64	249	35	113	726	173	361	137	186	180	603	A 9	—
41	676	77	116	36	114	369	183	153	136	187	582	26	172	188
42	677	76	124	42	115	419	182	152	—	188	270	433	171	95
43	371	141	128	50	116	405	181	147	135	189	786	204	378	—
44	681	80	117	49	117	348	178	155	152	190	885	352	496	—
45	675	81	129	46	118	657	171	363	138	191	666	406	533	176
46	673	79	130	47	119	933	408	532	139	192	667	407	534	177
47	213	463	99	57	120	930	405	531	130	193	882	354	492	169
48	35	490	7	13	121	629	175	368	147	194	—	439	542	195
49	672	73	123	43	122	630	339	466	148	195	939	440	543	196
50	177	602	120	23	123	785	163	367	153	196	187	610	175	97
51	192	605	126	—	124	883	332	470	154	197	70	503	17	81
52	107 a	538	51	16	125	736	172	366	140	198	116	558	65	83
53	49	604	127	24	126	881	341	469	141	199	14	504	19	86
54	316	69	252	27	127	—	176	364	151	200	57	505	18	84
55	122	607	134	25	128	? 920	337	472	155	201	968	456	558	98
56	186	430	135	26	129	769	177	365	149	202	? 986	455	559	—
57	233	431	156	91	130	874	344	480	150	203	751 / ? 649	—	379	—
58	80	543	52	17	131	637	199	373	164	204	744	214	381	187
59	—	—	54	56	132	638	342	478	165	205	271	211	174	186
60	176	—	A 4	—	133	645	200	372	162	206	545	24	311	189
61	762	154	350	113	134	646	347	477	163	207	576	32	313	229
62	354	142	136	106	135	732	197	369	159	208	613	104	490	184
63	? 375 a	144	137	51	136	848	346	482	160	209	30	507	20	85
64	577	143	138	52	137	777	196	371	166	210	142	559	66	82
65	679	82	131	48	138	859	345	479	167	211	109	442	545	199
66	670	145	348	53	139	739	194	374	168	212	951	445	544	197
67	775	146	349	54	140	97	555	63	71	213	941	443	546	198
68	195	462	254	55	141	92	544	53	63	214	946	444	548	201
69	201	464	100	62	142	—	—	61	68	215	942	441	547	200
70	200	472	103	61	143	128	546	62	72	216	535	216	384	192
71	111	545	55	—	144	130	548	57	64	217	283	31	312	191
72	783	155	355	108	145	134	550	56	65	218	585	33	314	236
73	557 / 558	156	142	101	146	135	551	59	66					

CWA	HdG	B 1935	B 1966	G 1968	CWA	HdG	B 1935	B 1966	G 1968	CWA	HdG	B 1935	B 1966	G 1968
219	511	71	262	190	297	53	519	29	—	375	367	—	225	379
220	619	355	497	193	298	384	130	400	304	376	291	297	224	298
221	845	356	498	194	299	261	128	199	261	377	709	126	427	375
222	136	565	69	89	300	593 b	41	399	301	378	554	51	330	376
223	139	554	74	217	301	532	256	398	280	379	556	52	331	380
224	140	560	68	87	302	—	380	510	281	380	569	53	333	389
225	141	561	67	88	303	489	119	410	319	381	562	54	332	381
226	74	562	70	203	304	944	454	554	344	382	720	118	522	382
227	93	563	71	205	305	143	583	83	269	383	715	113	521	396
228	5	508	22	202	306	133	584	84	—	384	193	306	227	377
229	971	458	561	290	307	299	378	270	284	385	366	261	245	395
230	642	217	385	230	308	330	377	269	285	386	664	315	428	400
231	643	357	499	231	309	399	266	204	299	387	753	277	425	338
232	559	27	315	237	310	39	611	202	282	388	—	298	432	393
233	550	34	316	238	311	453	263	402	306	389	782	299	433	394
234	949	446	549	265	312	292	267	206	305	390	46	530	37	351
235	948	451	550	266	313	363	269	203	283	391	146	597	—	352
236	620	409	536	234	314	580	42	322	308	392	121	594	92	353
237	734	218	386	232	315	628	268	404	307	393	82	596	93	350
238	860	360	501	233	316	413	478	207	286	394	407	300	435	392
239	609	108	264	226	317	41	521	31	271	395	—	627	228	378
240	331	359	265	224	318	950	543	555	345	396	162	628	229	368
241	239	219	176	225	319	269	275	408	317	397	164	629	241	369
242	728	358	500	235	320	712	276	405	309	398	157	630	240	360
343	227	476	105	206	321	536	43	324	310	399	168	615	235	366
244	27	509	23	204	322	721	111	512	311	400	—	—	237	362
245	38	511	24	207	323	717	112	513	318	401	170	617	236	361
246	926	410	537	239	324	309	387	272	279	402	190	307	232	386
247	555	37	319	253	325	440	274	407	314	403	194	616	234	365
248	565	36	317	240	326	502	384	276	—	404	183	619	238	364
249	605	109	503	241	327	879	371	277	315	405	575	59	338	403
250	40	513	25	213	328	506	381	274	312	406	175	304	233	387
251	230	435	177	222	329	439	270	210	313	407	173	614	231	359
252	747	222	390	246	330	442	131	406	302	408	189	397	283	367
253	437	229	183	242	331	507	383	275	303	409	498	396	526	388
254	457	185	165	243	332	315	385	279	292	410	380	285	431	391
255	960	450	553	268	333	528	44	325	320	411	208	480	280	294
256	104	566	72	208	334	306	437	278	289	412	441	309	239	402
257	746	235	184	244	335	702	120	411	325	413	—	319	242	370
258	735	265	391	250	336	191	308	205	300	414	336	310	539	390
259	850	365	505	—	337	268	279	211	287	415	225	482	108	354
260	752	237	392	—	338	972	417	562	291	416	393	314	429	383
261	861	369	506	249	339	118	586	85	276	417	857	394	523	384
262	364	236	190	254	340	101	589	87	273	418	863	395	524	385
263	438	239	185	247	341	100	588	86	272	419	852	398	527	398
264	757	221	387	245	342	18	523	33	275	420	744 a	311	438	397
265	547	38	320	262	343	17	524	32	274	421	376	324	247	—
266	324	367	507	248	344	22	525	34	277	422	784	312	439	405
267	327	368	268	228	345	927	414	538	326	423	781	313	437	401
268	64	514	26	209	346	725	281	415	327	424	928	415	540	404
269	85	569	76	210	347	703	293	417	328	425	217	483	244	371
270	94	570	73	211	348	741	287	416	—	426	210	479	281	293
271	90	572	77	212	349	854	389	516	331	427	772	255	440	410
272	77	575	78	216	350	716	116	518	339	428	185	618	248	363
273	78	574	79	215	351	238	122	418	335	429	705	289	434	406
274	2	515	27	214	352	704	123	419	330	430	540	60	340	399
275	943	452	552	267	353	202	114	282	288	431	218	484	284	373
276	197	474	104	270	354	652	391	519	336	432	207 a	639	285	374
277	55	516	28	221	355	454	282	220	333	433	503	400	520	337
278	88	576	80	220	356	178	612	221	295	434	929	416	38	356
279	876	362	508	264	357	169	613	217	296	435	48	531	39	357
280	365	250	396	260	358	—		284	297	436	560	61	341	419
281	362	249	395	259	359	—	—	219	332	437	658	321	441	407
282	627	252	397	263	360	392	283	218	334	438	780	322	443	408
283	749	251	394	251	361	36	526	35	—	439	220	485	286	372
284	865	370	509	252	362	750	278	409	316	440	776	320	442	413
285	305	110	266	227	363	553	48	327	329	441	829	—	444	409
286	144	579	—	219	364	581	49	326	324	442	743	323	445	414
287	145	578	82	218	365	539	45	328	—	443	779	327	446	411
288	154	577	81	223	366	563	50	329	343	444	880	402	528	412
289	159	620	194	255	367	—	290	421	342	445	755	326	447	417
290	161	621	195	257	368	756	294	422	340	446	869	401	529	418
291	—	625	197	256	369	774	295	423	341	447	113	598	94	355
292	—	623	198	—	370	212	481	106	278	448	931	457	541	416
293	163	624	212	321	371	65	520	30	348	449	551	55	339	415
294	—	—	213	322	372	102	—	91	349	450	527	62	342	420
295	158	622	215	323	373	13	528	36	346	451	? 81 d	600	95	358
296	160	626	196	258	374	25	527	226	347					

Other Rembrandtesque works formerly considered autograph by some critics or in public collections

The works listed below have been attributed to Rembrandt by some critics but cannot, in our opinion, be considered autograph. The abbreviations of publication references have been altered as follows: *AB* = B 1935; *AB2* = ibid., second edition; *BG* = BG 1969; *HdG* = HdG 1915; *KB* = B 1966. An asterisk following *AB* and *BG* indicates that, in BG 1969, the painting has been catalogued amongst those not attributable to Rembrandt.

Aix-en-Provence
Musée Granet
Self-Portrait (see no. 379)
panel 30 × 23 *c.* 1660
HdG 524; AB 58; KB 336

Formerly at Amsterdam
De Boer Collection
Zachariah in the Temple
Panel 58 × 47,5 *c.* 1630
AB 542

Formerly at Amsterdam
De Boer Collection
Portrait of an Old Man
Panel 23 × 18 *c.* 1643
HdG 433; AB 228*; KB 179

Amsterdam
Kleiweg de Zwaan Collection
Diana Bathing
Panel 18 × 17 *c.* 1631
HdG 199; AB 461

Amsterdam
Rijksmuseum
Still-Life
Panel 91 × 120 *c.* 1630

Amsterdam
Rijksmuseum
The Holy Family
Panel 60 × 77 *c.* 1638
HdG 91; AB 568

Antwerp
Musée Royal des Beaux-Arts
Portrait of Eleazar Swalmius
Canvas 132 × 109 1637
HdG 722; AB 213; KB 380

Baltimore (Ma.)
Museum of Art
Portrait of an Old Man
Canvas 68 × 56 1650
HdG 412; AB 258; KB 201

Baltimore (Ma.)
Museum of Art
Portrait of Titus
Canvas 78,5 × 67 *c.* 1660
HdG 707; AB 124; KB 430

Baltimore (Ma.)
Walters Art Gallery
Young Girl at a Window
Canvas 85 × 71 *c.* 1655
HdG 325; AB 386

Bayonne
Musée Bonnat
Study of Nude
Panel 22 × 17,5 *c.* 1647
HdG 60; AB 372*

Bayonne
Musée Bonnat
Head of an Old Man
Panel 25 × 22 *c.* 1660
HdG 172; AB 303

Formerly at Belgrade
Royal Collections
Quintus Fabius Maximus
Canvas 179 × 197 *c.* 1653
HdG 224; AB 477

Formerly at Berlin
Heilgendorff Collection
Female Figure
Panel 54 × 47 *c.* 1633
HdG 40A; AB 495; KB 255

Berlin
Staatliche Museen
The Good Samaritan
Canvas 29,5 × 36 *c.* 1650
HdG 110; AB 580*

Bremen
Kunsthalle
Portrait of a Man
Canvas 72 × 60,5 *c.* 1662
KB 436

Brunswick
Herzog Anton Ulrich-Museum
Scholar Reading
Panel 51 × 44 *c.* 1630
HdG 228; AB 429*

Brunswick
Herzog Anton Ulrich-Museum
Portrait of a Lady (see no. 76)
Panel 63,5 × 48 1633
HdG 849; AB 338; KB 465

Bucharest
Muzeul de Artă
The Condemnation of Haman
Canvas 232 × 188 *c.* 1654
HdG 47; AB 522; KB 40

Budapest
Szépmüvészeti Múzeum
The Angel Appearing to Joseph in his Dream
Canvas 105 × 83 *c.* 1650

Cambridge (Mass.)
Fogg Art Museum
Self-Portrait
Panel 23 × 19 1629
AB 4; KB 291

Cambridge (Mass.)
Fogg Art Museum
Portrait of Rembrandt's Father (?)
Panel 20 × 17 1629
HdG 682; AB 74; KB 114

Cassel
Staatliche Kunstsammlungen
Portrait of a Lady
Canvas 72 × 59 *c.* 1636
HdG 851; AB 353; KB 494

Cassel
Staatliche Kunstsammlungen
Study of a Head
Panel 20 × 16 *c.* 1645
HdG 374; AB 230; KB 187

Cassel
Staatliche Kunstsammlungen
Study of a Head
Panel 20 × 16 *c.* 1645
HdG 375; KB 188

Chapel Hill (N.C.)
University of North Carolina
Portrait of a Young Girl
Panel 52 × 39 *c.* 1632
HdG 695; AB 88; KB 463

Chicago (III.)
Art Institute
Portrait of a Man
Panel 56 × 47 c. 1665
AB 316*

Formerly at Chicago
Angell-Norris Collection
The Raising of Lazarus
Panel 41 × 36 c. 1630
HdG 107; AB 537*

Cincinnati (Ohio)
Art Museum
Little Girl with a Medal
Canvas 65.5 × 58 1640–3

Cincinnati (Ohio)
Taft Museum
Smiling Old Woman
Panel 66 × 52 c. 1652
HdG 496; AB 382; KB 271

Cleveland (Ohio)
Museum of Art
Young Scholar
Canvas 84,5 × 69 c. 1650
HdG 414; AB 246

Cologne
Wallraf-Richartz-Museum
Christ at the Column
Panel 33 × 28 c. 1644
HdG 125; AB 591; KB 192

Copenhagen
Statens Museum for Kunst
Profile of an Old Man
Panel 19,5 × 16 c. 1630
HdG 388; AB 136; KB 345

Copenhagen
Statens Museum for Kunst
Ox
Panel 48 × 69,5 c. 1650
HdG 970; AB 459*

Copenhagen
Statens Museum for Kunst
Man in Oriental Dress
Panel 25 × 21,5 c. 1660
HdG 347; AB 301*

Copenhagen
Statens Museum for Kunst
The Falconer
Canvas 66,5 × 50,5 1661–2
HdG 265; AB 318*; KB 243

Darmstadt
Hessisches Landesmuseum
Christ at the Column
Canvas 93 × 72 1658
HdG 124; AB 593; KB 90

Denver (Colo.)
Art Museum
Reading Woman
Panel 43,5 × 35 c. 1632
HdG 211; AB 465

Detroit (Mich.)
Backus Collection
Study of an Old Man
Panel 20,5 × 17 c. 1640
AB 244; KB 180

Detroit (Mich.)
Fisher Collection
Bust of a Young Man
Panel 40 × 34,5 c. 1660
HdG 787 H; AB 125; KB 230

Detroit (Mich.)
Institute of Arts
Portrait of an Old Man
Panel 56 × 40 c. 1630
KB 125

Detroit (Mich.)
Institute of Arts
Woman Crying
Panel 21,5 × 17 c. 1645
HdG 717 A; AB 366

Detroit (Mich.)
McAneeny Collection
Head of an Old Man
Panel 27 × 22 c. 1660
AB 305

Formerly at Detroit (Mich.
Whitcomb Collection
Portrait of Titus (?)
Canvas 52 × 40,5 c. 1660
HdG 708; AB 127*

Dortmund
Becker Collection
Scholars in Conversation
Panel 39 × 30,5 c. 1630
AB 424; KB 6

Downton Castle
Kincaid-Lennox Collection
Rest during the Flight into Egypt
Panel 76,5 × 64 c. 1630
HdG 87; AB 540

Dresden
Staatliche Kunstsammlungen
Portrait of an Old Man
Canvas 95,5 × 80,5 c. 1645
HdG 377; AB 240; KB 191

Dresden
Staatliche Kunstsammlungen
Portrait of an Old Man
Panel 102 × 78 1654
HdG 231; AB 272; KB 208

Dresden
Staatliche Kunstsammlungen
Self-Portrait
Canvas 85,5 × 65 1657
HdG 537; AB 46

Dublin
National Gallery of Ireland
Portrait of L. van Linden (?)
Panel 66,5 × 52 c. 1634
HdG 737; AB 198

Dublin
National Gallery of Ireland
Head of an Old Man
Panel 62 × 45,5 c. 1650
HdG 378; AB 231; KB 200

Edinburgh
National Gallery of Scotland
(Sutherland Collection)
Head of a Man
Panel 20 × 15 c. 1646
HdG 396; AB 247; KB 189

Eindhoven
Philips-de Jongh Collection
Self-Portrait
Panel 20 × 17 c. 1630
HdG 591; AB 13; KB 296

Eindhoven
Philips-de Jongh Collection
Landscape
Canvas 37 × 61 c. 1639
AB 449; KB 551

Enschede
Rijksmuseum Twenthe
Head of an Old Man
Panel 17 × 13 c. 1630
KB 122

Glasgow
Art Gallery and Museum
Self-Portrait
Panel 66 × 51,5 c. 1636
HdG 541; AB 28*

Glasgow
Art Gallery and Museum
Rembrandt Painting
Panel 51 × 61   c. 1643
HdG 335; AB 436'

Formerly at Glasgow
Beattie Collection
Portrait of C. Huygens (?)
Panel 22 × 19,5   c. 1629
HdG 571; AB 139; KB 346

Göteborg
Konstmuseum
The Adoration of the Magi
Panel 75 × 65   c. 1630
AB 541

Groningen
Museum voor Stad en Lande
Study of a Man
Panel 25,5 × 21   1654
HdG 381; AB 271; KB 209

Hartford (Conn.)
Wadsworth Atheneum
Portrait of Saskia
Panel 67,5 × 52,5   1636
HdG 611; AB 105; KB 493

Hartford (Conn.)
Wadsworth Atheneum
Portrait of Titus (?)
Canvas 97,5 × 84   c. 1655
KB 413

Helsinki
Ateneumin Taidemuseo
Portrait of a Woman
Panel 68 × 55,5   c.1630
HdG 499; AB 328'

Henfield
Salmond Collection
Portrait of a Man
Canvas 111,5 × 105   1644
HdG 232; AB 233'

Hoevelaken (N.J.)
Van Aalst Collection
People Reading by Candlelight
Panel 32 × 25   c. 1627
AB 421

Hoevelaken (N.J.)
Van Aalst Collection
A Head Operation
Panel 32 × 25   c. 1627
BG 421 A

Indianapolis (Ind.)
Clowes Fund Collection
Self-Portrait
Panel 43 × 33   c. 1628
HdG 549; AB 3; KB 289

Indianapolis (Ind.)
Herrington Collection
Portrait of a Woman
Panel 69 × 52   c. 1635
KB 481

Indianapolis (Ind.)
Herron Museum of Art
Portrait of a Woman
Panel 62 × 49   1634
AB 100; KB 483

Knowsley Hall (Liverpool)
Derby Collection
Head of an Old Man
Panel 71,5 × 55   c. 1635
HdG 398; AB 208; KB 169

Leeuwarden
Fries Museum
Portrait of Saskia
Panel 72 × 48   1633
HdG 618; AB2 634; KB 467

Leiden
Stedelijk Museum "De
Lakenhal"
Study of a Head
Panel 19,5 × 16   c. 1631
HdG 266; AB 135; KB 132

Leiden
Stedelijk Museum
De Lakenhal"
Man in Oriental Dress
Panel 72,5 × 59   1637
HdG 344; AB 210'; KB 173

Leipzig
Museum der Bildenden Künste
Portrait of an Old Man
Panel 20,5 × 17   c. 1630
HdG 390; AB 140'; KB 344

Leipzig
Museum der Bildenden Künste
Self-Portrait
Panel 26 × 21,5   c. 1650
HdG 548; AB 40

Leningrad
Hermitage
Lady at her Dressing-Table
Panel 41 × 31   c. 1637
HdG 310; AB 506

Leningrad
Hermitage
Seated Lady
Panel 61 × 49   1643
HdG 310; AB 361; KB 267

Formerly at Leningrad
Yussupof Collection
Portrait of a Child
Panel 19,5 × 16,5   1633
HdG 493; AB 187; KB 148

London
Buckingham Palace
The Adoration of the Magi
Panel 122 × 103   1657
HdG 84; AB 592; KB 88

Formerly at London
Borthwick Norton Collection
Portrait of a Young Girl
Canvas 77,5 × 66   c. 1660
HdG 497; AB 393; KB 525

London
Cevat Collection
Self-Portrait
Panel 22,5 × 19   c. 1628
KB 287

Formerly at London
Davis Collection
Portrait of a Woman
Panel 73,5 × 63,5   c. 1639
HdG 307; AB 107; KB 263

London
National Gallery
Diana Bathing
Panel 46,5 × 35,5   c. 1638
HdG 198; AB 473'

London
National Gallery
Portrait of a Jewish Merchant
Canvas 137,5 × 105   c. 1650
HdG 391; AB 257'

London
National Gallery
Portrait of a Woman
Canvas 68,5 × 59   1666
HdG 855; AB 399'

London
Schicht Collection
Portrait of an Old Man
Panel 57 × 47   c. 1632
HdG 436; AB 150; KB 145

Formerly at London
(Sotheby sale 24-6-1964)
Still-Life
Panel 73×56 *c.* 1638
HdG 988 (?); KB 560

London
Wallace Collection
The Centurion Cornelius
Canvas 182×221 *c.* 1655

London
Wallace Collection
Portrait of a Soldier
Panel 66×51 *c.* 1634
HdG 558; AB 193`; KB 160

London
Weitzner Collection
Portrait of a Man
Canvas 89×66 1648
HdG 288; AB 253; KB 193

London
Westminster Collection
Lady Holding a Fan
Canvas 114,5×98 1643
HdG 864; AB 363; KB 502

London
Westminster Collection
Man Holding a Falcon
Canvas 114,5×98 1643
HdG 748; AB 224; KB 388

Los Angeles (Calif.)
Cohn Collection
Portrait of an Old Man
Panel 64×45 *c.* 1632
HdG 443; AB 149; KB 144

Los Angeles (Calif.)
University Galleries
Portrait of a Woman
Panel 65×52 *c.* 1635
HdG 317A; AB 351; KB 260

Lugano
Thyssen Collection
Landscape
Panel 22×29,5 *c.* 1639
HdG 947; AB 447

Formerly at Lugano
Thyssen Collection
Portrait of an Old Man
Canvas 70×58 *c.* 1667
HdG 401; AB 325; KB 246

Melbourne
National Gallery of Victoria
Self-Portrait
Canvas 77×61 *c.* 1660
HdG 579; AB 56; KB 335

Milwaukee (Wis.)
Bader Collection
Scholar at his Desk
Copper 14×14 *c.* 1629
HdG 240; AB 425`; KB 118

Montreal
Bronfman Collection
Self-Portrait
Canvas 73,5×59 *c.* 1660
AB 57; KB 334

Munich
Alte Pinakothek
Portrait of Hendrickje
Panel 72,5×51,5 *c.* 1656
HdG 718; AB 115; KB 517

Formerly at Munich
Böhler Collection
Head of a Jew
Panel 24×21 *c.* 1651
HdG 370; AB 264`; KB 403

Formerly at New York
Borchard Collection
Study of a Head
Panel 18,5×16 *c.* 1650
HdG 461; AB 262`

New York
Brooklyn Museum
Portrait of Rembrandt's Father (?)
Panel 16,5×12,5 *c.* 1630
HdG 683; AB 75`

Formerly at New York
Cintas Collection
Portrait of a Rabbi
Panel 62,5×52 *c.* 1637
HdG 409; AB 209`

New York
Frick Collection
Portrait of a Painter
Canvas 99,5×89 *c.* 1645
HdG 763; AB 254`

New York
Historical Society
Portrait of a Man
Canvas 65,5×52,5 *c.* 1632
HdG 759; AB 158`

Formerly at New York
Heastand Collection
Portrait of Rembrandt's Father (?)
Panel 26,5×20 *c.* 1630
AB 72`

New York
Lamon Collection
Head of a Young Girl
Panel 26×21 *c.* 1650
HdG 494 C; AB 376`

New York
Lehman Collection
Portrait of a Seated Man
Canvas 105×81,5 1638
HdG 768; AB 215; KB 383

New York
Linsky Collection
Portrait of a Young Girl
Canvas 58×48 *c.* 1651
HdG 504; AB 379; KB 511

New York
Metropolitan Museum of Art
Head of an Old Man
Panel 21×17,5

New York
Metropolitan Museum of Art
Bellona
Canvas 123×96 1633
HdG 196; AB 467; KB 257

New York
Metropolitan Museum of Art
Portrait of Saskia with a Crown of Flowers
Canvas 67×51 *c.* 1633
HdG 204; AB 98; KB 256

New York
Metropolitan Museum of Art
The Sybil
Canvas 96×76 *c.* 1640
HdG 214; AB 438`

New York
Metropolitan Museum of Art
Portrait of a Rabbi
Panel 75×61 1642
HdG 425; AB 220

New York
Metropolitan Museum of Art
The Admiral
Canvas 121,5×98,5 *c.* 1643
HdG 765; AB 223; KB 389

New York
Metropolitan Museum of Art
The Admiral's Wife
Canvas   121 × 98   1643
HdG 871; AB 364; KB 504

New York
Metropolitan Museum of Art
Portrait of a Man
Canvas   94,5 × 78   1644
HdG 758; AB 234; KB 393

New York
Metropolitan Museum of Art
Old Woman Cutting her Nails
Canvas   126 × 102   1648

New York
Metropolitan Museum of Art
Portrait of Titus
Canvas   79 × 59   1655
HdG 706; AB 121; KB 412

New York
Metropolitan Museum of Art
Portrait of W. van Coppenol
Panel   36 × 28   *c.* 1657
HdG 636; AB 291; KB 424

New York
Metropolitan Museum of Art
Portrait of a Man in Red
Panel   38 × 31   1659
HdG 411; AB 296; KB 426

New York
Metropolitan Museum of Art
Pontius Pilate
Canvas   129 × 165   *c.* 1660
HdG 129; AB 595˙

New York
Metropolitan Museum of Art
Portrait of a Man
Canvas   73,5 × 64   1665
HdG 754; AB 317

New York
Prins Collection
High Priest
Panel   30 × 26,5   1657
KB 223

Formerly at New York
Van Diemen Collection
Portrait of a Man
Panel   19 × 16   *c.* 1643
AB 226˙

New York
Zedwitz Collection
Portrait of an Old Man
Panel   23,5 × 18,5   *c.* 1640
HdG 365 A; AB 242; KB 168

Nivaa (Denmark)
Malerisamlingen paa Nivagaard
Portrait of a Woman
Panel   76,5 × 59   1632
HdG 875; AB 334; KB 458

Formerly at Oldenburg
Landesmuseum
Portrait of an Old Man
Panel   61,5 × 47,5   *c.* 1632
HdG 416; AB 151˙

Oslo
Nasjonalgalleriet
Landscape
Panel   19,5 × 36,5   1639
HdG 945; AB 448; KB 556

Oslo
Nasjonalgalleriet
Study of a Head
Panel   19,5 × 15,5   *c.* 1645
AB 241˙

Oxford
Ashmolean Museum
Head of an Old Man
Panel   15,5 × 10,5   *c.* 1630
HdG 456; BG 138 A; KB 115

Paris
Bentinck-Thyssen Collection
Cupid
Panel   74,5 × 92   1634
AB 470; KB 157

Formerly at Paris
Bischoffsheim Collection
Portrait of a Jew
Panel   27 × 22,5   *c.* 1647
HdG 59; AB 248˙

Formerly at Paris
De Schickler Collection
Portrait of a Woman
Canvas   68,5 × 48   *c.* 1632
HdG 505; AB 83; KB 450

Formerly at Paris
Flersheim Collection
Portrait of a Man
Panel   21,5 × 16   *c.* 1632
HdG 773; AB 157˙

Paris
Musée du Louvre
Self-Portrait
Panel   80 × 62   1637
HdG 568; AB 29; KB 310

Paris
Musée du Louvre
Susanna Surprised by the Elders
Panel   62 × 48   *c.* 1647
HdG 58; AB 518˙

Paris
Musée du Louvre
The Good Samaritan
Canvas   114 × 135   1648
HdG 112; AB 581˙

Paris
Musée du Louvre
Portrait of Rembrandt's Brother Adriaen (?)
Canvas   80 × 67   1650
HdG 420; AB 129; KB 401

Paris
Musée du Louvre
Portrait of a Man
Canvas   83 × 66   1657
HdG 421; AB 286; KB 222

Paris
Musée du Louvre
Portrait of a Young Man
Canvas   73 × 61   1658
HdG 422; AB 292; KB 420

Paris
Musée du Louvre
Venus and Cupid
Canvas   110 × 88   *c.* 1662
HdG 2L5; AB 117; KB 107

Paris
Musée du Petit Palais
Self-Portrait with a Dog
Panel   81 × 54   1631
HdG 350; AB 16; KB 301

Paris
Weill-Schloss Collection
Portrait of an Old Man
Panel   64 × 67   1634
HdG 427; AB 184˙; KB 161

Philadelphia (Pa.)
Museum of Art
Man in a Turban
Canvas   83 × 64   *c.* 1631
HdG 345; AB 133; KB 133

Philadelphia (Pa.)
Museum of Art
The Finding of Moses
Canvas 47 × 59 c. 1634
HdG 23; AB 496; KB 12

Philadelphia (Pa.)
Museum of Art
Study of a Head
Panel 21 × 17,5 c. 1645
KB 186

Philadelphia (Pa.)
Zimbalist Collection
Portrait of a Woman
Panel 56,5 × 44,5 c. 1632
HdG 853; AB 329; KB 457

Raleigh (N.C.)
Museum of Art
Young Man with a Sword
Canvas 118 × 97 1635

Rennes
Musée des Beaux-Arts
Bathsheba
Panel 25 × 21 1632
HdG 42; AB 492; KB 8

Richmond (Va.)
Museum of Fine Arts
Portrait of a Young Girl
Canvas 58 × 45 1633
HdG 693; AB 90; KB 464

Richmond (Va.)
Museum of Fine Arts
Study of Saskia
Panel 21 × 17 c. 1633
HdG 886; AB 92; KB 487

Richmond (Va.)
Museum of Fine Arts
Study of an Old Man
Panel 21 × 17 1643
HdG 385; AB 232; KB 181

Rotterdam
Museum Boymans-van
Beuningen
The Return of Tobias
Canvas 108,5 × 143 c. 1628

Rousham (Oxfordshire)
Cottrell Dormer Collection
Self-Portrait
Canvas 75 × 63 c. 1653
HdG 537 (ref.); BG 47 A;
KB 323

San Antonio (Tex.)
Urschel Collection
Portrait of an Old Man
Panel 75 × 61 c. 1645
HdG 403; AB 245

San Diego (Calif.)
Fine Arts Gallery
Head of a Baby
Panel 24 × 18

San Francisco (Calif.)
Young Memorial Museum
Self-Portrait
Canvas 74,5 × 61 c. 1653
HdG 537 (ref.); AB 47

Sarasota (Fla.)
Ringling Museum of Art
*The Lamentation over the
Dead Christ*
Canvas 177,5 × 196,5 1650
HdG 137; AB 582

Shelburne (Vt.)
Shelburne Museum
Portrait of a Man
Canvas 112 × 91 1632
HdG 764; AB 168

Stockholm
Nationalmuseum
Portrait of a Young Girl
Panel 59 × 44 c. 1632
AB 91

Stockholm
Nationalmuseum
Portrait of an Old Woman
Canvas 87 × 73 1655
HdG 510; AB 388; KB 514

Stockholm
Nationalmuseum
Portrait of an Old Man
Canvas 89 × 73 1655
HdG 452; AB 280; KB 414

Stuttgart
Staatsgalerie
Self-Portrait
Canvas 68 × 56,5 c. 1661
KB 337

The Hague
Mauritshuis
*Portrait of Rembrandt's
Mother (?)*
Panel 17 × 13 c. 1630
HdG 686; AB 67; KB 449

The Hague
Mauritshuis
*Rest during the Flight into
Egypt*
Panel 38,5 × 34 c. 1635
HdG 89; AB 556; KB 50

The Hague
Museum Bredius
The Raising of the Cross
Panel 39 × 30 c. 1645
HdG 131; AB 564; KB 75

Warsaw
Muzeum Narodowe
Portrait of a Man
Panel 71 × 53 1634
HdG 778; AB 195; KB 370

Washington, D.C.
Corcoran Gallery of Art
Portrait of a Man
Panel 66 × 48 1633
HdG 760; AB 174; KB 362

**Formerly at Washington,
D.C.**
Lamont Belin Collection
Soldier in a Breast-Plate
Canvas 100 × 82,5 c. 1635
HdG 272; AB 434*

Washington, D.C.
National Gallery of Art
Old Housewife
Canvas 133 × 104,5

Washington, D.C.
National Gallery of Art
Study of a Head
Panel 28 × 21,5 c. 1645
HdG 448; AB 243*

Washington, D.C.
National Gallery of Art
The Mill
Canvas 87,5 × 105,5
c. 1650

Washington, D.C.
National Gallery of Art
Self-Portrait
Canvas 92 × 75 1650
HdG 574; AB 39; KB 321

Washington, D.C.
National Gallery of Art
*Portrait of a Jew
(The Philosopher)*
Panel 61,5 × 49,5 1656
HdG 469; BG 260 A*; KB 21*

Washington, D.C.
National Gallery of Art
Portrait of a Woman
Canvas 103 × 86 1656
HdG 878; AB 390; KB 515

Washington, D.C.
National Gallery of Art
Head of an Old Woman
Panel 21 × 17 c. 1657
HdG 508; AB 392; KB 373

Washington, D.C.
National Gallery of Art
*Head of an Old Man
(St Matthew (?))*
Panel 25 × 19,5 c. 1660
HdG 174; AB 302

Wassenaar
Van der Bergh Collection
Head of a Woman
Panel 21 × 17,5 c. 1650
HdG 501; AB 373

Weimar
Stadtmuseum (formerly)
Self-Portrait
Canvas 61 × 48 1643
HdG 578; AB 35; KB 318

Williamstown (Mass.)
Clark Art Institute
Portrait of a Reading Man
Canvas 66,5 × 58 1645
AB 238

Williamstown (Mass.)
Clark Art Institute
Christ on the Cross
Panel 32 × 29 1657
HdG 132B; AB 590; KB 89

Worcester (Mass.)
Art Museum
St Bartholomew
Panel 62 × 47 c. 1632
HdG 169 A (ref.); BG 606 A;
KB 154

Zurich
Bührle Collection
Portrait of Saskia
Canvas 78,5 × 66 1636
HdG 614; AB 106; KB 495

Zurich
Haab-Escher Collection
A Foot Operation
Panel 31,5 × 24,5 1628
AB 422; KB 98

Zurich
Labia Collection
Portrait of a Jew
Canvas 66 × 57 1656
AB 273˚

Private collection
Portrait of a Young Man
Panel 60 × 48 c. 1632
HdG 736; AB 153

Private collection
Susanna and the Elders
Panel 51 × 41 c. 1632
AB 493; KB 10

Private collection
Portrait of a Rabbi
Panel 48 × 36 c. 1660
HdG 408 A; AB 638˚

Basle
Private collection
*Portrait of Rembrandt's
Mother (?)*
Panel 19 × 11,5 c. 1627
AB 65˚

Great Britain
Private collection
Head of a Young Girl
Panel 22 × 19 c. 1650
HdG 509; AB 374

Holland
Private collection
Portrait of a Boy
Panel 46,5 × 41 c. 1633
AB 189˚

Los Angeles (Calif.)
Private collection
*Portrait of Rembrandt's
Father (?)*
Panel 18 × 16 c. 1633
AB 635˚

Los Angeles (Calif.)
Private collection
Landscape
Panel 30 × 44 c. 1655
KB 557

Paris
Private collection
Portrait of a Boy
Panel 23 × 18 c. 1657
HdG 434; AB 288˚

USA
Private collection
Scholar at his Desk
Panel 15,5 × 13,5 c. 1630
AB 426

USA
Private collection
Portrait of Saskia
Panel 9,7 × 7,7 c. 1634
AB 93; KB 484

USA
Private collection
Study of a Head
Panel 22,5 × 15,6 c. 1635
AB 636˚

USA
Private collection
Portrait of an Old Man
Panel 18,5 × 15,5 1643
AB 227˚; KB 178

USA
Private collection
Head of a Young Girl
Panel 20,5 × 17 c. 1650
HdG 495; AB 375˚

Formerly at London
Private collection
Christ at the Column
Canvas 74,5 × 63 c. 1628
HdG 126; AB 534; KB 45

Formerly at London
Private collection
Portrait of a Man
Panel 21 × 17 c. 1643
AB 225˚; KB 182

Formerly at Paris
Private collection
Self-Portrait
Panel 20,5 × 17,5 1630
HdG 572; AB 15˚

Formerly at Stockholm
Private collection
Self-Portrait
Panel 47 × 31 c. 1630
AB 14˚

Formerly at Zurich
Private collection
*Portrait of Rembrandt's
Mother (?)*
Panel 22 × 17 c. 1630
AB 66˚; KB 448

Appendix 1
Drawings by Rembrandt

Dr. 1

Dr. 3

Dr. 2

The thirty-one drawings reproduced in these pages are as follows: 1. *Seated Nude*, 262 × 186 mm., pen and watercolour, *c*. 1630, Paris, Louvre. 2. *The Raising of the Cross*, study for painting no. 144 (q.v.) 232 × 187 mm., watercolour, 1633, Vienna, Albertina. 3. *Woman at a Window*, 236 × 178 mm., pen and watercolour, *c*. 1633–4, Rotterdam, Museum Boymans-van Beuningen. 4. *Susanna Surprised by the Elders*, 235 × 364 mm., red chalk, *c*. 1635, Berlin, Kupferstichkabinett. 5. *The Abduction of Ganymede*, study for painting no. 178 (q.v.), 190 × 160 mm., pen and watercolour, *c*. 1635, Dresden, Kupferstichkabinett. 6. *Woman with a Weeping Baby*, 205 × 143 mm., pen and watercolour, *c*. 1635, Berlin, Kupferstichkabinett. 7. *Lady Having her Hair Dressed*, 238 × 184 mm., pen and watercolour, *c*. 1635, Vienna, Albertina. 8. *Saskia in Bed*, 228 × 165 mm., pen and watercolour, *c*. 1636, Munich, Staatliche Graphische Sammlungen. 9. *Elephant*, 230 × 340 mm., charcoal, signed and dated: "Rembrandt f 1637", Vienna, Albertina. 10. *Three Elephants*, 242 × 363 mm., charcoal, *c*. 1637, Vienna, Albertina. 11. *Pair of Horses*, 170 × 272 mm., charcoal, *c*. 1637, Muri (Berne), de Bruyn-van der Leeuw Collection. 12. *Negro Drummers on Horseback*, 230 × 170 mm., pen, pastel and watercolour, *c*. 1637, London, British Museum. 13. *Manoah and the Angel*, 175 × 190 mm., pen, *c*. 1637, Berlin, Kupferstichkabinett. 14. *The Repudiation of Hagar*, 185 × 224 mm., pen and watercolour, *c*. 1638, London, British Museum. 15. *Birds of Paradise*, 181 × 154 mm., pen and watercolour, 1640, Paris, Louvre. 16. *Manoah and the Angel*, study for painting no. 244 (q.v.), 233 × 203 mm.,

pen and watercolour, 1641, Stockholm, Nationalmuseum. 17. *Geertje Dircks*, 220 × 150 mm., pen and watercolour, *c*. 1642, Haarlem, Teylers Museum. 18. *Christ Preaching*, perhaps a study for the etching *Christ the Healer* (p. 137, no. 18), 198 × 230 mm., pen and bistre, *c*. 1642, Paris, Louvre. 19. *The Dream of Jacob*, 250 × 208 mm., pen and watercolour, *c*. 1642, Paris, Louvre. 20. *Landscape*, 298 × 452 mm., pen, red chalk and watercolour, 1644, London, British Museum. 21. *Landscape* 139 × 196 mm., pen and watercolour, *c*. 1645, Hamburg, Kunsthalle. 22. *Lady at a Window*, 195 × 140 mm., charcoal and watercolour, *c*. 1645, Bayonne, Musée Bonnat. 23. *Young Girl at a Window*, study for painting no. 267, 97 × 107 mm., pen, *c*. 1645, Dresden, Kupferstichkabinett. 24. *Portrait of Jan Six with a Dog*, study for an etching (p. 137, no. 21), 220 × 175 mm., pen and watercolour, 1647, Amsterdam, Six Collectie. 25. *Seated Nude*, 224 × 185 mm., pen and watercolour, *c*. 1650, Munich, Staatliche Graphische Sammlungen. 26. *The Repudiation of Hagar*, 172 × 224 mm., pen, *c*. 1650, Amsterdam, Rijksmuseum. 27. *St Jerome*, study for an etching (p. 137, no. 26), 265 × 190 mm., pen and watercolour, *c*. 1651–2, Hamburg, Kunsthalle. 28. *Christ amongst the Doctors*, 190 × 257 mm., pen, *c*. 1652, Paris, Louvre. 29. *Portrait of a Man*, 232 × 194 mm., pen and watercolour, *c*. 1660, Amsterdam, Six Collectie. 30. *Seated Nude*, 287 × 160 mm., charcoal, watercolour and white lead, *c*. 1660, London, British Museum. 31. *Nude Holding an Arrow*, study for an etching (p. 138, no. 40), 293 × 180 mm., pen and watercolour, *c*. 1661, London, British Museum.

Dr. 4

Dr. 5

Dr. 6

Dr. 7

Dr. 8

Dr. 9

Dr. 10

Dr. 12

Dr. 11

Dr. 13

Dr. 14

Dr. 15

Dr. 17

Dr. 16

Dr. 18

Dr. 19

Dr. 20

Dr. 21

Dr. 24

Dr. 25

Dr. 22

Dr. 27

Dr. 26

Dr. 28

Dr. 23

Dr. 29

Dr. 30

Dr. 31

Appendix 2
Etchings by Rembrandt

Rembrandt's intense graphic activity during the whole of his life is not to be considered as secondary to his painting but rather of parallel importance. His etchings reveal a very distinctive technique, sometimes heightened by drypoint, which Rembrandt went on perfecting and polishing, and which still remains obscure in some ways.

The most recent catalogue (Ludwig Münz, *The Etchings of Rembrandt*, complete edition, London, 1952, 2 vols.) lists 395 autograph etchings, from a *Rest during the Flight into Egypt* and a *Circumcision* which date back to 1626, to a *Portrait of Dr Van Linden*, which can be dated to 1665. Some of the artist's etchings have already been reproduced in the *Outline biography*.

We reproduce on this page and the two following, forty etchings which are amongst the most varied and representative of Rembrandt's corpus, and show the technique and style used from 1629 to 1661. They are as follows: 1. *Beggars*, first state, 112 × 81 mm., Signed "RL", c. 1629. 2 *Portrait of Rembrandt's Mother*, first state, 145 × 129 mm., signed and dated "RHL 1631". 3. *The Raising of Lazarus*, third state, 367 × 257 mm., signed "RHL v. Rijn", c. 1631–2. 4. *The Good Samaritan*, executed with help, first state, 258 × 219 mm., 1633. 5. *The Descent from the Cross*, second state, 530 × 410 mm., signed and dated "Rembrandt f cum pryvl 1633". 6. *Peasant*, 112 × 43 mm., with the words "tis vinnich hout" ("it is very cold"), signed and dated "Rembrandt f 1634". 7. *Peasant*, 111 × 39 mm., with the words "Dats niet" ("it doesn't matter", obviously an answer to the comment on the previous etching), signature and dated incomplete "Rembran.. f 163.", 1634. 8. *The Great Jewish Bride*, second state, 220 × 168 mm., signed and dated "R 1635". 9. *Christ Driving the Money-Changers from the Temple*, second state, 135 × 167 mm., signed and dated "Rembrandt f 1635". 10. *Christ before Pontius Pilate*, fourth state, 550 × 446 mm., signed and dated "Rembrandt f 1636 cum privile". 11. *Joseph Relating his Dreams*, second state, 108 × 81 mm., signed and dated "Rembrandt f 1638". 12. *ibid.*, third state, with the addition of shading on the face of the man in a turban, on the left, and on the hangings in the centre towards the top. 13. *The Death of the Virgin*, second state, 409 × 315 mm., signed and dated "Rembrandt f 1639". 14. *The Triumph of Mordecai*, 174 × 215 mm., c. 1639–40. 15. *The Presentation of Christ in the Temple*, second state, 213 × 290 mm., c. 1640–1. 16. *Portrait of the Receiver General Jan Uytenbogaert (The Weigher of Gold)*, 146 × 142 mm., signed "Rembrandt", c. 1640–2. 17. *The Three Trees*, 211 × 280 mm., signed and dated "Rembrandt f 1643". 18. *Christ the Healer* (the "Hundred Guilder Print"), first state, 278 × 396 mm., c. 1642–5. 19. *View of Omval*, first state, 185 × 225 mm., signed and dated "Rembrandt f 1645". 20. *Portrait of Dr Bueno*, second state, 240 × 177 mm., signed and dated "Rembrandt f 1647". 21. *Portrait of Jan Six*, third state, 245 × 191 mm., with the words "Jan Six AE 29" and the signature and date "Rembrandt f 1647". 22. *The Wedding of Creusa and Jason*, etching for the tragedy *Medea*, by Jan Six, first state, 240 × 177 mm., 1648. 23. *The Alms Money*, second state, 164 × 128 mm., signed and dated "Rembrandt f 1648". 24. *Jews in Synagogue*, first state, 71 × 129 mm., signed and dated "Rembrandt f 1648". 25. *Portrait of the Painter Jan Asselijn*, first state, 215 × 170 mm., signature and date incomplete: "Rembra... f 164", c. 1648. 26. *St Jerome*, second state, 260 × 207 mm., c. 1651–2. 27. *Trees and Landscape*, second state, 124 × 210 mm., signed and dated "Rembrandt f 1652'. 28. *Faust in his Study*, first state, 209 × 161 mm., with the words "INRI" in the centre of the disc, "ADAM TE DAGEREM" in the first circle and "AMRTET ALGAR ALGASTNA" in the second, c. 1652–3. 29. *The Three Crosses*, third state, 387 × 450 mm., signed and dated "Rembrandt f 1653" (see also no. 39). 30. "*Ecce Homo*", first state, 383 × 455 mm., 1655. 31. *Portrait of Dr Tholincx*, first state, 198 × 149, c. 1655–6. 32. *Portrait of the Goldsmith Jan Lutma*, second state, 197 × 148 mm., signed and dated "Rembrandt f 1656". 33. *Christ Preaching (The Small Tomb)*, 155 × 207 mm., c. 1656. 34. *The Presentation of Christ in the Temple*, 207 × 162 mm., c. 1657–8. 35. *Portrait of the Art Dealer Abraham Fransen*, first state, 152 × 208 mm., c. 1658. 36. *Ibid.*, fourth state, in which Fransen is sitting in an armchair and no longer on a stool; the curtain has been removed, a small painting has been added on the right of the tryptich, trees can be seen from the window, a drawing can be see on the sheet of paper which Fransen holds in his hands, and, finally the sitter's right hand appears altogether. 37. *Half-Nude Woman*, first state, 228 × 96 mm., 1658. 38. *Ibid.*, fourth state, in which the face and bust are more elaborately drawn and the shading more pronounced throughout; the handle of the stove has been added, the woman's cap has been removed and the signature and date "Rembrandt f 1658" have been added. 39. *The Three Crosses* (see no. 29), fourth state, completely altered: the group on the left has been removed, the thunderstorm's shadows added and the date and signature removed; c. 1660–1. 40. *Nude Holding an Arrow*, 203 × 123 mm., signed and dated "Rembrandt f 1661".

As can be seen, the initial pathos gives way to greater and ever growing dramatic effects, through the establishment of a "black style" (see the *Presentation in the Temple*, no. 34); the outline becomes thicker and the lines themselves more intense, achieving thereby, beyond monochrome and chiaroscuro effects, a veritable effect of colour and a feeling of space and brooding atmosphere which had hitherto never been found in etchings. We have published several of these etchings in various states in order to illustrate the different phases of Rembrandt's search towards an ultimate expression which is evident in all his works. Two well-known etchings deserve particular attention: the enigmatic *Faust in his Study* (no. 28), watching the apparition of a magical disc in which is written the word "INRI" surrounded by cabalistic words and whose symbolical or allegorical significance has appealed to the fantasy of dozens of scholars. The second etching is the famous "Honderguldersprent" or "Hundred Guilder Print" (called thus because it reached that very high price in Rembrandt's lifetime), which represents Christ the Healer (no. 18); this is a combination of etching and drypoint and was finished after three years of work; it represents perhaps the highest achievement ever reached in any etching, not only by Rembrandt himself.

As far as the present value of Rembrandt's etchings are concerned, the prices reached at the London sale (Christie's) of 13 May 1969, are representative enough: no. 32, third state, $655; no. 26, $1008; no. 23, $1890; no. 33, $2016; no. 18 (the "Hundred Guilder Print"), second state, $3654; no. 27, $30,240.

Et. 1

Et. 2

Et. 6

Et. 7

Et. 8

Et. 3

Et. 4

Et. 5

Et. 9

Et. 10   Et. 11   Et. 12   Et. 13

Et. 14   Et. 15   Et. 18

Et. 17   Et. 19   Et. 27

Et. 16   Et. 21   Et. 22   Et. 26

Et. 23   Et. 24   Et. 20   Et. 25

137

Et. 28

Et. 29

Et. 39

Et. 31

Et. 30

Et. 33

Et. 32

Et. 35

Et. 36

Et. 34

Et. 37

Et. 38

Et. 40

Appendix 3
Pupils of Rembrandt's

As has been mentioned elsewhere, one of Rembrandt's chief activities as far back as 1628, had been that of teaching. He gathered around him, usually for a period of three years, a great number of young men whom he trained to become painters. Arnold Houbraken (see p. 12) has described their mode of life in picturesque terms and has related some anecdotes of doubtful authenticity, supposed to have taken place in the Bloemgracht studio (see p. 85, c. **1635**). Sandrart had already mentioned the numerous apprentices who were present at the same time in the master's studio; each of these was supposed to have paid Rembrandt 100 florins a year, which, according to Sandrart's calculations, must have amounted to about 2,500 florins, including the money brought in by the sale of their works. It has not been ascertained whether these sums were correct. It is, however, known that at least fifty painters, both Dutch and foreign, were apprenticed to Rembrandt, that they were all more or less influenced by what they had learnt from him and that they passed it on. Besides, quite apart from all these, there was not, in Amsterdam and indeed in the whole of Holland, during the height of Rembrandt's fame and for some decades after, a single painter who did not feel — whether consciously or not — Rembrandt's influence.

Below is a list of thirty-two seventeenth-century artists, not all Dutch, whose work seems close to that of Rembrandt's, and not only stylistically: twenty-three of these were undoubtedly his pupils; the others less certainly. The list includes Rembrandt's friend and associate in Leiden, Jan Lievens.

Jacob Adriaensz. Backer
(Harlingen, 1608–9 – Amsterdam, 1651)

One of Rembrandt's first pupils in Amsterdam, in 1632–3, he then became his friend and collaborator until at least 1640. His subsequent works (historical subjects and hunting scenes) link him with Bartholomeus van der Helst. He in turn had many pupils, amongst whom was his nephew Adriaen.

Leendert Cornelisz. van Beyeren
(Amsterdam, c. 1620–49)

Rembrandt's pupil in 1635–7, he painted great historical compositions.

Ferdinand Bol
(Dordrecht, 1616 – Amsterdam, 1680)

Rembrandt's pupil in 1632–5, he then became his friend and continued to learn from him until c. 1640. He was a successful painter, draughtsman and etcher and later on turned to the manner of Van der Helst, although he continued to acknowledge the influence of Rembrandt, indeed emphasising its characteristics in his paintings and etchings.

Benjamin Gerritsz. Cuyp
(Dordrecht, 1612–52)

Perhaps a pupil of Rembrandt's in 1630–2, he was a painter of religious and genre scenes in the manner of Adriaen van Ostade, although his work shows some of the luminous chromatic characteristics of Rembrandt's own work in his Leiden days.

Abraham van Dijck
(?, c. 1635 – Amsterdam, c. 1672)

A pupil of Rembrandt's in 1650. His few Biblical and genre scenes are more reminiscent of Barent Fabritius, with vague Rembrandtesque touches.

Lambert Doomer
(Amsterdam, 1622–3 – Alkmaar, 1700)

A pupil of Rembrandt's between 1640 and 1645; after which he went on a long voyage, to various villages, castles and cities of Europe from which he brought back some very fine sketches of landscape which show a striking and serene originality.

Gerrit (Gérard) Dou
(Leiden, 1613–75)

Dou was Rembrandt's first pupil, while still at Leiden, between 1628 and 1631. He attended Rembrandt's studio after being first taught by his father, Jan Dou, a painter of stained-glass windows. He was an associate in the studio shared by Rembrandt and Lievens and imitated Rembrandt's style. He remained in Leiden after Rembrandt had moved to Amsterdam and gradually moved away from the Rembrandtesque style, turning more and more to the tradition of still-lifes prevalent in Leiden and finally to small scenes of bourgeois interiors with candlelight, which subsequently became fashionable. He had several pupils, amongst whom was Gabriel Metsu.

Willem Drost
(?, c. 1630 – Dordrecht, 1687)

Perhaps a pupil of Rembrandt's in 1654–6, after a voyage in Italy from his native Germany. He was a painter of portraits and history scenes.

Heyman Dullaert
(Rotterdam, 1636–84)

A pupil of Rembrandt's in 1653; he had probably been introduced to Rembrandt through Philips Koninck. A poet of repute, his limited pictorial activity was restricted to still-lifes.

Gerbrandt van Eeckhout
(Amsterdam, 1621–74)

A pupil of Rembrandt's between 1635 and 1640. Rembrandt's influence is manifest in his paintings to the very last works, and he remained a close friend of the master's all his life. His works, which are excellent in quality, encompass mainly mythological, historical and religious subjects.

Barent Fabritius
(Middenbeemster, 1624 – Amsterdam, 1672)

Perhaps a pupil of Rembrandt's between 1643 and 1646. He travelled to England towards 1654, then to various places in the Low Countries, where he was commissioned to execute history paintings. His work shows a pleasing clarity.

Carel Fabritius
(Middenbeemster, 1622 – Delft, 1654)

A pupil of Rembrandt's in 1641–3; he was one of his most brilliant and faithful followers, even though his output was rather small and mostly attributed to Rembrandt himself. Only in the last three years of his life did he acquire any personal characteristics.

Govaert Flinck
(Cleves, 1616 – Amsterdam, 1660)

A pupil of Rembrandt's in 1633–6, after an apprenticeship in the studio of Lambert Jacobszoon. He was one of the most famous painters of his time and a follower of Rembrandt's, whose influence is evident throughout his work. In 1656–7 he was given the responsibility of supervising the decoration of the Burgerzaal in the Nieuwe Stadhuis, for which Rembrandt painted the *Oath of the Batavians* (no. 415); after Flinck's death the supervision was passed on to Jacob Jordaens, Jan Lievens, Ferdinand Bol and Jüngen Ovens.

Abraham Furnerius
(Amsterdam, c. 1628 – Rotterdam, 1698)

A pupil of Rembrandt's at the same time as Samuel van Hoogstraten. He was a landscape artist and several drawings by him are known.

Aert de Gelder
(Dordrecht, 1645–1727)

A pupil and assistant of Rembrandt's from 1661 to 1667, after an apprenticeship in the studio of Samuel van Hoogstraten. He was Rembrandt's most faithful pupil and the one pupil indeed who remained true to the master's style. Nevertheless his powerful portraits and his mythological and Biblical compositions, painted with broad brushstrokes, are a far cry from the master's breadth of vision.

Samuel van Hoogstraten
(Dordrecht, 1627–78)

A pupil of Rembrandt's for a year, between 1640 and 1642. One of the most famous characters of his time, he was a painter, a poet, an architect and a writer of treatises. He praises Rembrandt repeatedly in his treatise *Inleyding tot de Hooge der Schilder-Konst . . .*, published the very year of his death. The style of his own paintings was very much influenced by Rembrandts. Van Hoogstraten made frequent and long visits to Vienna, Germany, Rome and England. He in turn had many pupils amongst whom were his brother Jan, Carel Fabritius, Aert de Gelder and Jan Victors.

Isaac de Jouderville
(Leiden, 1613 – Amsterdam, c. 1645)

A pupil of Rembrandt's in 1629–31, in Leiden, he followed the master when he moved to Amsterdam. He produced few and small Biblical scenes where the influence of the early Rembrandt is evident.

Bernhardt Keil
(Elsinore, 1624 – Rome, 1687)

A pupil of Rembrandt's in 1642–4. He was of Danish origin and known in Italy as "Monsù Bernardo". He first arrived in Italy in 1651 after a stay in Amsterdam and never left the country after that. It was Keil who gave Baldinucci all the information regarding Rembrandt (see pp. 9–10). At first fairly close in manner to Rembrandt, he later became more and more attracted to the style of Strozzi and Feti.

Philips Koninck
(Amsterdam, 1619–88)

Perhaps a pupil of Rembrandt's in 1641. One of the most important Dutch landscape painters, he also painted portraits, genre, Biblical and historical scenes in which a certain Rembrandtesque touch is unmistakable, slightly less so in his last few years.

Salomon Koninck
(Amsterdam, 1609–56)

Perhaps not a proper pupil of Rembrandt's, but was nevertheless much influenced by the early Rembrandt, in his paintings and etchings, even down to the subject-matters and the use of exotic costumes, but above all in his use of chiaroscuro.

Paulus Lesire
(Dordrecht, 1611–c. 1656)

Not definitely known to have been Rembrandt's pupil, he nevertheless imitated his style particularly successfully, especially that of the "Passion" cycle which Rembrandt painted for Prince Frederick Henry (see no. 144 etc.).

Jan Lievens
(Leiden, 1607 – Amsterdam, 1674)

Lievens is not known definitely to have been Rembrandt's pupil, although he was his associate in the Leiden studio from 1624–5 to 1631. The son of an embroiderer, he had before he joined Rembrandt, been a pupil of Pieter Lastman's. The two young painters decided to join forces (even actually collaborating on some works) when they first started on their independent careers, because of the many links they had: the same native city, the same age, the same social background and artistic education. When, however, their partnership came to an end and Lievens went to England, then, after his return settled in Antwerp and later in Amsterdam, his style underwent a complete transformation: the likeness to Rembrandt's stopped and was replaced with a likeness to the style of Anthonie van Dijck.

Nicolaes Maes
(Dordrecht, 1634 – Amsterdam, 1693)

A pupil of Rembrandt's in c. 1648, from which his first works date; in these the master's influence is evident. Later he was influenced by the style of Jacob Jordaens but he finally reached a style of his own in the numerous decorative and rich portraits which he painted exclusively from 1660 onwards.

Johann Ulrich Mayr
(Augsburg, 1630–1704)

A pupil of Rembrandt's in c. 1660, a portrait-painter and an etcher, he was well known amongst the German artists of his time.

Jürgen Ovens
(Tönningen, 1623 – Friedrichstadt, 1678)

A pupil of Rembrandt's after 1642 when he moved from his native Germany to Holland. His entire work is influenced by Rembrandt and includes historical paintings, portraits and etchings.

Christoph Paudiss
(?, Saxony, 1618 – Freising, c. 1666)

A pupil of Rembrandt's from 1640 to 1642. He was

successful in several German courts and was a painter of historical scenes and portraits.

Carol van der Pluym
(Leiden, 1625–1672)

Perhaps a pupil of Rembrandt's c. 1647, he was a member of the Guild of St Luke in Leiden subsequently. His few works reveal to some extent the influence of Rembrandt.

Willem de Poorter
(Haarlem, 1608 –
Amsterdam, 1648)

He was a pupil of Rembrandt's both in Leiden and Amsterdam, in 1630–3, although only two years younger than the master. He copied Rembrandt's style as well as his subject-matters and his favourite characteristics, heightening their dramatic effects.

Constantijn Daniel van Renesse
(Utrecht, 1626 –
Eindhoven, 1680)

A pupil of Rembrandt's in 1649–52. A painter, draughtsman and etcher in the Rembrandt manner, his style was so close to that of Rembrandt, especially in his etchings, that many of his works have been attributed to the master.

Jan Victors
(Amsterdam, 1620 –
Indian seas, 1676)

A pupil of Rembrandt's in 1632–5, he always reproduced extremely well Rembrandt's manners in both the subject and structure of his compositions, yet relieving them to some extent of their dramatic content and achieving an entirely personal chromatic clarity.

Simon Jacobsz. de Vlieger
(Rotterdam, 1601 –
Wesp, 1653)

Perhaps a pupil of Rembrandt's after 1643, although five years Rembrandt's senior. He was above all his friend and one of the most famous artists of his time, both as a painter and as an etcher.

Jacob Willemsz. de Wet
(Haarlem, 1610–71)

A pupil of Rembrandt's in Leiden, 1630–2, he returned in 1635 to Haarlem where he settled for good. His mythological, historical and religious scenes show the Rembrandtesque elements present in de Poorter's work.

Indexes

Index of subjects

Abraham 274, 376
Absalom 245
Actaeon 70
Ahasuerus 6, 390
Alexander the Great 411, 426
Allegories 12–3, 161, 243, 324, 332, 337
Andromeda 68
Anna 4, 35, 268, 371
Anslo, Cornelius Claesz 236
Aristotle 316
Artemis 70
Artemisia 160
Athena, see Minerva
Avarice (allegory) 13
Backer, Jacob Adriaenz. 127
Balaam 5
Balthazar 180
Bas, Agatha 237
Bathsheba 91, 250, 317
Baucis 370
Bible (episodes from the Old Testament) 2, 3, 4, 5, 6, 20, 35, 48, 103, 177, 179, 180, 181, 182, 183, 184, 197, 199, 200, 209, 228, 244, 245, 268, 274, 277, 288, 297, 342, 343, 344, 361, 371, 373, 374, 376, 390
Bible (characters from the Old Testament) 17, 23, 34, 53, 54, 91, 148, 161, 250, 251, 276, 284, 310, 313, 317, 434, 435
Bilderbeeck, Margaretha 122
Bockenolle, Mary 134
Bol, Ferdinand 73
Brutus 3
Bruyningh, Nicolaes 315
Bueno, Ephraim 282
Burchgraeff, Willem 121
Buys, Petronella 167
Callisto 70
Caullery, Joris de 75
Children 104–5, 151, 201–2, 240, 267, 307–8
Christ (other than in composition groups) 59, 289–96, 395–8
Civilis, Julius 413
Cocq, Frans Banningh 216, 246
Coopal, Anthonis 172
Coppit, Oopjen 132
Cornelia (daughter of Henrickje and Rembrandt) 448
Cuyper, Aelbert 99
Daey, Maerten 131–2
Danae 276
Daniel 103, 297
David 2, 48, 245, 310, 361
Deborah 161
Delilah 20, 184
Democritus 17, 436
Deyman, Jan 345
Diana 71
Dircks, Geertje 266

Doomer, Herman 230
Doomer, Lambert 230
Dou, Gerrit (Gerard) 19
Elijah 17
Elison, John 133
Esther 6, 91, 390
Europa 69
Flora 159, 162, 353
Floris V (Count of Holland) 413
Frederick Henry, Prince of Orange-Nassau, Stadtholder of the United Provinces 203
Frederick II (of Swabia) 413
Ganymede 178, 370
Geer, Margaretha de 417–8
Gheyn III, Jacob de 78
Goliath 2
Good Samaritan, The 71, 211
Group portraits 81, 119–20, 165, 191–2, 236, 246, 345, 424, 434, 448
Hagar 228, 285
Haman 6, 390, 435
Hannah 4, 35, 268, 288, 371
Haring, Thomas Jacobsz 368
Heraclitus 17, 436
History (characters from) 17, 160, 316, 411, 413, 425–6, 431, 439
History (scenes from) 3, 415
Hollaer, Ariaentje 284
Homer 316, 425
Hooghsaet, Catrina 354
Huygens, Constantijn 125
Huygens, Maurits 77
Isaac 181–2, 376, 434
Jacob 313, 344, 373
Jacobs, Jacomijntje 259
Jeremiah 53
Jonah 3, 245
Jonghe, Clement de 258
Joseph 199, 342–3
Judas 32
Jupiter 178, 370
Krul, Jan 118
Lairesse, Gérard de 437
Landscapes 194–5, 211–5, 234–5, 255, 275, 304, 318
Lazarus 52
Levy Monteyra, Haham Saul 410
Liberty (allegory) 337
Literature (characters from) 91, 337, 370
Looten, Maerten 80
Lucasz Philips 166
Lucretia 431, 439
Manoah 244
Martens, Baartgen 231
Mary Magdelene 210
Melancholy (allegory) 161
Mercury 370
Minerva 106, 411, 426
Monk 336, 384, 402
Moses 374
Music (allegory) 12
Mythology (characters from) 68, 106, 159, 161–2, 276, 411, 426, 432
Mythology (scenes from) 47, 69, 70, 178, 370
Nun 408
Decker, Jeremias de 440
Pellicorne, Caspar 191
Pellicorne, Eva Susanna 192
Pellicorne, Jan 191
Pellicorne, Susanna 192
Philemon 370
Portraits 10, 11, 19, 23, 24, 25, 36, 40, 41, 42, 50, 53, 54, 66, 73, 74, 75, 77, 78, 80, 83, 84, 85, 86, 87, 83, 89, 90, 98, 99, 100, 101, 109, 110, 111, 113, 118, 121, 123, 124, 125, 126, 127, 128, 129, 130, 131, 132, 133, 134, 135, 136, 137, 138, 139, 149, 150, 158, 159, 161, 162, 163, 166, 167, 168, 169, 170, 171, 172, 187, 188, 189, 190, 193, 203, 205, 208, 216, 219, 220, 221, 230, 231, 237, 238, 239, 242, 249, 258, 259, 260, 261, 266, 282, 283, 284, 285, 298, 299, 300, 301, 302, 303, 315, 319, 320, 322, 323, 328, 329, 330, 331, 334, 335, 346, 347, 348, 349, 350, 351, 352, 353, 354, 360, 368, 376, 377, 382, 383, 384, 386, 408, 410, 413, 416, 417, 418, 419, 427, 429, 433, 437, 438, 440, 442, 443, 444, 445, 446
Prodigal Son, the 447
Pronck, Cornelia 100
Proserpina 47
Rabbi 360, 410
Rachel 276
Raman (family) 139
Rebecca 434
Rembrandt, Neeltje (Cornelia Willemsdr. van Zuytbroeck) 23–5, 40, 54, 140, 219
Rihel, Frederick 427
Rijn, Adriaen van 10, 36, 205, 298–9, 330
Rijn, Gerrit van 10
Rijn, Harmen Gerritsz. van 10, 11, 41–2, 50, 53
Rijn, Lijsbeth van 85–90, 109
Rooleeuw, Hendrick Jacobsz. 354
Ruts, Nicolaes 66
Samaria (woman from) 340–1, 372
Samson 20, 179, 184, 209
St Anastasius 56
St Thomas 147
St Bartholomew 257, 399
St Francis of Assisi 196, 336, 384
St James 401
St John the Baptist 93, 140
St John the Evangelist 404
St Joseph 269
St Matthew 406–7
St Paul 16–17, 50, 60, 186, 356, 376, 405
St Peter 17, 21, 49, 55, 94, 392
St Simon 400
St Stephen 1
Sarah 276, 285
Saul 2, 48, 361
Schouten, Aeltje Gerritse 236
Self-portraits 3, 8, 19, 26, 27, 28, 29, 30, 31, 37, 38, 39, 73, 74, 112, 140, 144, 145, 152, 153, 154, 155, 156, 164, 165, 187, 188, 206, 207, 209, 217, 218, 232, 233, 246, 247, 248, 265, 300, 314, 321, 333, 363, 364, 365, 366, 378, 379, 380, 381, 405, 430, 436, 449, 450
Simeon 45
Six, Jan 258, 320
Slaughtered ox 229, 338
Sophonisba 160
Soolmans, Maerten 131
Sorgh, Hendrick Maertensz 283
Spinoza, Baruch 445
Still-Lifes 201–2, 217, 229, 338
Stoffals, Hendrickje 285, 317, 322–3, 334, 350, 353, 382–3, 433
Uylenburch, Saskia van 85–90, 110–11, 158–9, 161–3, 165, 208, 239, 240
Uzziah 177
Virgin Mary 408
Women (other than in portraits and as historical or mythological characters) 91–2, 107–8, 279, 324, 326–7, 332, 402

Index of titles

Abduction of Europa, The 69
Abduction of Ganymede, The 178
Abduction of Proserpina, The 47
Abraham and the Angels 274
Adoration of the Shepherds, The 272, 273
Ahasuerus, Esther and Haman at the Table 390
Allegory of the Concord of the State 243
Alexander the Great 411, 426
Anatomy Lesson of Dr Deyman, The 345
Anatomy Lesson of Dr Tulp, The 81
Andromeda 68
Angel leaving Tobias, The 197
Apostle at Prayer 403
Apostle Peter Denying Christ, The 21, 392
Aristotle Contemplating a Bust of Homer 316
Artemisia 160
Artist in the Studio, An 19
Ascension of Christ, The 185
Ass of Balaam, The 5
Bald-Headed Old Man 95
Bareheaded Boy 151
Bathsheba at her Toilet 250
Bathsheba with David's Letter 317
Bearded Old Man in a Cap 116
Bearded Old Man with a Gold Chain 97
Belshazzar's Feast 180
Biblical Character 435
Biblical Scene with a Woman on a Donkey 228
Biblical Scene with an Old Woman and a Child 288
Biblical Scene with Two Figures Embracing 245
Boy in a Cap and Embroidered Cape 105
Boy in a Cap, with an Earring 104
Bust of a Man in Oriental Costume 117, 176
Bust of a Young Man 72
Christ 289–96, 395–7
Christ and his Disciples in the Storm 102
Christ and the Woman of Samaria 341–2, 372
Christ and the Woman Taken in Adultery 256
Christ appearing to Mary Magdelene 210
Christ Driving the Money-Changers from the Temple 7
Christ on the Cross 59
Circumcision, The 393
Concert, The 12
Clemency of Titus, The 3
Danae 276
Daniel and Cyrus before the Idol of Bel 103
David Playing the Harp before Saul 48, 361
David Presenting the Head of Goliath to Saul 2
Descent from the Cross, The 145, 146, 306
Dream of Joseph at Bethlehem, The 269
"Ecce Homo" 143
Entombment of Christ, The 223
Equestrian Portrait of Frederick Rihel 427
Evangelist Writing 404
Family Portrait 448
Female Figure in a Cape, with Musical Instruments 106
Female Figure with a Laurel Crown 161
Flight into Egypt, The 14, 142
Girl at a Window 308
Girl with a Broom 307
Girl with Dead Peacocks 201
Girl with Still-Life 202
Good Samaritan, The 71
Happy Couple, The 165
Head of an Old Man 406
Hermit Reading, A 51
Holy Family, The 141, 227, 270, 271
Homer 425
Incredulity of St Thomas, The 147
Jacob 313
Jacob Blessing Joseph's Children 344
Jacob Wrestling with the Angel 373
Jeremiah Foreseeing the Destruction of Jerusalem 53
Jewish Bride, The 434
Joseph Accused by Potiphar's Wife 342–3
Joseph Relating his Dreams 199
Judas Returning the Thirty Pieces of Silver 32
Juno 432
Jupiter and Mercury Visiting Philemon and Baucis 370
King David 310
King Uzziah Stricken with Leprosy 177
Lamentation over the Dead Christ, The 222
Landscape with a Baptism 194
Landscape with a Castle 255
Landscape with a Church 234
Landscape with a Coach 235
Landscape with an Arched Bridge 212
Landscape with an Obelisk 213
Landscape with a Stone Bridge 195
Landscape with Huts 318
Landscape with Ruins 214
Landscape with Storm 215
Landscape with Swans 304
Landscape with the Good Samaritan 211
Last Self-Portrait 450
Laughing Soldier 36
Lucretia 431, 439
Man Frowning 358
Man Holding a Letter 369
Man Holding a Pair of Gloves 264
Man in a Cloak and a Large Beret 420
Man in a Fanciful Costume 301
Man in a Fur-Lined Coat 362
Man in a Tall Hat 423
Man in Oriental Costume 175
Man Sitting in Front of a Stove 388
Man Standing in a Doorway 252
Man with a Goatee Beard 76
Man with a Falcon 413
Man with a Gold Chain 359
Man with a Long Beard 412
Man with Arms Akimbo 367
Man with Dishevelled Hair 174
Man with Folded Arms 387
Man with the Golden Helmet, The 299
Manoah and the Angel 244
Money-Changer, The 13

Monk Reading 402
Monk with Folded Hands 336
Moses with the Tables of the
  Law 371

Night Watch, The 246
Noble Slav, The 82
"Noli Me Tangere" 305

Oath of the Batavians, The 415
Officer, An 206
Old Man in a Beret 253
Old Man in a Cap, with a Gold
  Chain 65
Old Man in a Fur Hat 281
Old Man in a Fur-lined Coat
  262
Old Man in a Large Beret 355
Old Man in an Armchair 312
Old Man in a Sumptuous
  Costume 254
Old Man in Formal Dress 204
Old Man in Sumptuous Dress
  309
Old Man in the Costume of a
  Rabbi 173
Old Man Seated 325
Old Man with a Walking-Stick
  263
Old Man with a White Beard 96
Old Man with Gold Chains and
  Cross 43
Old Man with his Hand on his
  Breast 115
Old Man with his Hand on his
  Breast 311
Old Man with White Hair 375
Old Soldier with an Earring 44
Old Woman in a Cap 92
Old Woman Reading 332
Old Woman Seated, with a
  Veil 327
Old Woman with a Book and
  Spectacles 279
Old Woman with a Shawl on
  her Head 25
Old Woman with Folded Hands
  326
Old Woman with Folded Hands
  409
Oval Self-Portrait 265

Parable of the Workers in the
  Vineyard, The 198
Portrait of a Bald Man 10
Portrait of a Bareheaded Man
  298
Portrait of a Bearded Man in a
  Large Hat 139
Portrait of a Child 303
Portrait of a Couple in Black
  120
Portrait of a Dark Young
  Woman 259
Portrait of a Fair Young Man
  258
Portrait of a Forty-Year-Old
  Man 98
Portrait of a Lady Holding a
  Carnation 446
Portrait of a Lady Holding a
  Handkerchief 261
Portrait of a Lady Holding a
  Poppy 419
Portrait of a Lady Holding an
  Ostrich-Feather Fan 444
Portrait of a Lady in a Lace Cap
  128
Portrait of a Lady in a Large
  Ruff 130
Portrait of a Lady in a Ruff and
  a Cap 193
Portrait of a Lady with a
  Brooch on her Collar 169
Portrait of a Lady with a Gold
  Chain 109
Portrait of a Lady with a Gold
  Chain and a Lace Collar 136
Portrait of a Lady with a Tassel
  in her Hair 138
Portrait of a Lady with a
  Trinket in her hand 84
Portrait of a Man at a Window
  300

Portrait of a Man Holding a
  Magnifying Glass 445
Portrait of a Man Holding a
  Pair of Spectacles 260
Portrait of a Man in a Tall Hat,
  with Gloves 443
Portrait of a Man in a Wide-
  Brimmed Hat 129
Portrait of a Man in Polish
  Costume 205
Portrait of a Man Rising from
  a Chair 125
Portrait of a Man Sharpening
  a Quill 74
Portrait of a Man Standing
  before a Doorway 216
Portrait of a Man with a Flat
  White Collar 127
Portrait of a Man with a Fur
  Collar 41
Portrait of a Man with a Gold
  Chain 187
Portrait of a Man with a
  Ribbon on his Sleeve 168
Portrait of a Man with a
  Tasselled Hat 137
Portrait of a Man with a Wide-
  Brimmed Hat and a Lace
  Ruff 135
Portrait of a Man with his
  Hand at his Breast 83
Portrait of a Middle-Aged
  Woman 101
Portrait of a Nobleman 203
Portrait of a Paunchy Old Man
  441
Portrait of a Rabbi 360
Portrait of a Richly Dressed
  Boy 150
Portrait of a Richly Dressed
  Young Woman 433
Portrait of a Seated Lady with
  Gloves in her Hand 124
Portrait of a Seated Man 442
Portrait of a Seated Man with
  Gloves in his Hand 123
Portrait of a Shipbuilder and
  his Wife 119
Portrait of a Standard-Bearer
  319
Portrait of a Standard-Bearer
  with a Moustache 188
Portrait of a Writer 368
Portrait of a Young Girl in a
  Beret 85
Portrait of a Young Girl in an
  Embroidered Robe 88
Portrait of a Young Girl with
  a Gold Necklace 86
Portrait of a Young Girl with
  Earrings and an Embroidered
  Robe 87
Portrait of a Young Lady
  Holding a Carnation 349
Portrait of a Young Lady with
  a Fan 89
Portrait of a Young Man in a
  Large Beret 347
Portrait of a Young Man in a
  Pearl Embroidered Beret 348
Portrait of a Young Man with
  a Gold Chain 73
Portrait of a Young Man with a
  White Collar 438
Portrait of a Young Woman at
  a Door 266
Portrait of a Young Woman
  with a Fan 126
Portrait of an 83-Year-Old
  Woman 149
Portrait of an Old Lady with
  Folded Hands 328
Portrait of an Old Man in a
  Fur Hat 42
Portrait of an Old Man Seated
  170
Portrait of an Old Man with a
  White Beard 11
Portrait of an Old Woman in a
  Veil 331
Portrait of an Old Woman
  Seated 171
Portrait of an Old Man in a
  Beret 330

Portrait of an Old Man with
  Folded Hands 329
Portrait of an Old Man with a
  Goatee Beard 376
Portrait of an Old Rabbi 410
Portrait of Aelbert Cuyper 99
Portrait of Agatha Bas 238
Portrait of Alotte Adriaensdr.
  Trip 220
Portrait of Amalia van Solms 90
Portrait of Anna Wijmer 242
Portrait of Anthonis Coopal 172
Portrait of Ariaentje Hollaer 284
Portrait of Baartgen Martens
  231
Portrait of Catrina Hooghsaet
  354
Portrait of Cornelia Pronck 100
Portrait of Cornelis Claeszoon
  Anslo with a Woman 236
Portrait of Dirck van Os 386
Portrait of Dr Bueno 282
Portrait of Dr Tholincx 346
Portrait of Frans Coopal 189
Portrait of Gérard de Lairesse
  437
Portrait of Hendrick
  Maertenszoon Sorgh
Portrait of Hendrickje as Flora
  353
Portrait of Hendrickje at a
  Window 350
Portrait of Hendrickje in a Stole
  323
Portrait of Hendrickje in Bed
  285
Portrait of Hendrickje in
  Sumptuous Dress 322
Portrait of Hendrickje Seated
  383
Portrait of Hendrickje with her
  Hand on her Breast 382
Portrait of Herman Doomer 230
Portrait of Jacob de Gheyn III
  78
Portrait of Jacob Trip 416
Portrait of Jan Krul 118
Portrait of Jan Pellicorne with
  his Son Caspar 191
Portrait of Jan Six 320
Portrait of Jan Uytenbogaert
  113
Portrait of Jeremias de Decker
  440
Portrait of John Elison 133
Portrait of Maerten Looten 80
Portrait of Joris de Caullery 75
Portrait of Margaretha
  Bilderbeeck 122
Portrait of Margaretha de Geer
  417–8
Portrait of Maria Trip 221
Portrait of Mary Bockenolle 134
Portrait of Maurits Huygens 77
Portrait of Nicolaes Bruyningh
  315
Portrait of Nicolas Ruts 66
Portrait of Nicolaes van
  Bambeck 237
Portrait of Ooppen Coppit 132
Portrait of Petronella Buys 167
Portrait of Philips Lucasz 166
Portrait of Rembrandt's Mother
  with a Stick 219
Portrait of Saskia as Flora 159
Portrait of Saskia in Arcadian
  Costume 162
Portrait of Saskia in a Beret
Portrait of Saskia in a Hat 158
Portrait of Saskia Laughing 111
Portrait of Saskia with a Pearl
  Necklace 110
Portrait of Saskia with a Pink
  239
Portrait of Saskia with a Veil
  163
Portrait of Susanna van Collen
  with her daughter Eva
  Susanna 192
Portrait of Titia van Uylenburch
  190
Portrait of Titus Dressed as a
  Monk 384
Portrait of Titus in a Beret 429

Portrait of Titus in a Small Beret
  371
Portrait of Titus Reading 351
Portrait of Titus Studying 335
Portrait of Titus with a Chain
  and a Pendant
Portrait of Willem Burchgraeff
  121
Posthumous Portrait of Saskia
  249
Presentation of Christ in the
  Temple, The 15, 58
Profile of an Old Man in a
  Fanciful Costume 421
Prophetess Anna, The 54

Raising of Lazarus, The 52
Raising of the Cross, The 144
Rembrandt's Mother as a
  Prophetess 40
Rembrandt's Mother Praying 23
Rembrandt's Mother Reading
  24
Repentant St Peter, The 49
Resurrection of Christ, The 225
Rest during the Flight into
  Egypt 277
Return of the Prodigal Son 447
Riding Figure 337
Risen Christ, The 398
Risen Christ at Emmaus, The
  22, 286, 287, 391

Sacrifice of Isaac, The 182
St Bartholomew 357, 399
St Francis at Prayer 196
St James 401
St John the Baptist 93
St John the Baptist Preaching
  140
St Matthew and the Angel 407
St Paul 60, 186, 356
St Paul in Meditation 50
St Paul in Prison 16
St Peter 94
St Peter in Prison 55
St Simon 400
Sampling Officials of the
  Drapers' Guild, The 424
Samson Betrayed by Delilah 20
Samson Blinded by the
  Philistines 184
Samson's Wedding Feast 209
Samson Threatening his
  Father-in-Law 179
Scholar at his Desk 241
Scholar in a Lofty Room, A 18
Scholar in his Study, A 148
Scholar in Meditation 57, 251
Scholar Reading 56
Seated Young Man with a
  Sword 256
Self-Portrait 37
Self-Portrait as St Paul 405
Self-Portrait at the Easel 380
Self-Portrait Bareheaded 39
Self-Portrait in a Cloak 164
Self-Portrait in a Frilled Shirt
  233
Self-Portrait in a Fur Collar 154
Self-Portrait in a Gorget and
  Plumed Cap 156
Self-Portrait in a Helmet 155
Self-Portrait in a Large Beret
  365, 381
Self-Portrait in a Large Hat 79
Self-Portrait in a Plumed Cap
  30
Self-Portrait in a Small Cap 38
Self-Portrait in a Stand-Up
  Collar 363
Self-Portrait in a Wide Brimmed
  Beret 364
Self-Portrait Laughing 436
Self-Portrait Turned towards
  the Left 378
Self-Portrait in a Beret and
  Gold Chains 321
Self-Portrait with a Chain and
  Pendant 430
Self-Portrait with a Dead
  Bittern 217
Self-Portrait with a Fur Collar
  and Gold Chains 232

Self-Portrait with a Gold Chain
  28
Self-Portrait with a Gold Chain
  and Cross 218
Self-Portrait with a Gorget 29
Self-Portrait with a Gorget and
  a Beret 152
Self-Portrait with a Moustache
  112
Self-Portrait with a Moustache
  and a Cap 153
Self-Portrait with a Scarf 26
Self-Portrait with a Stick 366
Self-Portrait with a White
  Collar 27
Self-Portrait with an Earring
  247
Self-Portrait with an Earring
  and a Gold Chain 333
Self-Portrait with Cap Pulled
  Forward 31
Self-Portrait with Dishevelled
  Hair 8
Self-Portrait with Folded
  Hands 449
Self-Portrait with Gold Chains
  248
Self-Portrait with his Hand on
  his Breast 207
Self-Portrait with his Hand on
  his Hips 314
Self-Portrait with Palette and
  Brushes 379
Simeon Holding the Infant
  Jesus 451
Slaughtered Ox 229, 338
Soldier in a Great Cloak 45
Soldier in a Plumed Hat 46
Soldier with a Sword 9
Stoning of St Stephen, The 1
Stories of Diana 70
Study of a Bareheaded Old
  Man 114
Study of an Old Man in a Beret
  385
Susanna Surprised by the
  Elders 200, 271

Tobit, Anna and the Kid 4, 268
Tobit Asleep 34
Tobit Healed by his Son 183
Tribute Money, The 33, 339
Two Negroes 414
Two Scholars Disputing 17

Virgin Mary, The 408
Vision of Daniel 297
Visitation, The 226

Waiting of Tobit and Anna, The
  35, 371
Winter Landscape 275
Woman in a Fanciful Costume
  302
Woman with a Lace Collar 108
Wrath of Ahasuerus, The 6
Writer at his Desk 67
Writing Evangelist 428

Young Girl at a Window 267
Young Girl at the Window-Sill
  240
Young Jew in a Waistcoat 280
Young Jew with a Fastened
  Collar 394
Young Man in a Turban 62
Young Man with a Broad
  Collar 61
Young Man with a Gold Chain
  64
Young Man Seated 389
Young Man Seated, with his
  Hand on his Hip 422
Young Soldier in a Plumed Cap
  157
Young Soldier in a Small Cap
  63
Young Woman at her Mirror
  324
Young Woman Bathing in a
  Stream 334
Young Woman Having her
  Hair Dressed 91
Young Woman Seated 107

Topographical Index

AERDENHOUT
Loudon Collection 39

ALLENTOWN (Pa.)
Art Museum 86

AMSTERDAM
Rijksmuseum 4, 37, 53–4, 110, 176, 195, 199, 201, 221, 246, 282, 345, 384, 392, 405, 424, 434

Six Collectie 242, 320

BASLE
Oeffentliche Kunstsammlung, Kunstmuseum 2

BENNBROCK, HAARLEM
Von Pannwitz Collection 274

BERLIN
Staatliche Museen, Gemäldegalerie 13, 20, 47, 106, 140, 154, 156, 179, 212, 236, 249, 262, 268–9, 277, 280, 295, 297, 299, 313, 343, 350, 358, 373–4

BEVERLY HILLS (Calif.)
Loew Collection 127

BIRMINGHAM
City Museum and Art Gallery 65
Cotton Collection 375

BOSTON (Mass.)
Isabella Stewart Gardner Museum 30, 102, 120, 213
Museum of Fine Arts 19, 49, 87, 133–6, 248, 362, 404

BREMEN
Kunsthalle 60

BRUNSWICK
Staatliches Herzog Anton Ulrich-Museum 76, 215, 305, 448

BRUNSWICK (Maine)
Bowdoin College Museum of Art 257

BRUSSELS
Mérode – Westerloo Collection 55
Musées Royaux des Beaux-Arts 237

BUDAPEST
Szépművészeti Múzeum 251

BUSCOT PARK (Berkshire)
Faringdon Collection 258–9

BYWELL (Northumberland)
Allendale Collection 339

CAMBRIDGE
Fitzwilliam Museum 96, 294

CASSEL
Staatliche Kunstsammlungen, Gemäldegalerie 8, 10, 43, 74, 95, 97, 118, 155, 158, 216, 271, 275, 304, 315, 321, 344

CHATSWORTH (Derbyshire)
Devonshire Collection 177, 309

CHICAGO (Ill.)
Art Institute 45, 266

CINCINNATI (Ohio)
Taft Museum 125, 300

CLEVELAND (Ohio)
Museum of Art 73, 169, 403

COLOGNE
Wallraf-Richartz-Museum 260, 436

COLUMBUS (Ohio)
Gallery of Fine Arts 196

COPENHAGEN
Statens Museum for Kunst 286, 326, 348–9

COWDRAY PARK (Sussex)
Cowdray Collection 441

DETROIT (Mi.)
Institute of Arts 226, 290
Wilson Collection 157

DRESDEN
Staatliche Kunstsammlungen, Gemäldegalerie 111, 121, 165, 178, 209, 217, 239, 244, 421

DRUMLANRIG CASTLE, Thornhill (Dumfrieshire)
Buccleuch Collection 332

DUBLIN
National Gallery of Ireland 278

EDINBURGH
National Gallery of Scotland 138, 285, 288, 363

ÉPINAL
Musée Départemental des Vosges 408

ESSEN
Von Bohlen und Halbach Collection 40

FLORENCE
Galleria degli Uffizi 152, 365, 410, 430

FRANKFURT
Stadelsches Kunstinstitut 48, 122, 184

FULLERTON (Calif.)
Norton Simon Foundation 303, 323

GLASGOW
Art Gallery and Museum 79, 229, 411
Hunterian Museum and University Art Collection 223

GLENS FALLS (N.Y.)
Hyde Collection 396

GOTEBORG
Konstmuseum 413

GREENWICH (Conn.)
Neumann de Végvár Collection 172

HAMPTON COURT
Royal Collection 173

THE HAGUE
Mauritshuis 29, 36, 41, 58, 68, 81, 200, 206, 298, 361, 414, 425, 450
Museum Bredius 289

HAMBURG
Kunsthalle 15, 77

HANOVER
Niedersächsisches Landesmuseum 194

KRAKOW
Muzeum Czartoryski 211

LEIDEN
Stedelijk Museum "De Lakenhal" 3

LE MAS-D'AGENAIS (Lot-et-Garonne)
Parish church 59

LENINGRAD
Hermitage 44, 67, 137, 146, 150, 159, 181, 198, 231, 245, 253, 270, 276, 324–5, 328–9, 372, 412, 435, 440, 447

LISBON
Fundaçao Calouste Gulbenkian 263, 426

LIVERPOOL
Formerly in Heywood-Lonsdale Collection 207
Walker Art Gallery 26

LONDON
Buckingham Palace Royal Collection 119, 210, 238
Dulwich College Picture Gallery 78, 267, 429
Kenwood House, Iveagh Bequest 379
Morrison Collection 383
Mountain Collection 46
National Gallery 18, 35, 143, 149, 162, 166, 180, 222, 233, 256, 272, 313, 334, 336, 360, 376, 416–8, 427, 449
Victoria and Albert Museum 228
Wallace Collection 71, 105, 191–2, 232, 235, 352
Weitzner Collection 161
Westminster Collection 283–4
Wharton Collection 142

LOS ANGELES (Calif.)
Ahmanson Collection 52
County Museum of Art 80, 93

LUGANO
Batthyany Collection 9

LUGANO CASTAGNOLA
Thyssen Collection 129

LYONS
Musée des Beaux-Arts 1

MADRID
Alba Collection 234
Museo del Prado 160

MELBOURNE
National Gallery of Victoria 17, 442

MENTMORE (Buckinghamshire)
Rosebery Collection 113

MERTOUN (Scotland)
Sutherland Collection 204

METZ
Musée Central 116

MILAN
Pinacoteca di Brera 88

MILWAUKEE (Wis.)
John Collection 395

MINNEAPOLIS (Ind.)
Institute of Arts 439

MONTREAL
Museum of Fine Arts 318, 433
Van Horne Collection 394

MOSCOW
Pushkin Museum 7, 147, 327, 330–1, 390

MULGRAVE CASTLE (Yorkshire)
Normanby Collection 32

MUNICH
Alte Pinakothek 27, 117, 141, 144–5, 182, 185, 224–5, 273, 398

NEW YORK
Columbia University 367
Fleitman Collection 61
Frick Collection 66, 337, 366
Houghton Collection 114
Kaplan Collection 310
Klotz Collection 69
Lehman Collection 437
Metropolitan Museum of Art 31, 82–4, 98, 101, 171, 203, 230, 250, 264, 296, 316, 319, 340, 353, 368, 381–2, 387, 397, 401, 445–6
Meyer Collection 167
Middendorf Collection 432
Payson Collection 347
Straus Collection 409
Whitney Collection 385

NUREMBERG
Germanisches Nationalmuseum 50

OMAHA (Neb.)
Joslyn Art Museum 386

PARIS
Musée Cognacq-Jay 5
Musée du Louvre 51, 57, 99, 100, 112, 115, 153, 197, 227, 255, 287, 317, 322, 338, 377, 380, 391, 407
Musée Jacquemart-André 22, 90, 346
Rothschild Collection 131–2, 188

PENRHYN CASTLE (Wales)
Douglas-Pennant 354

PHILADELPHIA (Pa.)
John G. Johnson Art Collection 293

PRAGUE
Národni Galerie 148

RALEIGH (N.C.)
North Carolina Museum of Art 6

RHEDE (Westphalia)
Zu Salm-Salm Collection 70

ROCHESTER (N.Y.)
George Eastman Collection of the University 389

ROSSIE PRIORY (Perthshire)
Kinnaird Collection 193

ROTTERDAM
Museum Boymans-van Beuningen 243, 281, 335, 428
Stichting W. van der Vorm 220, 371

SALZBURG
Residenzgalerie 23

SAN DIEGO (Calif.)
Fine Arts Gallery 63
Timken Gallery of Art, Putnam Foundation 357

SAN FRANCISCO (Calif.)
California Palace of the Legion of Honor 359
M.H. de Young Memorial Museum 359

SANTA BARBARA (Calif.)
Converse Collection 108

SÃO PAULO
Museu de Arte 187

SARASOTA (Fla.)
John and Mable Ringling Museum of Art 302

St LOUIS (Mo.)
City Art Museum 420

STOCKHOLM
Nationalmuseum 38, 56, 89, 94, 308, 415, 451

STUTTGART
Staatsgalerie 16, 183

SUTTON PLACE, New Guildford (Surrey)
Getty Collection 399

TILBURG
Weyers Collection 292

TISBURY (Wiltshire)
Margadale Collection 252

TOKYO
Bridgestone Museum of Art, Ishibashi Foundation 21

TOLEDO (Ohio)
Museum of Art 64

TURIN
Galleria Sabauda 34

TORONTO
Art Gallery 261, 419

TOURS
Musée des Beaux-Arts 14

VANÅS, SKÅNE (Sweden)
Wachtmeister Collection 72, 311

VIENNA
Akademie der bildenden Kunste, Gemäldegalerie 107
Kunsthistorisches Museum, Gemäldegalerie 123–4, 186, 219, 314, 333, 351, 364

WASHINGTON D.C.
Corcoran Gallery of Art 170
National Gallery of Art 163, 175, 205, 279, 306–7, 342, 356, 370, 388, 393, 422–3, 431, 443–4

WASSENAAR
Kohn Collection 139
Private collection 214
Van der Bergh Collection 11

WELBECK ABBEY (Nottinghamshire)
Portland Collection 151

WILTON HOUSE Salisbury (Wiltshire)
Penbroke and Montgomery Collection 24

WINDSOR
Royal Collection 25, 62, 247

WINTERTHUR
Sammlung Oskar Reinhart 388

WOBURN ABBEY (Bedfordshire)
Bedford Collection 218, 254

ZURICH
Buhrle Collection 189, 202
Kunsthaus 400
Wiederkehr Collection 85

Anonymous Private collections 92, 103–4, 109, 128, 130, 174, 190, 208, 214, 369, 406

Whereabouts unknown 12, 28, 164, 240–1, 291